# Journal of Beat Studies

Volume 6, 2018

PACE UNIVERSITY PRESS • NEW YORK

Copyright © 2018 by
Pace University Press
41 Park Row, 15th Floor
New York, NY 10038

All rights reserved
Printed in the United States of America

ISSN 2165-8706
ISBN: 978-1-935625-27-8 (pbk: alk.ppr.)

Member

Council of Editors of Learned Journals

♾ Paper used in this publication meets the minimum requirements of
American National Standard for Information
Sciences–Permanence of Paper for Printed Library Materials,
ANSI Z39.48–1984

## Editors

Ronna C. Johnson — Tufts University
Nancy M. Grace — The College of Wooster

## Editorial Board

Ann Charters — University of Connecticut–Storrs (emerita)
Maria Damon — Pratt Institute of Art
Terence Diggory — Skidmore College (emeritus)
Tim Gray — CUNY Staten Island
Oliver Harris — Keele University, United Kingdom
Allen Hibbard — Middle Tennessee State University
Tim Hunt — Illinois State University
Cary Nelson — University of Illinois
A. Robert Lee — The University of Murcia, Spain
Jennie Skerl — West Chester University (retired)
David Sterritt — Long Island University (emeritus)
Tony Trigilio — Columbia College–Chicago
John Tytell — CUNY Queens College
John Whalen-Bridge — National University of Singapore, Singapore

## Production Staff

Stephanie Hsu — Production Editor, Pace University
Elliane Mellet — Graduate Assistant, Pace University Press
Bryan Potts — Graduate Assistant, Pace University Press

# Journal of Beat Studies

Volume 6, 2018

|  | 1 | Letter from the Editors |
|---|---|---|
| *Jolie Braun* | 3 | A History of Diane di Prima's Poets Press |
| *Mary Paniccia Carden* | 23 | Joanne Kyger's Travel Chapbooks: A Poetics of Motion |
| *Terence Diggory* | 53 | Big Sur Breakdown: Lew Welch and "Ring of Bone" |
| *Jane Falk* | 75 | Michael McClure: A Filmography |
| *Sara Villa* | 89 | Le Club Jack Kérouac and the Renaissance in Beat Scholarship on Kerouac's French Canadian Background |

## THE BEAT INTERVIEW

| *Jennie Skerl* | 109 | Ed Sanders |
|---|---|---|

## REVIEWS

| *Nancy M. Grace* | 125 | *Love, H: The Letters of Helene Dorn and Hettie Jones* by Helene Dorn and Hettie Jones (Duke University Press, 2016) |
|---|---|---|
| *Kurt Hemmer* | 132 | *The Poetry and Politics of Allen Ginsberg* by Eliot Katz (Beatdom Books, 2015) |
|  | 141 | The Beat Index |

**163** Essay Abstracts

**166** Notes on Contributors

**168** Editorial Policy

# Letter from the Editors

As we introduce volume 6 of the *Journal of Beat Studies*, we are grateful to our colleagues in the field for their diligent resistance to the resistance of integrating Beat Studies into the U.S. literary critical discourse. We hope that our readers will be engaged by the range of essays presented in this issue, as well as the thoughtful new works that we review, the lengthy list of new scholarship in Beat Studies recorded in our Beat Index, and the insightful interview with Ed Sanders, which is our featured Interview of the year. These all document the advancement of the field, further evidenced by developments such as the two Beat-focused panels at the 2018 MLA annual convention, one of them sponsored by the Beat Studies Association; the introduction in 2017 of the first-ever Beat Studies book series sponsored by Clemson University Press and Liverpool University Press; annual European conferences on Beat writers and cultures.

In particular, we're pleased to feature several essays focused on archival work in Beat Studies. Jolie Braun's "A History of Diane di Prima's Poets Press" draws on di Prima documents from archives throughout the United States; Sara Villa's discussion "Le Club Jack Kérouac and the Renaissance in Beat Scholarship on Kerouac's French Canadian Background" complements the recent and significant new research on Jack Kerouac's French Canadian heritage; and Jane Falk's "Michael McClure: A Filmography" itemizes McClure's involvement and explorations with avant-garde cinema. In addition, volume 6 includes Mary Carden's "Joanne Kyger's Travel Chapbooks: A Poetics of Motion," a detailed study of Joanne Kyger's numerous travel journals and an homage to an audacious voice in Beat philosophical and literary experimentation. Terence Diggory's discerning "Big Sur Breakdown: Lew Welch and 'Ring of Bone'" expounds on the wide-ranging and interdisciplinary nature of Beat poetics, spirituality, and Welch's literary and personal life. Several of these texts are accompanied by archival and vintage images, which add period authenticity to the scholarship and, by their publication here, contribute greater access to the historical record.

Although the journal has already announced the addition of Matt Theado of Kobe City University of Foreign Studies as our first-ever Book Review Editor, we wish to do so once again, thanking him for joining the journal's editorial board and bringing his extensive Beat studies scholarly interests to bear on our shared enterprise.

Finally, we thank, first, Stephanie Hsu, our production editor, for shepherding us through the process with good humor and professionalism, and, second, Victoria McCaslin, a history and English double major at The College of Wooster and our research assistant, for her stellar contributions to the Beat Index.

Onward!
Ronna C. Johnson and Nancy M. Grace

# A History of Diane di Prima's Poets Press
Jolie Braun

From 1965 to 1969, Diane di Prima's Poets Press published more than two dozen volumes by major poets of the 20th century—including Allen Ginsberg, Robert Creeley, and Frank O'Hara—and helped launch the careers of young writers such as Audre Lorde, David Henderson, and A.B. Spellman. Examining the press's output reveals an important intersection of the major underground literary movements of the mid-20th century, key countercultural concerns of the era, and a vibrant network of poets and artists. This essay draws on archival materials to construct a history of the press and the books it published.

By 1965, Diane di Prima had been writing and promoting her work and that of other underground writers and artists for several years. In 1961, she and LeRoi Jones began *The Floating Bear,* a mimeographed literary newsletter for young, experimental poets that, according to Jones, "was meant to be 'quick, fast and in a hurry'" and aimed to capture the "zigs and zags of the literary scene as well as some word of the general New York creative ambience" (Baraka 169). That same year, di Prima and a group of friends (James Waring, John Herbert McDowell, LeRoi Jones, Alan Marlowe, and Freddie Herko [*Recollections* 255]) founded the experimental theatre company New York Poets Theatre. She also had established herself as a poet, publishing in little magazines and producing collections such as *This Kind of Bird Flies Backward* (1958) and *Dinners and Nightmares* (1961). As these activities suggest, di Prima had a network that extended beyond one particular literary scene, and her involvement with a wide variety of projects brought her into contact with an exceptionally diverse group of writers.

She also spent the late 1950s and early 1960s gaining publishing knowledge and skills that helped prepare her to run Poets Press (di Prima, *Recollections* 252). In addition to editing, typing, and printing *The Floating Bear*, two experiences stand out. In 1958, di Prima was approached by two individuals who planned to start a press and offered to publish a collection of her poetry as their first book. While she was in the process of preparing the manuscript for *This Kind of Bird Flies Backward*, however, they changed their minds. Although they decided not to pursue publishing, they offered to do the press run if she did the other work involved (*Recollections* 182-184). Di Prima not only typeset the book, but also "learned such arts as dummying a book for printing four-up, and stripping and opaquing negatives" and became captivated with the work (*Recollections* 182). Soon thereafter, Totem Press, run by LeRoi and Hettie Jones, published *This Kind of Bird Flies Backward* as their first book. (It was also during this time that di Prima and LeRoi Jones were having an affair.) Another formative experience was assisting LeRoi and Hettie Jones with *Yugen* and Totem Press books during the late 1950s and early 1960s.

In a 2014 interview, Hettie Jones recalled having stapling parties for the earliest issues of the magazine, stressing the importance of friends and community in the production process, a common practice that di Prima employed with her projects as well (Anderson 80-1). Di Prima sometimes visited the couple for dinner, and the routine of assisting with their projects afterward was instructive: "we would work together on *Yugen* magazine or one of the early Totem Press books...we would type and proof and paste till almost midnight. I learned some of the production skills I later used at Poets Press while working with Roi and Hettie" (*Recollections* 218).

It was within this context of productivity and experimentation that di Prima launched Poets Press. In her 2001 memoir *Recollections of My Life As a Woman*, she recalls her motivation: "owning a press and printing books seemed a natural next step after mimeographing *The Floating Bear* for so many years, and most recently turning out programs and flyers for the theatre on the Gestetner [copy machine]" (410). By the mid-20th century, it had become possible to print one's own work relatively cheaply and easily, and the technological innovations of the period played a crucial role in making projects such as di Prima's feasible: "direct access to mimeograph machines, letterpress, and inexpensive offset made these publishing ventures possible, putting the means of production in the hands of the poet. In a real sense, almost anyone could become a publisher" (Clay and Phillips 14). Di Prima purchased a Fairchild Davison offset press that came with one week of classes (*Recollections* 410). It was expensive—$1,200—and she raised the funds by securing donations from artist friends after telling them of her vision for the press and the kinds of books she wanted to publish (*Recollections* 411). In March 1965, she rented a storefront on the Lower East Side across the street from the Poets Theatre to print Poets Press books (di Prima and Baraka xvii).

Di Prima's New York City base also was an important factor in the press's founding. As a native New Yorker, she had a deep knowledge of the city and an extensive social network. Moreover, rents were cheap and equipment and supplies readily available and often inexpensive (Clay and Phillips 14). While di Prima and her contemporaries' projects were a world apart from the major publishing houses, they benefited from their physical proximity. In a November 22, 1967, letter to Lawrence Ferlinghetti, di Prima's then-husband Alan Marlowe said of New York, "this is the world printing center, all practically within walking distance: paper, printers, binders, stats, Xerox, etc" (City Lights Records, Box 8, Folder 20).[1] She herself noted that "New York in those days was full of stores that sold broken cartons and odd lots of paper," enabling her to find the paper used for the first Poets Press book in a remnant shop (*Recollections* 412).

The press was di Prima's vision, but she did not work alone. During the first few years of *The Floating Bear* she regularly recruited help to produce the issues, a strategy she also employed while running Poets Press (di Prima and Baraka xii).

# DIANE DI PRIMA'S POETS PRESS             *Braun*

Friends assisted with whatever needed to be done: proofreading, printing, collating, stapling, and mailing (*Recollections* 418). In a letter to artist George Herms, di Prima mentioned a friend who "used to spend 36 hours at a streth [sic] addressing envelopes & now sends out Poets Press books, and proofreads whatever I typeset" (George Herms Papers, Box 5, Folder 9, no date). Collaboration of this nature was typical for small presses and little magazines of the era. As scholar Linda Russo has observed, during the mimeo revolution, "where friends assembled[,] materials were assembled" (249).

In addition to di Prima's friends, Marlowe played an integral part. In a letter dated June 24, 1965, he wrote to inform Lawrence Ferlinghetti of the new press, describing his own role as a partner in the project:

> Diane and I have a shop set up and a photo offset press. We will be printing and publishing books at the rate of one a month...Diane sets the proofs up on the IBM, I do paste up, and run the press. I will also try and see that there is proper distribution of the books around the country. This is a family operation. (City Lights Records, Box 8, Folder 20)

Di Prima wanted Marlowe to be an active participant in her world and also encouraged him to write and edit. In a March 29, 1968, letter to him she said, "your letters are fantastically beautiful—I want to make them into a book—yr letter and my journal for the NY scene side by side day by day—Please keep up your journal—you are in unique position at a unique moment in history" (Diane di Prima Papers 1934-1992, Box 4, Folder 10). That same year, Marlowe selected poems for di Prima's *Earthsong: Poems 1957-1959,* and in 1969, Poets Press released a collection of his poetry called *John's Book*, dedicated to John Wieners and John Braden (a friend of di Prima and Marlowe's, and Marlowe's sometime lover). Yet di Prima's collaboration with Marlowe—an actor, director, and fellow cofounder of the New York Poets Theatre with no previous writing or publishing experience—was different from her work with Jones on *The Floating Bear* and from other male/female collaborations of the period, as she had far more expertise than her partner and was decidedly the initiator and architect of the project.[2]

In mid-1965, the press published its first book, *The Beautiful Days* by A.B. Spellman, poet, music critic, and founding member of the Black Arts Movement (see fig. 1). Spellman's work had appeared in *The Floating Bear* and prior to Jones and di Prima beginning the newsletter, Spellman and di Prima had planned to start a literary journal together (Meltzer 13). The collection, which was Spellman's first, included an introduction by Frank O'Hara and illustrations by African American artist William White. The press produced a first run of 750 copies of the softcover edition that sold for $1.00 and 10 copies of a hardbound limited edition for $15

*Fig. 1. Front cover of* The Beautiful Days *by A.B. Spellman, Rare Books and Manuscripts Library, The Ohio State University.*

(*Recollection*s 412; City Lights Records, Box 8, Folder 20, 4 November 1965). Reviews were enthusiastic. In *The East Village Other*, poet Carol Bergé declared Spellman "a modern man who speaks with today's language" with a "voice sharp and clean," and in *Paper,* poet and activist John Sinclair called the volume "a rare delight" (12-13). A review in *Work* urged readers to "please get this book" (Moore 104).

An examination of the Poets Press catalog reveals a fascinating intersection of the major underground literary movements of the mid-20th century: writers spanned the Beat Generation, the Black Arts movement, the New York School, Black Mountain, and San Francisco Renaissance. The books also reflect major countercultural concerns of the era, including the sexual revolution, drug use, and the anti-war movement. Examples of publications include a pirated translation of a Jean Genet poem, a Timothy Leary adaptation of Book One of the Tao Te Ching, and an anthology of poetry protesting the Vietnam War. In its holograph series, it published limited editions of some of the most important poets of the second half of the 20th century, including Allen Ginsberg, Robert Creeley, and John Ashbery. Perhaps more important was the press's dedication to championing new writers and publishing first collections. Eight of nearly 30 books in the press's catalog were by new poets, the Press helping to launch the careers of poets such as Audre Lorde, Clive Matson, Kirby Doyle, A.B. Spellman, and David Henderson. Several of the individuals the press published were young poets whose work had appeared in *The Floating Bear* and other little magazines, but who had not yet released a collection, a position that di Prima could likely sympathize with, having faced challenges getting her own work in print (Grace and Johnson 97).

How many books did Poets Press publish? This seemingly simple question is surprisingly difficult to answer. One reason is because of what remains; there is no Poets Press collection held at any public or academic archive, as there are for publications such as *The Floating Bear* and *Yugen*. Furthermore, di Prima's archives are dispersed across the country at several institutions, none of which has a clearly defined series of Poets Press materials within their collections.[3] Poets Press is often mentioned in writing about di Prima, but examining this information reveals discrepancies. For example, Russo noted that the press published 12 books between 1965 and 1968 (252), and Amy Friedman counted a total of 29 books during its run (29). Sharon Slate Gibson's unpublished biography available in the University of Louisville special collections includes notes addressed to di Prima asking if the press published 23, 28, or 29 books. The total number of books Poets Press published, however, appears to be 27. There are also inconsistencies about when the press started, likely because di Prima's own date for its founding oscillated between 1964 and 1965. For example, the "Diane di Prima Chronology" in *Pieces of a Song* lists 1964 as the year she began Poets Press, founding it with Alan Marlowe (198), whereas in the introduction to the 1971 collection of *The Floating Bear*, di Prima recalled setting up her print shop in 1965 (di Prima and Baraka xvii). Furthermore, there is limited information available about what books were published by the press, some of which is inaccurate. *Freddie Poems* was first published in 1974 by di Prima's later press, Eidolon Editions, but is commonly cited as a Poets Press book, sometimes as *Poems for Freddie*. *New Mexico Poem*, a fine press volume designed and printed by Igal Roodenko and published in 1968, is often attributed to Poets Press but includes no bibliographic information linking it to the press and, perhaps more tellingly, bears no resemblance to either the softcover or limited edition Poets Press books. Additionally, the bibliographic information in the Poets Press books changes throughout the course of the press: some volumes provide the press name, location, print run; others do not. To some extent, these discrepancies are not surprising from a small press, and the variations speak to both improvisation and a lack of interest in standardization. Collectively, however, these issues likely have contributed to the lack of attention the press has received in the intervening years.

Poets Press produced some significant publications during its existence and highlighting a few examples is essential to appreciating di Prima's project. *Huncke's Journal* by Herbert Huncke contained stories and recollections written between 1948-1964 along with illustrations by Erin Matson. A Times Square hustler, Huncke and his "lifestyle undoubtedly provided the very model of what it meant to be Beat and to struggle against a system that stymied any alternative phenomenon that deviated from the mainstream" (Niski). An associate of William S. Burroughs and a mentor to Allen Ginsberg, he appears in a fictionalized form in *Junkie*, *Howl*, and *On the Road*, and it was his use of the word "beat" that was adopted and circulated by Burroughs, Kerouac, and Ginsberg (Charters xvii-xviii). In his autobiography, *Guilty of Everything*, Huncke remembered his first book's genesis: "I ran into Diane di Prima on the street…[she] asked me if I had anything she could publish….I finally grabbed a whole lot of stuff at random I'd had in various places and gave them to her….She published one or two things in her *Floating Bear* journal, and then she put together my first book" (180).

*Huncke's Journal* was Poets Press's second release and its only volume of prose, likely because of the labor-intensive process of preparing it for publication. In *Recollections*, di Prima described the slow, painstaking method of creating the book's justified right-hand margin:

> The way to do that with an "executive" typewriter was to count the hairline spaces that were needed to even out the margin of a particular line, … writing the numbers onto your typewritten copy. Then you retyped the whole page, adding the tiny spaces with the space bar as you went along. Each line was different, of course—it was a nerve-wracking process. (412)

Until the 1965 publication of *Journal* at age 50, Huncke had remained unpublished. His presence on the scene, influence on Beat writers, and honesty and skill in writing about taboo topics and documenting life on the margins all make *Huncke's Journal* a noteworthy publication. Scholar Rob Johnson called it "one of the more important memoirs by a male writer from the Beat Generation," stating that the "first edition of 1,000 copies sold quickly" (145). In a letter to Huncke, Ginsberg expressed his admiration of the work, noting, "Your own book is the most interesting new truthful word-text I've read in recent years-era" (Morgan 314).

Another important Poets Press book is Audre Lorde's *The First Cities*, the debut collection of the feminist writer and civil rights activist, who had attended Hunter High School with di Prima. According to Lorde, the 1968 volume was the result of di Prima's encouragement:

> she said, "You know, it's time you had a book." And I said, "Well, who's going to print it?" I was going to put these poems away, because I had found I was revising too much instead of writing new poems...Diane said, "You have to print these"...and the Poets Press published *The First Cities*. (Lorde and Rich 720)

In her introduction for the book, di Prima portrayed Lorde not only as an old friend, but also, like herself, a lifelong poet: "I have known Audre Lorde since we were 15, when we read our poems to each other in Home Room" (Welch). The publication was a major turning point in Lorde's career. The book garnered invitations for readings and positive reviews, notably including one by poet and publisher Dudley Randall, whose influential Broadside Press later released two of Lorde's collections (De Veaux 99).[4] In his review, Randall declared *The First Cities* "a quiet, introspective book" with poems that "attract you by their fresh phrasing, which draws you to return to them and discover new evocations" (13-14). Randall also observed that Lorde "does not wave a black flag, but her blackness is there, implicit" (13). It would not be until later collections that Lorde would hone the radical voice of dissent for which she is known today, using her poetry to explore lesbianism, feminism, racism, and social injustice. Lorde had worked as a librarian until 1968, when she accepted the position of poet-in-residence at Tougaloo College in Mississippi (Lorde and Rich 720). The publication of *The First Cities*, combined with the residency, launched her career as a poet. After Tougaloo, she was offered a teaching position in the City College of New York's SEEK Program subsequent to the director of the writing program being given a copy of *The First Cities* (De Veaux 101-02).[5] It was only a few years later, in 1974, that a writer in *Margins* declared Lorde's first book "now a collector's item" (Welburn 41).

There is a casualness to both of these stories that should not obscure di Prima's perceptiveness, willingness to take risks, and commitment to emerging writers. Di Prima herself put it most succinctly in a letter to Marlowe, in which she reflected on her strengths and the press's future: "I am a good hustler" (Diane di Prima Papers, 1934-1992, Box 4, Folder 10, March 29, 1968). With both Huncke and Lorde, her advocacy and resolve were integral to bringing works to light that otherwise may not have been published.

Lastly, *War Poems*, edited by di Prima and published in 1968, is an important document of 1960s counterculture poetry and political engagement. One of the earliest anthologies to protest the Vietnam War, the collection comprised works by 11 poets, making it considerably longer than most of the other books the press produced. *War Poems* was a substantial undertaking, and di Prima was proud of the book and what it meant for the future of the press. In a March 29, 1968, letter she told Marlowe, "I have started setting it—80 pages or so—I'll take an ad in all the peace journals and the *Voice* and perhaps some college papers…I feel the press is about to get off the ground and take off" (Diane di Prima Papers, 1934-1992, Box 4, Folder 10). She published the book in the midst of successful mainstream anthologies such as Walter Lowenfels's *Where Is Vietnam? American Poets Respond* (1967). With 87 contributors, Lowenfels's anthology had a broad scope, featuring Ginsberg and Ferlinghetti alongside Robert Lowell and James Dickey. Though *Where Is Vietnam?* positioned itself against the Vietnam War, Lowenfels made clear in his introduction that the collection was not antiwar: "few of our contributors are pacifists; many are veterans, including one who has served in Vietnam. It is this particular war that has aroused them" (x). By comparison, *War Poems* was firmly entrenched in the culture and politics of the underground, and featured some of its most significant poets, including Gary Snyder, Joel Oppenheimer, Gregory Corso, Robert Creeley, Philip Whalen, Robert Duncan, and LeRoi Jones. The collection was not simply protesting U.S. involvement in Vietnam but was a condemnation of America and its history and perpetuation of violence, oppression, and racism. The anthology features some particularly important protest poems, including Michael McClure's "Poisoned Wheat," which denounces the U.S. wartime tactic of poisoning wheat fields in Cambodia, and the famous anti-war lament "Wichita Vortex Sutra" by Allen Ginsberg, who worked with di Prima to select poems for the anthology. *War Poems* also contains one of di Prima's best-known poems, "Rant, from a Cool Place," which provides numerous examples of the U.S. government's corruption and in the process reveals the poet's skepticism and outrage about the state of the country.

In addition to publishing both new and established writers, Poets Press also was a venue for di Prima to promote her own writing. In an interview for his 2001 book *San Francisco Beat*, David Meltzer asked di Prima what a poet could do to reach an audience. Her answer was remarkably consistent with her attitude 50 years before:

## DIANE DI PRIMA'S POETS PRESS

"it's important to self-publish and make your work available" (Meltzer 21). Since she had been warned years before that "nobody in the world would publish [*This Kind of Bird Flies Backward* ]," the importance of having unmediated access to a press and the ability to print her own work liberated di Prima (Moffeit 97). During the press's existence, she published three volumes of her own poetry: *Earthsong: Poems, 1957-1959* (1968), *Hotel Albert* (1968), *L.A. Odyssey* (1969); a volume of translations, *Seven Love Poems from the Middle Latin* (1965); a reprint of *The New Handbook of Heaven* (first published by Auerhahn Press in 1963); and included her work in *War Poems* (1968).[6]

Di Prima had been drawn to publishing for its democratizing and radical potential, as indicated in part by her tendency to refer to herself as a printer rather than publisher. In a journal entry dated May 30, 1965—the outset of Poets Press—she declared, "I shall type and write and print—Printing books shall eventually be my trade" (Diane di Prima Papers, 1934-1992, Box 7, Folder 5). Reflecting on how she came to establish the press, di Prima later said, "the anarchist dream of being a printer had long been with me" (*Recollections* 410). She often cited her grandfather, the anarchist Domenico Mallozzi to whom *Revolutionary Letters* was dedicated, as a major influence. In a 2010 interview, she observed, "[d]oing a press is a very big pleasure, not only for the people [whose work] you're getting out, but it also creates a community—and that in itself is very important" (Jackson). Like other small press publishers of the era, she recognized publishing as a way to engage with and support a group of like-minded writers and artists.

This perspective inevitably informed Poets Press's aesthetic. Typically, the books were less than 40 pages and lacked page numbers and a table of contents, aspects that made them easier and cheaper to produce.[7] Nearly all had saddle-stitched binding, some done with the very stapler di Prima had used to assemble her own earliest books (*Recollections* 412). The printer's device—a woodcut of a basilisk from Horapollo's *Hieroglyphica* (1597), a nod to di Prima's interests in alchemy and the classics—appeared on the back of many of the softcover editions.

As might be expected of a new small press, some of the books had imperfections in design or execution. For example, the font in Frank O'Hara's *Odes* is uncomfortably small and the juxtaposition of images and text in Margaret Danner's *Iron Lace* is awkward. Yet the books were not devoid of artistry, and several include artwork, some by important artists of the era. Abstract expressionist Michael Goldberg created the cover for Frank O'Hara's *Odes*, visionary arts co-founder and *San Francisco Oracle* art director Michael Bowen designed Timothy Leary's *Psychedelic Prayers*, and California collagist and close friend of di Prima George Herms provided cover art for her works *Earthsong: Poems 1957-1959* and *L.A. Odyssey*. Several editions by new writers included introductions by established poets, a significant coup for any young poet that was possible because of di Prima's extensive network. Ginsberg introduced Herbert Huncke, LeRoi Jones introduced David Henderson, John Wieners introduced Clive Matson, and Robert Creeley introduced Alan Marlowe.[8] A 1966 ad for the press in issue 32 of *The Floating Bear* noted that it planned to release a new title every month (di Prima and Baraka 414a). This was an ambitious goal for a fledging publisher, and the closest di Prima would come to realizing this aim would be to publish 10 titles in 1968.

Di Prima began the press with the intention to publish books in two editions. An undated press release noted that one would be "a low-priced paperback edition of two thousand copies, the other, a limited hardbound signed edition of twenty-five copies, specially designed for college libraries and collectors" (Ted Wilentz Collection, Box 1, Folder 2). Print runs for the books ranged widely, with the smallest (non-limited editions) consisting of 150 first edition copies and the largest 2,500. By 1968, this plan had given way to publishing inexpensive, softcover editions of books by new writers and holograph limited editions of well-known writers, as the latter were more economically viable than the softcovers and easier to produce than the hardcover limited editions. In a February 7, 1968, letter aimed at persuading Ferlinghetti to become a dealer of these limited editions, Marlowe explained: "We make 150 copies, signed by the author....We are issuing one a month. Last month Corso. Next month Creeley. Hope to get a piece of the personality of the Poet into each book. The limiteds are supporting us and the press" (City Lights Records, Box 8, Folder 20).[9] Between 1967 and 1969, Poets Press published seven of these holograph limited editions: Allen Ginsberg's *Scrap Leaves: Hasty scribbles* (see figs. 2 and 3), Michael McClure's *Little Odes Jan-March 1961*, di Prima's *L.A. Odyssey* and *Hotel Albert*, John Ashbery's *Three Madrigals*, Robert Creeley's *5 Numbers*, and Robert Duncan's *Play Time Pseudo Stein*. Multiple volumes in the series featured earlier works by major poets. For example, Ashbery's *Three Madrigals* was comprised of work he had written in 1958, and the cover of Robert Duncan's book notes that the writing within is from "the laboratory records notebook of 1953." More pointedly, the subtitles of Ginsberg and Corso's volumes read like disclaimers. Ginsberg's book states on the cover that the poems included within are "hasty scribbles from Journals hither too puzzling for me to publish," and Corso's notes that the works were "collected at random from 2 suitcases filled with poems—the gathering of 5 years." These softbound volumes, typically 12 pages long, were facsimiles in the poets' hand. One advantage for di Prima was that this format meant there was no need to worry about typesetting or access to equipment, a concern because she made several moves during the years she maintained the press. For readers, the holograph editions provided an intimate and informal perspective, and Ginsberg's, di Prima's, and Duncan's volumes included not only text, but also artwork or doodles by the writers.

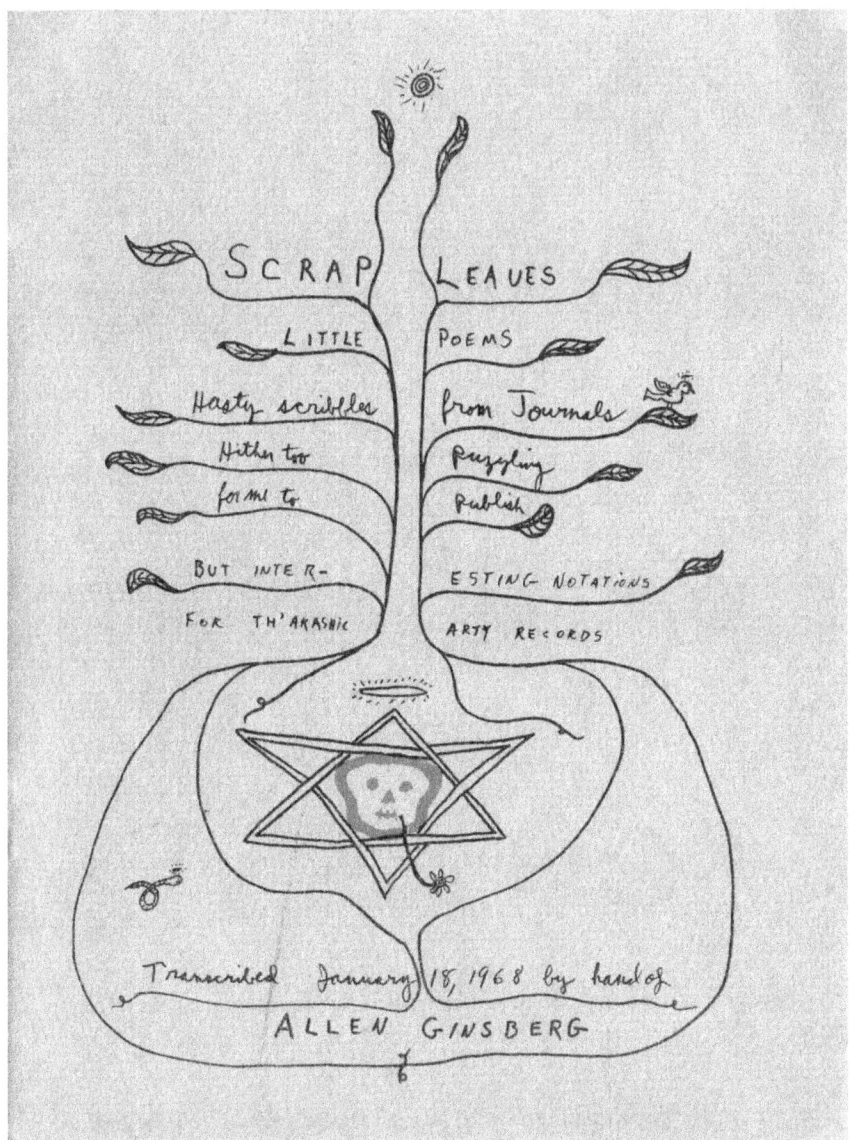

*Fig. 2. Front cover of* Scrap Leaves *by Allen Ginsberg, Rare Books and Manuscripts Library, The Ohio State University.*

*Fig. 3. Back cover of* Scrap Leaves *by Allen Ginsberg, Rare Books and Manuscripts Library, The Ohio State University.*

# DIANE DI PRIMA'S POETS PRESS

According to di Prima, Poets Press books did not have trouble finding an audience. In *Recollections*, she remembered:

> I had begun to build up a list of libraries and bookstores which had standing orders for everything I printed....At the height of the Press...I was mailing out six hundred copies as soon as a book was ready, and I had to up the first printing of each book from one to two thousand copies, to have enough for the stores. (417)

Notices about the books appeared in little magazines and underground newspapers such as *LA Free Press, Olé, Margins, Quixote, The Berkeley Barb,* and *The Paper*, often receiving positive reviews. The press also was recognized by the then-newly established National Foundation of the Arts and Humanities (later the National Endowment for the Arts), which awarded di Prima three grants during its five-year run. In an August 2, 1967, letter to di Prima, the foundation recognized Poets Press for championing "authors of significant works who have difficulty in being published through the usual commercial channels," acknowledging its efforts "in advancing the cause of the unknown, obscure or difficult writer, and in the publication of books visually and typographically distinctive, thereby helping to advance the cause of the best in American art" (Ted Wilentz Collection, Box 1, Folder 2).

Readers acquired Poets Press books in a variety of ways. One method was to purchase directly from di Prima. In 1966, a full-page advertisement in *The Floating Bear* 32 included a list of current and forthcoming titles with an order form. The books also were available from several of the important bookstores of the era, some of which also acted as regional distributors for the press. In a letter negotiating the terms of such an arrangement, Marlowe told Ferlinghetti, "We would be pleased to have you act as a distributor in your area. 50% OK" (City Lights Records, Box 8, Folder 20, 23 September 1965). Other bookstores that carried Poets Press included the Phoenix Book Shop (where di Prima had worked), Eighth Street Bookshop in New York City, the Tenth Muse Bookshop in San Francisco, the Student Book Shop next to the University of Buffalo, and Indica Bookshop in London. As these shops "provided a meeting place for the literary community as well as an outlet for selling new writing," they played a crucial role in supporting and publicizing small presses such as di Prima's and writers such as the ones she published (Birmingham, "Floating Bear").

Despite the successes, Poets Press also experienced publishing setbacks and financial problems. Evidence of these troubles is apparent in the discrepancies between the press's catalog and ads. For example, an advertisement in issue 32 of *The Floating Bear* noted several forthcoming volumes, including a collection of short stories called *A Quiet Sunday at Home* by Joel Oppenheimer, *The Calculus of Variation* by di Prima, *Braincandy* by Philip Whalen, and poetry collections by Harold Carrington and Arnold Weinstein, none of which Poets Press released. Issue 35 still listed the di Prima, Weinstein, and Whalen titles as upcoming releases, adding Robin Blaser's *The Faerie Queene,* which also was not published by the press. Of all of these titles, Whalen's *Braincandy* is perhaps the most notorious. Di Prima later said of this work, "It was a thick book and took a dreadfully long time to set. It had to go to Japan and back to be proof-read by Phil Whalen, and by the time it came back, Phil had signed a contract with Harcourt, Brace and World to do *On Bear's Head*, a great big book…a large chunk of which is *Braincandy*" (di Prima and Baraka 571). In an interview years later, di Prima recalled, "it was just about ready to go to press when Philip found a publisher who could give him money and he needed money" (Hadbawnik). Although di Prima did not explicitly say so, it is evident that Whalen's decision to profit from signing with a major publisher was a financial loss for her.[10]

Another example is Robert Duncan's *Play Time Pseudo Stein,* which was intended to be part of the limited edition holograph series. Only 35 copies were printed for subscribers and an unspecified number of lettered "author's copies" were produced. Printing of the work was cut short due to a disagreement between di Prima and Duncan about the number of author copies he would receive. He had expected "twenty-six lettered copies, decorated by him, as the 'author's edition,' which—because of her prior arrangement with Robert Wilson of the Phoenix Book Shop—di Prima could not give him (the production of the holograph series was to be financed through the sale of the manuscript to Wilson and the strict limitation of the edition)" (Quartermain 790). Duncan subsequently published a second edition with bookseller Julia Newman's Tenth Muse. In it, he included "A Little History of This Edition," explaining the story behind the aborted first edition. Duncan's anger at di Prima, whom he saw as exploiting her connections for financial gain, is apparent: "At the beginning of this year, 1969, Diane di Prima and Alan Marlowe asked me for a book for their Poet's Press series. 'We need bread Creeley and Alan [sic] gave us books and we want you to give us one'…Time had come and my payment due for the existence of that remarkable Lady Pirate."[11]

As Duncan's preface and the loss of *Braincandy* suggest, money was a perpetual problem in di Prima's personal and professional life, her letters and journal entries from this period foregrounding lack of money as one of the most consistent themes. In an undated (but likely 1967) letter to Herms, she said, "we are lootless," and a notebook entry dated "December 10, Saturday" (possibly 1969) recorded that she was "looking for things to sell, because no money at all in sight" (George Herms Papers, Box 5, Folder 9; Diane di Prima Papers, 1955-2008, Folder 566). Most notably, di Prima wrote *Memoirs of a Beatnik* during this period because of an urgent need for money (192). One factor was that as an underground poet who worked odd jobs, di Prima had a limited and unpredictable income. Another issue was Marlowe's behavior. In *Recollections*, di Prima cited his extravagant spending as the source of their financial troubles and described selling personal papers and prized books from her collection for quick cash (408, 348). Compounding these issues was di Prima's sizeable household, which comprised her husband and children as well as an "extended family" (*Recollections* 273). In a February 19, 1968, letter to Ferlinghetti, Marlowe stressed the profitability of the limited editions the press was producing, noting, "In New York this counts. We are now supporting six adults and five children" (City Lights Records, Box 8, Folder 20). Bookshop owner and friend Bob Wilson complicated Duncan's view of di Prima as a "Lady Pirate," recalling in his memoir that she was the primary provider for her family as well as a fluctuating number of musicians, artists, and writers who lived with them: "virtually none of them had jobs or could in any way contribute money to the communal establishment, but somehow Diane always managed to supply food and shelter for anyone who came knocking at her door" (101).

During the period that di Prima ran Poets Press, she and her family moved multiple times, which also affected her finances and ability to publish. According to Brenda Knight:

> The last half of the sixties saw Diane very much on the move—living at an upstate New York ashram; staying at Timothy Leary's experimental, psychedelic community at Millbrook; and traveling on an epic 20,000-mile journey, kids in tow, across America in a Volkswagen bus, reading poetry at dance halls, bars, storefronts, colleges, and galleries. She finally settled in San Francisco. (126)

A photograph album Marlowe kept from 1965-1967 documents their extensive cross-country road trip—including stays in Massachusetts, Michigan, Colorado, British Columbia, California, and New Mexico, among other locales—and makes apparent why in a November 1967 Poets Press notice di Prima stated, "Poets Press is back in business after a year's lull" (Diane di Prima Papers, 1955-2008, PA-12002/1; di Prima and Baraka 477). (The press produced only three titles in 1967: David Henderson's *Felix in the Silent Forest*, Jay Wright's *Death as History*, and the limited edition *10 Times a Poem* by Gregory Corso.) Furthermore, the publisher location of Poets Press volumes (when this information is included) shows evidence of di Prima's multiple moves. During its existence, Poets Press was located in New York City (at multiple addresses); Kerhonkson, New York; Millbrook, New York; and San Francisco.[12]

In a letter to a friend dated September 7, 1969, di Prima announced that she was "getting rid of Poets Press, forever this time, I think" (Diane di Prima Papers, 1948-1971, Box 1). The following week, di Prima wrote to Marlowe about divesting her remaining stock, expressing relief about ending a project that had become a burden:

> I brought all the remaining Poets Press books to Julia Newman, who will sell them on consignment—very slowly, no doubt, that's the way of it here, but small monies will come in handy in the months ahead. It was like I had lost hundreds of pounds—I was walking off the ground after I got rid of the books. (Diane di Prima Papers, 1955-2008, Folder 328, 13 September 1969)

By the end of the 1960s, di Prima had several reasons for wanting to shut down the press. In 1969 di Prima and Marlowe divorced. Their relationship had been turbulent from the outset, and Marlowe's homosexuality, the couple's unstable finances, and frequent arguments contributed to their breakup. Di Prima also had decided to relocate to Northern California, where printing equipment and supplies were harder to come by and more expensive than in New York (Gibson 90). Perhaps most importantly, she saw her move to the West Coast as a way to start a new chapter of her life and to explore different opportunities and interests (*The Poetry Deal* 2).

Given di Prima's contributions, it may be surprising that she and Poets Press have not garnered greater recognition. Part of the reason rests with her position as a woman writer associated with the Beat Generation. Amy Friedman has observed that "for decades women writers associated with the Beat Generation have been an ignored presence, only glancingly acknowledged as the critical fascination with the Beats continues to grow" (230). In "Mapping Women Writers of the Beat Generation," Ronna C. Johnson demonstrates that the neglect of their male contemporaries within the scene, as well as that of critics, academics, and media outlets of the era, had a lasting impact on scholarship about and the legacy of the women writers: "to study women Beat writers has meant to track dispersed, uncollected, and sometimes unpublished sources, a body of work that in this disarray does not readily present itself as a coherent field of writing" (4). Di Prima herself has cited gender as a reason, and also the particular kind of woman she was: neither sad nor quiet, and decidedly unapologetic for her transgressions (Waldman 29). Additionally, aspects of di Prima's press have contributed to its neglect. One factor is the objects it produced. Russo has contended that small-run chapbooks such as the ones Poets Press published have been "mere ephemera in the eyes of the custodians of literary history, easily effaced"

(246). Furthermore, archival absences and misinformation have posed challenges for recovering the press's history.

Although Poets Press was short-lived and plagued with financial troubles, its output and di Prima's accomplishments are significant, and its history helps reveal a more complete picture of small press publishing of the period. An examination of the press's catalog reveals remarkable variety, a vital cross section of underground literary movements and counterculture concerns, and multiple first collections by important poets. Some of Poets Press's publications remain in print today, a testament to the longevity of the writing and di Prima's selections. For example, Clive Matson's *Mainline to the Heart* and Timothy Leary's *Psychedelic Prayers* are still available in their entirety, and poems that appeared in Poets Press editions are now available in the collected or selected poems of Audre Lorde, Allen Ginsberg, and di Prima, just to name a few. Poets Press provides a window into the life of Diane di Prima, a major underground poet during a period of experimentation and advocacy, when she created an influential outlet for her writing and that of other emerging poets.

## Notes

[1] Di Prima and Marlowe were married from 1962-1969 (di Prima, *Pieces of a Song* 198-99).
[2] Russo has noted that di Prima, Margaret Randall, Rosemarie Waldrop, Anne Waldman, and Bernadette Mayer all edited with a husband or lover (246).
[3] The major repositories of di Prima's papers include Syracuse University, the University of North Carolina, the University of Connecticut, and the University of Louisville.
[4] Randall's review appeared in *Negro Digest*, a publication that regularly reviewed Poets Press releases by African American poets.
[5] "Search for Education, Elevation, and Knowledge" (SEEK) Program: A pre-baccalaureate program established in 1965 and still in existence today.
[6] Jed Birmingham observed, "In 1963, Auerhahn printed di Prima's *The New Handbook of Heaven*. Haselwood got burned on the printing costs, and then further burned when di Prima bootlegged the book on her own Poets Press imprint" ("Auerhan Press Archive").
[7] Two exceptions are *Huncke's Journal* and *War Poems*, both of which included a table of contents and page numbers.
[8] Ginsberg's introduction appeared in the second edition.
[9] Gregory Corso's *10 Times a Poem* was published in 1967, and Robert Creeley's *Mazatlan: Sea* was published in 1969.
[10] Lew Welch's 1969 review of *On Bear's Head* makes clear both the advantage and drawback of Whalen's decision to publish with Harcourt, Brace and World rather than Poets Press. Welch said, "Until now, the poetry of Philip Whalen could be found only in Little Magazines or in editions so small they quickly sold out. *On Bear's Head* is a one-volume collection of nearly all his work, more than 20 years of it. One of this century's most brilliant poets is at last accessible to all." However, he also lamented the cost of the volume, which, at $17.50, was "outrageous."

[11] A reference to two of the holograph volumes from Poets Press in 1968: Allen Ginsberg's *Scrap Leaves: Tasty scribbles* and Robert Creeley's *5 Numbers*.
[12] Di Prima's essay "The Holidays at Millbrook–1966" in Ann Charters's *Portable Sixties Reader* discusses the experience of living at Leary's estate.

## Works Cited

Anderson, Stephanie. "An Interview with Hettie Jones." *Chicago Review*, vol. 59, no. 1/2, 2014, pp. 79-90.
Baraka, Amiri. *The Autobiography of LeRoi Jones*. Freundlich Books, 1984.
Bergé, Carol. "Voyeu Rama." Review of *The Beautiful Days* by A.B. Spellman. *The East Village Other*, July 15-Aug. 1, 1966, p. 12.
Birmingham, Jed. "Auerhahn Press Archive." *Reality Studio*, 29 Jan. 2017, realitystudio.org/ bibliographic-bunker/auerhahn-press-archive.
——. "Floating Bear." *Reality Studio*, 3 Oct. 2006, realitystudio.org/bibliographic-bunker/floating-bear.
Charters, Ann, editor. *The Portable Beat Reader*. Penguin Books, 1992.
City Lights Books Records, 1953-1970. Bancroft Library, University of California, Berkeley, Berkeley, CA.
Clay, Steven, and Rodney Phillips. *A Secret Location on the Lower East Side: Adventures in Writing, 1960-1980: A Sourcebook of Information*. New York Public Library, 1998.
De Veaux, Alexis. *Warrior Poet: A Biography of Audre Lorde*. W.W. Norton, 2004.
di Prima, Diane. *Memoirs of a Beatnik*. Penguin Books, 1998.
——. *Pieces of a Song*. City Lights, 1990.
——. *The Poetry Deal*. City Lights, 2014.
——. *Recollections of My Life As a Woman: The New York Years*. Viking, 2001.
——. *This Kind of Bird Flies Backward*. Totem Press, 1958.
——, editor. *War Poems*. Poets Press, 1968.
Diane di Prima Papers, 1934-1992. Ekstrom Library, University of Louisville, Louisville, KY.
Diane di Prima Papers, 1948-1971. Special Collections Research Center and University Archives, Syracuse University, Syracuse, NY.
Diane di Prima Papers, 1955-2008. Louis Round Wilson Special Collections Library, University of North Carolina, Chapel Hill, NC.
di Prima, Diane, and Imamu Amiri Baraka. *The Floating Bear: A Newsletter, numbers 1-37, 1961-1969*. Laurence McGilvery, 1973.
Duncan, Robert. *Play Time Pseudo Stein*. Tenth Muse, 1969.
Ellis, Jackson. "Interview: Diane di Prima." *Verbicide*, 29 July 2010, www.verbicidemagazine. com/2010/07/29/interview-diane-di-prima.

Friedman, Amy L. "Being Here As Hard As I Could: The Beat Generation Women Writers." *Discourse*, vol. 20, no. 1/2, 1998, pp. 229-44.

Gibson, Sharon Slate. "With the Grace and Gentleness of the Warrior: Diane di Prima and the Literary Underground." Unpublished diss. No date but after 1989.

Grace, Nancy M., and Ronna C. Johnson. *Breaking the Rule of Cool: Interviewing and Reading Women Beat Writers.* UP of Mississippi, 2004.

Hadbawnik, David. "Diane di Prima, in Conversation." *Jacket Magazine,* no. 18, Aug. 2002, jacketmagazine.com/18/diprima-iv.html.

George Herms Papers, 1890-2009. The Getty Research Institute, Los Angeles, CA.

Hoagland, Everett. "Samuel W. Allen (Paul Vesey), 1917-2015." *James Madison University News*, 7 Jul. 2015, www.jmu.edu/news/furiousflower/2015/07/07-sam-allen.shtml.

Huncke, Herbert. *Guilty of Everything: The Autobiography of Herbert Huncke.* Paragon House, 1990.

———. *Huncke's Journal.* Poets Press, 1965.

———. "Song of Self." *Huncke Tea Company*, huncketeacompany.com/song-of-self.

Johnson, Rob. "*Huncke's Journal.*" *The Encyclopedia of Beat Literature*, edited by Kurt Hemmer, Infobase Publishing, 2010, pp. 145-47.

Johnson, Ronna C. "Mapping Women Writers of the Beat Generation." *Breaking the Rule of Cool: Interviewing and Reading Women Beat Writers*, by Nancy M. Grace and Johnson, UP of Mississippi, 2004, pp. 3-41.

Knight, Brenda. *Women of the Beat Generation: The Writers, Artists, and Muses at the Heart of a Revolution.* Conari Press, 1996.

Lorde, Audre. *The First Cities.* Poets Press, 1968.

Lorde, Audre, and Adrienne Rich. "An Interview with Audre Lorde." *Signs*, vol. 6, no. 4, Summer 1981, pp. 713-36.

Lowenfels, Walter. *Where Is Vietnam? American Poets Respond.* Anchor Books, Doubleday & Co., 1967.

Meltzer, David. *San Francisco Beat: Talking With the Poets.* City Lights, 2001.

Moffeit, Tony. "Pieces of a Song: Diane di Prima." *Breaking the Rule of Cool: Interviewing and Reading Beat Women Writers*, by Nancy M. Grace and Ronna C. Johnson, UP of Mississippi, 2004, pp. 83-106.

Moore, Charles. Review of *The Beautiful Days* by A.B. Spellman. *Work*, no. 2, Fall 1965, pp. 103-04.

Morgan, Bill, editor. *The Letters of Allen Ginsberg.* Da Capo Press, 2008.

Niski, Marcus. "The Writer's Notebooks of Herbert Huncke." *Reality Studio,* 26 Mar. 2012, realitystudio.org/criticism/the-writers-notebooks-of-herbert-huncke.

Quartermain, Peter. *Robert Duncan: The Collected Early Poems and Plays*. U of California P, 2012.

Randall, Dudley. Review of *The First Cities* by Audre Lorde. *Negro Digest*, vol. 17, nos. 11-12, Sept./Oct. 1968, pp. 13-14.

Russo, Linda. "The 'F' Word in the Age of Mechanical Reproduction: An Account of Women-Edited Small Presses and Journals." *Talisman, A Journal of Contemporary Poetry and Poetics,* nos. 23-26, 2002, pp. 243-84.

"SEEK Program." *The City College of New York*, www.ccny.cuny.edu/seek.

Sinclair, John. "Fire Music." Review of *The Beautiful Days* by A.B. Spellman. *Paper*, no. 13, Feb. 1967, p.13.

Waldman, Anne. "An Interview with Diane di Prima." *The Beat Road*, edited by Arthur and Kit Knight, California, PA, 1984, pp. 27–33.

Welburn, Ron. "Broadside & Otherwise." *Margins*, no. 13, Aug.-Sept. 1974, pp. 40-41.

Welch, Lew. "Whalen's Poetry Swings Like Jazz." Review of *On Bear's Head* by Philip Whalen. *San Francisco Chronicle.* 22 June 1969. *Jacket Magazine,* no. 11, Apr. 2000. http://jacketmagazine.com/11/whalen-rev-by-welch.html.

Ted Wilentz, Diane di Prima, and Barbara Guest Correspondence Collection. Special Collections, Western Michigan University, Kalamazoo, MI.

Wilson, Robert A. *Seeing Shelley Plain*. Oak Knoll Press, 2001.

# Joanne Kyger's Travel Chapbooks: A Poetics of Motion
## Mary Paniccia Carden

> Maybe if I change the point / of departure.
> —Joanne Kyger, *Desecheo Notebook* (9/113)[1]

> To see is always to see from somewhere, is it not?
> —Maurice Merleau-Ponty, *Phenomenology of Perception* (69)

Joanne Kyger's long and productive career as a poet was distinguished by her periodic publication of chapbooks associated with journeys she undertook from the early 1970s through the late 1990s. *Desecheo Notebook* (1971), *Trip Out and Fall Back* (1974), *Mexico Blondé* (1981), *Phenomenological* (1989), and *Pátzcuaro* (1999) do not simply record Kyger's travels, nor do they offer purely imaginative representations of life on the road. Instead, they comprise an alternative genre that merges poetry, travelogue, and dream diary, seamlessly combining historical and mythic themes with memory and sensory impression, all interspersed with spiritual and philosophical inquiry. Kyger's chapbooks constitute new textual places, and "a new place," as travel scholar Frances Bartkowski suggests, "is always an opportunity for sanctioned cross-thinking," and "inter-speaking,…out of which something may emerge that transforms, transvalues, translates" (xxv-xxvi). In their rich, layered, free-associative structure, Kyger's chapbooks reproduce the felt experience of travel itself in ways that express her belief that "the 'psyche' is not / a personal but a world existence" (*Desecheo* 10/114).[2]

This fusion of text, travel, and "psyche" marks a significant development in both the shape and the focus of Kyger's life-writing, which *Journal of Beat Studies* readers may have encountered in her better-known *Japan and India Journals*. In these detailed and far-ranging notebooks, composed between 1960 and 1964, Kyger recorded her daily experiences and experimented with poetic form and content. Commentators often describe *The Japan and India Journals*—published in 1981 and reissued in 2000 as *Strange Big Moon*—as a combination diary/writer's workbook. The text chronicles Kyger's years-long stay in Asia, her marriage to Gary Snyder, her struggle to master Zen meditation techniques, and her aspirations as a budding poet. In contrast, the travel chapbooks are products of single, shorter trips. But even though they are more bounded in terms of duration, Kyger's shorter travel texts are more open in other ways—unstructured, fluid, and mobile.

An essentially unclassifiable subgenre of the life-writing that takes place in journals, Kyger's travel chapbooks follow the movement of her mind in conjunction with her movement through different geographical and cultural locales. While *The*

*Japan and India Journals* does examine the discontinuities and pleasures of life as a visitor in a strange land, they in large part concern Kyger's attempts to establish stability, to build at-homeness in her new household in Japan and in her relationship with the poet Gary Snyder. The chapbooks, on the other hand, focus intently and intensely on the sensations and stimuli of travel; they explore away-ness for its own sake and as its own purpose, rather than as a function of a larger project such as maintaining a marriage or studying Zen Buddhism. A key distinction between Kyger's *Journals* and her travel chapbooks, then, comes down to the difference between "seeing" from a relatively stable "somewhere" and seeing from multiple, shifting, and uncertain somewheres.

In Kyger's travel chapbooks, ongoing movement shapes modes of self-representation. Although her *Japan and India Journals* demonstrates a genre-bending aesthetic, the journals tend to maintain clearer lines between poems, dreams, and expository diary entries than do the travel chapbooks.[3] I will suggest that the chapbooks' heightened disregard of generic, disciplinary, and existential boundaries proposes an ethics and aesthetics of selves in motion, even selves *as* motion. During her years as a poet/traveler, Kyger developed the travel chapbook into a personal genre of expression aimed at forming new "points of departure" for conceptualizing human being in the world; *Desecheo Notebook*, *Trip Out and Fall Back*, *Mexico Blondé*, *Phenomenological*, and *Pátzcuaro* deploy travel as a metaphor for human consciousness. Rather than a condition the self finds itself in, travel seems analogous with the self.

As in the experience of travel, the chapbooks offer occasion for, even necessitate, "translations" and "transvaluations" of internal and external worlds. Perceptions flash past in shifting, overlapping moments of both discovery and dislocation, offering multi-faceted geographic, cultural, and sensory stimuli, invoking memory and reverie, and compelling self-examination. The travel chapbooks process the new through the already-known and probe the limits of individual consciousness. In travel, Kyger seeks and achieves varying degrees of integration with "world existence," undergoes experiences of de- and re-familiarization, and contemplates questions about how and why identity forms and reforms in different spaces and places, in different relations and proximities to others.

With its simultaneously inward- and outward-reaching ethos, Kyger's travel aesthetic reflects a sensibility shared by many of her Beat compatriots, who also shared her affinity for Mexico. For Beat writers, "movement and pursuit of freedom" are often "inextricably linked conceptually, often in an antithetical relationship to stasis, boredom, oppression, and authoritarianism" (Hibbard 15). Writers including Jack Kerouac, Gary Snyder, Philip Whalen, and Allen Ginsberg sought liberation, openness, and spiritual renewal in movement, pursuing unexpected truths in unexpected places. Travel spurred their evolution as writers, and their travel narratives, like Kyger's, embrace the uncertainties and ambiguities of perceiving self and world through the new lenses of new locales. For Kyger and many other Beat-associated writers, regenerating clarity of vision was often a function of an "experience of reality characterized by nonlinear time and by the intersection of the mythical with the modern" (Belgrad 36). Kyger's impulse to reconnect aspects of life commonly perceived as opposite and opposed—especially inner and outer, familiar and strange, mundane and transcendent—resonates with the work of Beat writers including Ginsberg and Kerouac, who reject dualistic binaries in favor of "a sense of communion with others or with the cosmos" (Belgrad 38).[4]

Similarities aside, however, Kyger resisted being designated a Beat poet, in large part due to her feeling that "Beat Generation" writers constituted a "brotherhood" in which she was not fully welcome ("Places" 140). Her poetry and journal writing evince a sense of simultaneous community with and alienation from her well-known male colleagues, writers who enjoyed the "rock-starish" prestige and authority afforded literary "gurus" (Shaw 77, 80).[5] In her earlier travel chapbooks especially, Kyger ties the searching uncertainties of travel to her own uncertainty about her identity as a poet. It was not "until I was about thirty," she said, that "poetry became an identity I was within. Before that, it was my own longings for it" (qtd. in Berkson 327). When Kyger joined the San Francisco literary scene in 1957, a great many of her friends and fellow writers were men, most of them with emphatic opinions about worthwhile poetic endeavor. She pursued her craft within the poetry circle of Robert Duncan and Jack Spicer, and formed relationships with artists including Snyder, Whalen, John Wieners, and Lew Welch. Her *Japan and India Journals* describes the uneven differentials of gender, artistry, and authority she experienced as a bohemian woman abruptly thrust into a traditional role as a "housewife" (xii). Chafing at her secondary position as Snyder's wife and frustrated by her difficulty carving out the time and space needed to nurture her poetic development, she briefly wished she "had never known writing"—"then I'd be more content with what I am doing now instead of wishing I was proving myself by writing" (36).

Kyger also struggled with male-focused definitions of poets and poetry. Her *Journals* record her response to "old crabby daddy" Ezra Pound's pronouncement that in order to be "*great*" a poet must "write an epic...have the command of a world / universal view" (225). In his formulation, Kyger observes, "a woman" cannot be "great" because "her craft seems to deal with parts, particulars" (226). Nevertheless, she composed most of the poems in her first book, *The Tapestry and the Web* (1965), during her time in Japan, material that grippingly and tangibly incorporates into a loosely woven representation of Homer's Penelope the "parts" and "particulars" of her life as a woman, an artist, and a sojourner in an unfamiliar land.[6]

In her review of Kyger's second book *Places to Go* (1970), Alicia Ostriker calls Kyger "a genius, though a weird one," and remarks that "handling her poetry is like handling a porcupine traveling at the speed of light" (qtd. in Knight 198). Kyger's writing is infused with movement and spontaneity—she intended her "pages" to "look alive" and "hold…energies" ("Energy" par. 49, 47).[7] Her aesthetic brings "stray and often extraneous seeming bits of image and fact...to bear upon a loosely scattered area which is the poem"; she viewed "the linear aspect of the poem" as "merely a suggested voice line to take you from the beginning to the end, but suggesting no such consecutiveness in thought. The area of the poem is able to contain all elements" (qtd. in Opstedal ch. 10). These qualities (and others discussed below) characterize most of Kyger's poetry; they appear in intensified and amplified forms in the travel chapbooks, which explore a consciousness testing its borders and boundaries.

Consider, for instance, the sensory detail characterizing the first poem in *Pátzcuaro* (1999):

> A car sinks in a muddy pothole,
> disappears.  Neat rows of roses.  Lagoon baby
> crocodiles, yellow fish exotica.  The painting
> of rabbit and coyote by Oaxaca's Francisco Toldeo
> plus the hair and the plumbing
> is a problem   deep chapel bells   a version
> of visions in lovey sponged blue cupids (7/695)[8]

As external phenomena infuse the traveler's consciousness in the form of sound waves, particles of light, and variations in color and shadow, they intersect with internal phenomena such as preoccupation with "problem" plumbing, a porousness that implies, in Maurice Merleau-Ponty's terms, "inspiration and expiration of Being" (qtd. in Wiskus 24). Kyger's travel poetry seeks connections between individual human lives and the life of the world, conceptualizing "consciousness itself" as "a project of the world…destined to a world that it neither encompasses nor possesses, but toward which it never ceases to be directed" (Merleau-Ponty lxxxii). Her understanding of human being in the world, as Jin Park and Gereon Kopt note about Merleau-Ponty himself, was "grounded in the notion of the 'life-world' instead of the 'transcendental ego.'" Like Merleau-Ponty, Kyger "embrace[d] the ambiguity between body and mind, self and the world, and sensor and the sensible" (3).[9]

Her work also renders ambiguous distinctions between significant and insignificant experiences, major and minor aspects of existence. Fellow poet David Meltzer remarks that Kyger's poetry "demands and awakens attention to the extraordinary ordinary" and "make[s] the pleasures and particulars of the 'everyday'…luminous and essential and central" (xvii, xviii). In *Pátzcuaro*, she admonishes herself:

# A POETICS OF MOTION

*Carden*

> Don't forget to write about
>
> > the two white plastic spoons
> > from the San Francisco Airport
> > coffee shop now used everyday
> > throw-aways (21/709)

The everyday, even the "throw-away," Kyger holds, are instruments of life, and thus appropriate and necessary subjects of poetry. Because she views "the self as a phenomenon" (Russo, "Introduction" par. 9), no element or aspect of the self is more relevant or meaningful than another:

> Your dreams are important, your humorous life is important, your cooking life is important, your friendships, the dialogues you assume, the news that comes from within, the news that comes from out there. There's such a wide variety of "things" that go on. It's important not to get stuck on any one of these as being the "I" that writes. Being able to report, as it were, from all these areas of life and see that they're equally "valid" and "important"....An egalitarian sense of what it's like to be a human. What being alive is like. ("Energy" par. 20)

Composed of various and varying phenomena, individual being-in-the-world is relational, experiential, and multi-layered. "Several selves...move one self around, thousands / jiggling," Kyger asserts in *Trip Out and Fall Back* (1974). "It is so inappropriate" to deny this multiplicity, "to be unfound, whine / around, hesitant, lock up the window again"; instead, the poet describes herself as the experience of now—"this space in time, this focus, of articulation, that hears / the bee buzz round and round" (15/143).[10] Kyger resists classification as a certain sort of woman, kind of poet, or adherent to a particular literary movement, and in their "inter-speaking" and "cross-thinking," her travel chapbooks mirror this drive toward flexibility and open-endedness.

The challenge that Kyger's embrace of ambiguity offers readers is quite literally visible on the cover of *Desecheo Notebook* (1971), her first published travel chapbook. Sixteen lines of a poem that describes Desecheo—an island "off    West Coast    Puerto Rico" only "1 ½ miles long / 1 mile wide" (n. pag./108)—appear on the outside back cover, but the final three lines are situated inside, at the front of the book.[11] The poem ends on the bottom of a page following the title page, a spot usually reserved for a dedication or an epigraph (see figs. 1, 2, and 3). In addition to this disorienting layout, the poem poses a thematic challenge that coincides with its shift from the outside to the inside of the chapbook; while the material on the

*Fig. 1.* Desecheo Notebook *front cover*

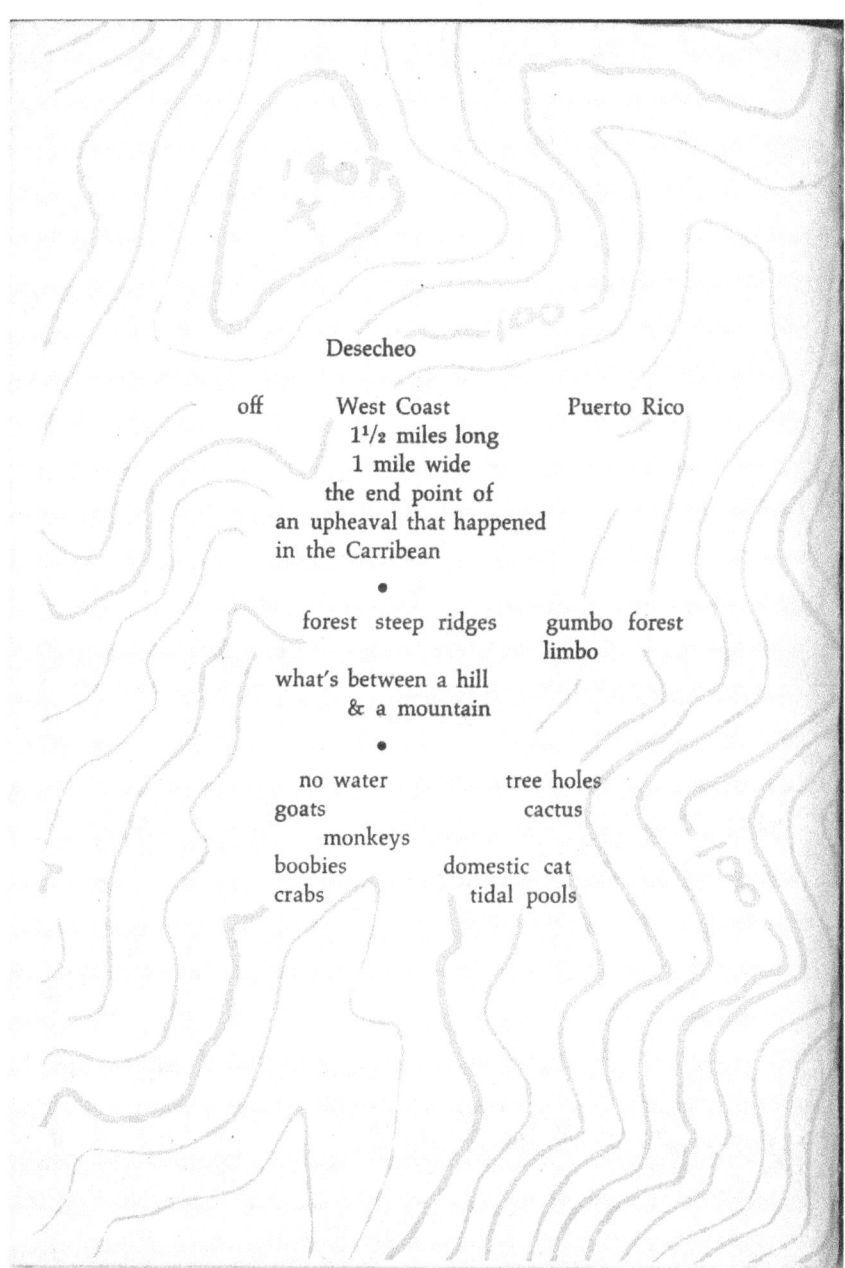

*Fig. 2.* Desecheo Notebook *back cover*

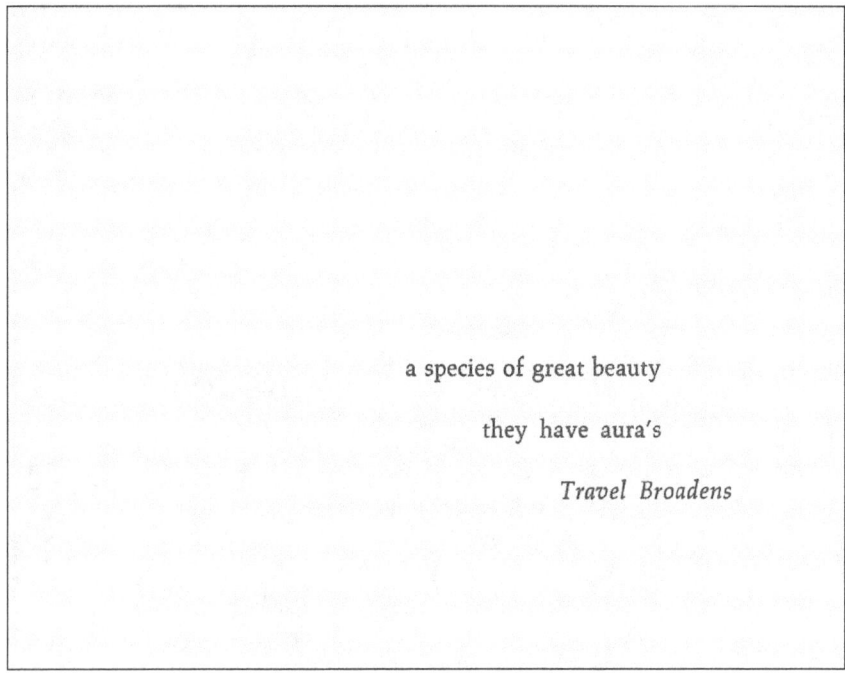

*Fig. 3.* Desecheo Notebook *front matter*

back cover provides a concrete "point of departure" for *Desecheo Notebook*—a specific geography dominated by "steep ridges" and tidal pools, and occupied by goats, monkeys, and crabs (n. pag./108)—the lines on the inside offer a less specific conclusion to the poem and/or introduction to the text:

> a species of great beauty
> they have aura's [sic]
> *Travel Broadens* (1/108)

What species? And what does it have to do with travel's broadening effects? These ambiguities preview the poetics of travel that unfolds over the course of Kyger's career—she grounds her travel chapbooks in the concrete particulars of her daily experience as a traveler, but renders the personal and everyday "point[s] of departure" for more transcendent possibilities and felt moments of truth that model the movements of a consciousness productively engaged with the world.

Many other poem/entries in *Desecheo Notebook* and in subsequent travel chapbooks return to the question of how and what travel broadens. Mulling over "the creation of life," the "Sun, the night, this / earth with its finely gathered garment" on Desecheo Island, Kyger considers that perhaps she and her companions are a "new race being born" and feels she is "no longer in waiting as this world [she] call[s] / [her] own open[s] out" (15/118). In *Trip Out and Fall Back*, she reports that as her vehicle passes under "clouds over Indiana," she has "large dreams of beautiful patterns" (16/143) and experiences "union" with the open world (17/144). Traveling in Mexico in the early 1980s, Kyger devoted a journal entry to an ancient belief system that consolidates the individual with the universe:

> Each person was bound to earth
> by his totemic animal & bound to
> heaven by the positions of Sun,
>    Moon, stars, planets & constellations
> at his birth. (*Mexico Blondé* 18)[12]

In *Pátzcuaro*, travel offers her the opportunity to "dream / too much" and become "completely pensativo" (11/699).

Kyger's focus on moments that broaden individual consciousness and awareness of "what being alive is like" highlights her preoccupation with the lenses and filters through which human beings encounter a world that "tirelessly announces itself within us" (Merleau-Ponty lxxxii). To return to the outside-in *Desecheo* poem cited above, her attribution of "aura" to an unspecified "species" draws attention to her own idiosyncratic modes of perception and response. Kyger looks at crabs, cacti, and monkeys, and assigns auratic beauty to *something* that broadens not just her view of the island but the parameters of her consciousness.

Aura, Miriam Bratu Hansen notes, "is a medium that envelops and physically connects—and thus blurs the boundaries between—subject and object, suggesting a sensory, embodied mode of perception" (351). Something similar could be said about Kyger's travel aesthetic: her chapbooks convey a sensory, embodied mode of perception rooted in her "total belief" in "the capacity of what [she] see[s]" (*Desecheo* 17/119).[13] In *Desecheo Notebook*, she asserts:

>    Concepts promise protection
> from experience.
>              The spirit does
> not dwell in concepts (10/114)

Her travel notebooks strip experience of the protection afforded by the abstract thinking that relies for its meaning on conceptual structures organized around exclusion, separation, and opposition.[14]

In fact, *Desecheo Notebook* itself is the product of Kyger's attempts to transform conditions of dislocation and alienation into opportunities for integration and wholeness. She had journeyed to Desecheo Island with Peter Warshall (with whom she lived in Bolinas, California, for a period in the 1970s) and a group studying "rhesus monkeys that had been left there a few decades earlier"; the students hoped to determine how the monkeys "had adapted and survived on essentially a desert island, an island with no water and very little rain" ("Conversation" 95). Alone in this harsh environment with six men engaged in scientific investigation, Kyger formulated her "own 'course of study'" centered in "investigating the 'self'" ("Conversation" 95). Accordingly, she resolves to both center and expand her sense of self by using her time on the island to "have a talk with [her] unconscious." In so doing, she imagines, a "figure will come up that [she] will commune with. / Maybe the king of the monkeys" (12/115). Positing an alternative approach to understanding the island monkeys and the mystery of their survival, Kyger couples contact with her self with connection to the entities with whom she shares a world.

Not coincidentally, she also identifies openness to the larger life-world as the basis of her poetic voice:

> I know I do not suffer more than anyone
>     in the whole world
> But this morning I had to have first thing
>     2 cigarettes, half a joint,
>       a poached egg and corned beef hash, 1 piece toast,
>           2 cups tea
>
> Jung, Williams, shells, stones,
>   2 slugs rum, depression, rest of joint,
>   cigarette, 7 Up, and it's only 10 o'clock
> Because I wanted to write a poem
> Because I want something to come out of me
> You can't try. I believe in life, I am living
>   now and for a moment the landscape
>     becomes clear. (21/122)

Moving from what the poet sees, feels, and takes in—food, drink, drugs, texts—to what "come[s] out of [her]," the poem links everyday urges toward pleasure and fulfillment to the immanence of life and to the world's announcement of itself within her: "I believe in life, I am living / now." The entry constitutes a kind of poetic manifesto, attesting that it is when she opens herself to "life" and the sensation of "living now" that "the landscape / becomes clear." Although the poem expresses the frustration of an individual artist struggling to express "something" authentic, it pivots on the shared values of her artistic community. Before she left Bolinas for Desecheo Island, Robert Creeley advised her "you can't try" to write, leading her to conclude "whatever is going to happen is going to come of its own volition" ("Conversation" 96); "inter-speaking" and "cross-thinking" with Creeley, Kyger affirms participation in all of life as the source of poetic clarity.

The poem/entry that concludes *Trip Out and Fall Back* offers a similar view of the poet's role, asserting that Kyger is "a poet"

> Because I write
> this down. I want bullet-like speed and precision
> to show that this mind connects in ways of delight, and
> also says truth way beyond this individual voice.
> Thus I speak from the holy story, the ordinary story.
> Thus I am married to the household gods, thus I aspire
> to be the consort of heaven. Thus I am sad when the earth
> is from me. We sleep together again. In no way will I
> part from this union. (17/144)

Her desire for "bullet-like speed and precision" evokes the sensation of travel, imaginatively aligning the consciousness of the poet with the consciousness of the traveler whose movement through the world empowers her to speak "beyond" her "individual voice" and achieve fuller "union" with the totality of life, ordinary and holy, heavenly and earthly. Similarly, a *Pátzcuaro* poem entitled "Trying to Write" identifies phenomenal connection to the earth as the poet's "point of departure":

> All of a sudden these leaves
> popped out
> of the tree reaching up from the beautiful
> patio garden
> under the bedroom window
>
> This is what happened. (17/705)

For her, "trying to write" means trying to express the seen and felt energy of life.

Kyger's travel texts imagine multiple modes and means of participation in the life of the world, interweaving, for example, locales of travel with her home in Bolinas and making frequent references to friends and companions, those traveling with her and those left behind. *Desecheo Notebook* conveys a sense of simultaneous, interpenetrating presence on "the island" of Desecheo and on what is essentially the island of Bolinas, a northern California town cut off from "the rest of the world," "perched upon the southernmost tip of the Point Reyes Peninsula" (Opstedal ch. 1). Entries in *Desecheo Notebook* merge concerns about housing in Bolinas and housing among "all these men" on Desecheo Island (7/112, 19/120), or shift from the specifics of a morning spent on the island to remembered details of a conversation with Kerouac (21/122). In *Phenomenological* (1989), the chapbook associated with Kyger's 1985 journey through the Yucatan Peninsula, evidence of commercial development in Mexico leads her to worry "what's to become of Bolinas?" (9), and multiple poem/entries intersperse thoughts of her Bolinas community with observations of Yucatan geographies and details of her group's activities.[15]

The travel texts draw in and on beloved others as mental signposts, sounding boards, and artistic collaborators; poems/entries incorporate friends' texts and speech, include drawings provided by travel companions, and invoke poets such as Creeley, John Thorpe, and Bill Berkson. In *Trip Out and Fall Back*, Kyger answers the question "Are you all this self awareness and ego?" by tempering the "transcendental ego" with references to material connections signified by friends' gifts,

> Whether it was in my purple
> mini skirt from Lynn and my blue sandals from
> Phoebe, or the yellow beads from Bill, or
> Joe's brown silk bandana. (5/138)

One entry in her 1981 journal *Mexico Blondé* consists entirely of her identification of "Dotty's gift of this / maroon and light purple polk-a-dot / Bandanna" as "one of the favorite things / [she] wear[s]" (16). In *Phenomenological*, Kyger explicitly links her internal states to those of others, attributing her own feeling of anxiety to "a little inferma" felt by her close friend Bill McNeill, back in California suffering from a terminal disease (8).

*Trip Out and Fall Back*, her chapbook about a 1972 trip to New York, found its impetus in creative collaboration (see figs. 4 and 5). Kyger suggested to illustrator Gordon Baldwin that he "'draw the East, and [she would] write about it.' He did a series of drawings, and gave them to Kyger, who used the drawings as inspiration for her words" (Opstedal ch. 10). Her husband Donald Guravich provided illustrations for *Mexico Blondé*—his last name appears with hers on the cover (in fact, it appears first), and in many entries his drawings take up at least as much space as her text (see figs. 6 and 7). In addition to these immediate, personal partnerships, Kyger also finds ways of collaborating with other writers while on the road. During her 1997-98 stay in Mexico, she explains at the opening of *Pátzcuaro* (see fig. 8), she took Pablo Neruda's *Memoirs*, "fortuitously given" to her, as a "close reading companion" (n. pag.). *Pátzcuaro* draws to a close with a poem celebrating Neruda's "beautiful adjectives and magnificent metaphors" (23/710), using his text to demonstrate:

*Fig. 4.* Trip Out and Fall Back *front cover*

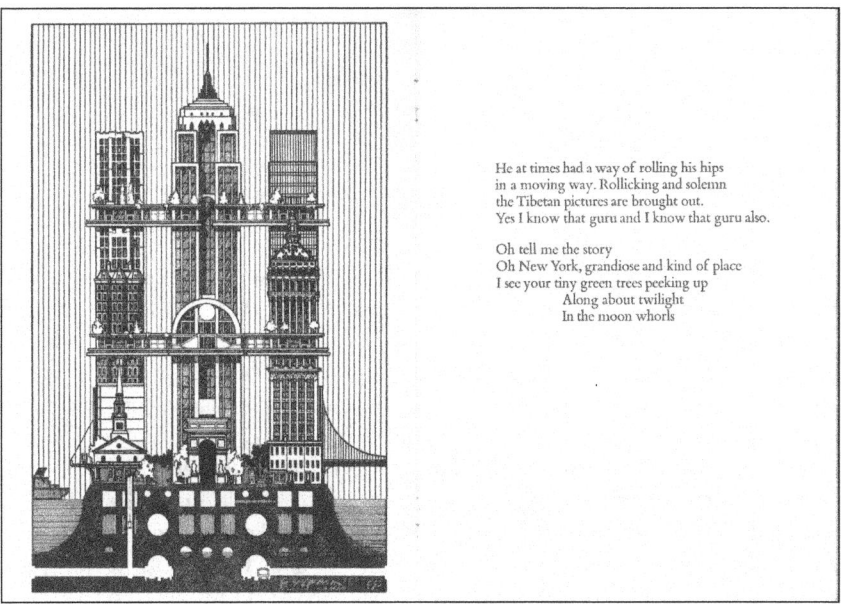

*Fig. 5.* Trip Out and Fall Back *entry*

*Fig. 6.* Mexico Blondé *front cover*    *Fig. 7.* Mexico Blondé *entry*

> "Words that have a crystalline texture, vibrate
>   are ivory, vegetable, oily like fruits, like algae
>   like agates, like olives...wander
>     from country to country
>       very ancient, very new" (25-26/711)

This poem is constructed almost entirely of quotes from Neruda's *Memoirs*, in which he articulates a poetics rooted in the geographies of his homeland and describes and praises the work of writers he knew and loved. Kyger likely found a number of elements of similarity with Neruda, who also spent time in Pátzcuaro, and saw "no country...more profoundly human than Mexico....In its brilliant achievements, as well as its gigantic errors, one sees the same chain of grand generosity, deep-rooted vitality, inexhaustible history, and limitless growth" (*Memoirs* 151). Quoting Neruda's commentary on poets including Frederico García Lorca, Paul Eluard, and César Vallejo, Kyger recreates his investment (so like her own) in productive artistic community, his "wholehearted brotherhood" and "warmth of...feelings and language for his fellow poets" (*Pátzcuaro* n. pag.). Neruda's resonant voice and his concern for everyday working people subtly infuse *Pátzcuaro*, the most politically

# A POETICS OF MOTION                                    Carden

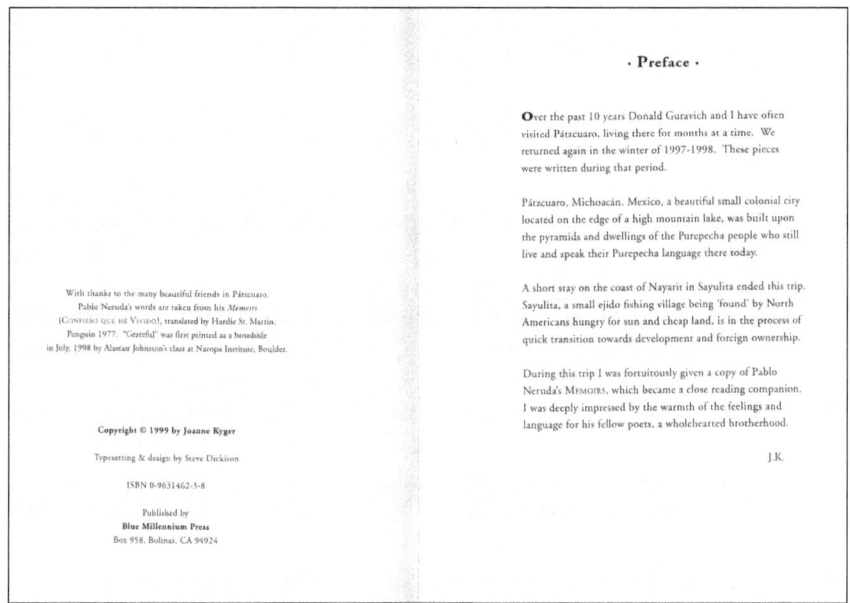

*Fig. 8.* Pátzcuaro *front matter*

engaged of the chapbooks, in poem/entries such as "You are not permitted the Sexual Act" (9/697) and "Dead in Acteal, Chiapas" (13/701).[16]

In *Phenomenological*, Kyger collaborates with another "great poet"—Juana Ines de Asbaje, a figure "from colonial / times in Mexico"—who "struggle[d] thru / her life with compassion and talent in / intellectual pursuits, not granted to women" (4, 5). Kyger occupies a similar, albeit less restricted position as a Beat- and Bolinas-associated writer, a woman living and working in male-dominated communities, a poet determined to distinguish herself as a writer while also "keep[ing] memory compassionate of all the / interconnections of people [she] has loved / and known" (20). Juana and Joanne share other areas of coincidence as well. Like Kyger, Juana is interested in the intertwined nature of human belief systems; in her time, she provoked the Catholic Church's opprobrium by arguing that "the Mexican corn god...anticipates the Christian symbolism / of the death and resurrection of Christ and / the Sacrament of Communion" (5). Kyger describes Juana as a poet who "blend[s] the Old World and the New" (5) in a poem/entry that combines old and new worlds, in a chapbook that explores both "the pyramids of antiquity" and the "contemporary" cultures of Mexico (1). The seventeenth-century poet also shares Kyger's concern with the ego. Juana, Kyger explains,

> becomes a nun, but runs into trouble
> with her mind, "I thought to flee from myself
> but wretch that I am
> I took myself with me." (5)

Kyger, too, "runs into trouble" with the stubborn structures of individual consciousness that frame and limit her capacity for pure, unfiltered "knowledge" of and "union" with the wide world, a predicament she has in common with Juana, and with all human beings (5).

Kyger experiences aspects of Mexico through what she reads and imagines of Juana's experience, viewing, for instance, a sky "filled / with swallows catching early morning breakfast" through Juana's poem of a "little bird who gets / eaten by a hawk for breakfast" (6). At other moments, she filters her perceptions through Charles Olson's *Mayan Letters*, a text that causes her to "muse about the Yucatan 30 / years ago," when it was "so much / emptier, no big tours from Florida" (8), and to acknowledge the inaccessibility of the more distant past. Riding to Chichen Itza in a "very comfortable" "first class bus" (9), Kyger finds herself surrounded by "tourists from all over the world," caught up in a "hilarious" cacophony of "people with / their comments in many languages" (10). Having read about the history of this site—over a thousand years marked by takeover and appropriation—she recognizes its reenactment in the present day by "teenagers of U.S. galloping / up and down on / history's past conquests." Nevertheless, she "immediately challenge[s] [her] self to El / Castillo's top":

> And once there, weak legged, wind blowing
> terrified to walk around the temple at the
> top for fear I'll fall off
>
> want immediately to descend while I can. What
> vertigo! Holding on to the chain, praying
> and trembling I descend backwards down the
> narrow steps, remember the human sacrifice
> practiced by the Itzas. (10-11)

Travel opens the world to exploration, but does not afford the traveler unrestricted entry or understanding, let alone equilibrium. Unable to navigate the ancient pyramid, Kyger retreats to the familiar, visiting a conveniently located "refreshment stand" and composing a postcard before returning to her hotel for "early bed / and easy fiction" (11). As in the case of an earlier visitor who leapt into "the Sacrificial Pool" only to be "knocked deaf and dumb for three days" (9), Chichen Itza makes

Kyger feel her limits, leaving her with "rubber legs for the next four days" (11), a tangible reminder of the barriers to union with "world existence."

Such barriers are implicit in the title of *Mexico Blondé*, which, accented "e" aside, points to Kyger's visible otherness as a blonde Anglo-American in Mexico; despite her frequent travels to Mexico and love for its landscapes and cultures, she remains a visitor, well aware she is not *of* Mexico. In this chapbook, her sense of difference emerges early and forcefully on a crowded train, where, aware "the whole / car is watching," she suffers what she describes as a "gringo / nervous breakdown" due to conditions native passengers seem to take in their stride (4). She had come to Mexico hoping to connect with "human / treasures of existing people in / past time" (19), but finds her access limited. "Our Lady of Soledad," she reports, seems "very remote" in "her / basilica....A far off / blur, thru the power of the church." Unable to achieve a sense of ease or inclusion, she finally feels compelled to leave—"I have to cough and go out" (7). Similarly, as she records her difficulty understanding the "structure" of the town of Zapotec, where "everybody is so / seemingly modern" and where she "[hasn't] been in / anybody's home," she recognizes that in order to more directly participate in the life of the place she would "have to make / a serious decision to study spanish: / obviously from   the heart" (21). These textual moments of disconnection and difference demonstrate that Kyger does not shrink from acknowledging the inevitable and at points unspecifiable impediments—internal and external—the traveler runs up against in her quest for integration.

At other junctures, however, the chapbooks suggest that travel does facilitate moments of coincidence during which some level of fusion with "world existence" might be achieved. Reflecting on shared elements of human experience in *Pátzcuaro*, Kyger declares that in the "completely / focused" act of "chopping...tomatoes, chilies, and onions," one "could be   anywhere / on Earth       and Time" (10/698). The mind, she observes, "genuflects / to age-old themes of anywhere" (20/708), and during her 1998 sojourn in Mexico she actively seeks such themes in manifestations of the "old Mother God...transformed / into the Virgin" Mary; in one incarnation she appears as the "Virgin of Health...fashioned from corncob / and orchid honey paste," "dwell[ing] still in her towering pyramid rebuilt / as a   basilica" (8/696). Multiple *Pátzcuaro* poems/entries examine meldings of "the indígena" and "the María of Spain's conquest," the "Ancient Goddess" and "the sacred new Virgin of now / Catholic Mexico" (15/703). A poem entitled "Noche Buena," or "Christmas Eve," mulls over and participates in shifting yet intertwined modes of relationship between humanity and divinity:

> When María gives birth
>      to the *son* of god
>           but somehow
>  becomes the *mother* of *god himself*

> During which miraculous
> ecclesiastical transformation
>
> We eat carefully prepared
>    chicken, cheese and mushroom crepes
>
> Where is He?
> He is here in your poem.
>
> Santa has his foot in the door.
> The old ways still for the birth of the innocent
>
>    victor, Christ.  And before that,
>  Before *that*…?    We start again. (14/702)

Part of the "we" who endlessly "start again," Kyger's witnessing of spiritual traditions draws God into the here and now of her poem, merging the modern and the mythic, and making the chapbook akin to pyramids-turned-basilicas—another site where the human spirit recognizes its continuity through time and space.

    In her travels, Kyger is drawn to artifacts and experiences that mark encounters of individual spirit and world spirit. Jonathan Skinner suggests "the occasion of travel is a retreat from ego possible only in fronting ego's desire, curiosity, generous impulses" (par. 13). A *Desecheo Notebook* poem captures this dilemma:

>   Generosity: I allow
>       your existence
>   equal weight with mine
>         \*
> I kick the rock
>     Rock spirit come out
>       damn it
>        \*
> slowly a string
> of beautiful figures drift
> from the cave
>    high up on the rocks
>  riding through the mists
> their diaphanous clothes
>     flutter
>   in the grey breeze
>       \*
> There was a time
>    when I wanted

# A POETICS OF MOTION  Carden

> to learn the knowledge
> out there
> possessed by the world
> \*
> it helps on this island
> to do exercise
> thoughts stay
> in the mind close
> to the home camp (23/124)

By turns respectful and demanding, oriented inward and outward, focused on the auratic beauty of the world and on daily rituals of self-care, the poem reflects on the act of reflecting, moving without judgment through various stances individual consciousness might assume in relation to the world, its multitudinous phenomena, its mysteries and its gifts. Integration with the life-world, Kyger consistently acknowledges, may not be fully possible, but the urge toward it, she suggests, shapes the human psyche and constitutes the primary engine of creative expression.

In *Phenomenological*, Kyger's questioning of the parameters of individual consciousness emerges most obviously and urgently in her search for her "dear friend" Bill McNeill, who, as she set out for Mexico, was dying in a California hospital, "suffering from the / last terminal stage of his illness" (1). The chapbook opens with Kyger's explanation that she and McNeill had "made / an agreement that [they] would somehow 'meet'/ down there, 'between the real and the apparent,'" and she describes *Phenomenological* as "a record of that journey" (1). In a gesture reminiscent of the outside-in poem that greets the reader of *Desecheo Notebook*, Kyger's statement about her planned meeting with her deceased friend presents travel as the agent of a heightened awareness capable of activating new modes of interaction with the world. It also signals her engagement with ongoing philosophical debates about the extent to which human beings are capable of discerning what phenomena are actually "real" and which are only "apparent," those whose position on the surface of the perceptible world might mask some more fundamental truth.[17]

*Phenomenological* does not portray Kyger meeting with or otherwise "feel[ing]" Bill McNeill's "new birth" (4), but it does track her deeply felt participation in the life of the world, expressed in sensory, embodied encounters with "living ruins" (19) and "deep and lush and green" Yucatan geographies (14/230). Kyger's depictions of these spaces and entities vibrate with an auratic intensity that suggests heightened sensitivity to and receptivity of a world that infiltrates and inhabits her consciousness. The world around her, she writes, "look[s] thru this mind" (15), and its phenomena, including "birds nest fern / bromeliad, ceiba tree, and an arm / thick vine," "reflect [her] attempt / to display them / in the form of this body watching"

(14/230). While recognizing the filters of the eye/I and her subjective stance as an embodied observer—"little Releases in time-space," she allows, are "personal to all, I suppose" (13)—poems/entries detailing the parts and particulars of Mexico do not render them separate objects viewed from a distance. Instead, internal and external phenomena look and live through each other; the poet and the world around her engage in the "cross-thinking" and "inter-speaking" that render boundaries between inside and outside worlds flexible and porous.

As Kyger "mak[es] a place / in the doorway of the Jaguar / Temple in the jungle," she undergoes an almost synesthesiac experience:

>            The Temple behind
>                         my back
>            The room in which I sit
>        flashes gold
>                thru the satiny silver air (14/230)

In its evocation of the numinous halo or "elusive phenomenal substance" associated with aura, with something that "look[s] back at us" and blurs lines between me and not-me (Hansen 339), this gold and silver moment gestures toward the ineffable richness of open intersection between the individual "psyche" and "world existence." Later, Kyger presents Bill McNeill's new life in much the same terms—she dreams of him

>                        showing a canvas
>            painted in two parts
>                        of a Moon light path
>            across the waters in silver and gold,
>            from one existence into another. (29)

These depictions of silver- and gold-hued boundary crossings recall brief but immeasurably enriching moments of coincidence with the wider world. Such moments, it seems, constitute the primary aim and reward—the desired destination—of Kyger's travels.

In *Phenomenological*, vivid sensory encounters continue at the Temple of the Cross in Palenque, where Kyger's group is greeted by a butterfly she identifies as "the Ambassador" and "Guardian" of the place. The butterfly "sits on [her] hand,"

>            A wonderful jeweled ornament...
>                on the very finger
>                        that writes this now.

# A POETICS OF MOTION

> The continuing embellishment
> of Life in this ancient
> Epitome of grace (16/232)

An accompanying drawing by Donald Guravich portrays the butterfly in front of the Temple, in a perspective that imbues the butterfly with significance equivalent to that of the ancient edifice: the butterfly's small, transient being and the monumental, enduring temple appear equally relevant dwelling-places of world spirit (see fig. 9). The butterfly hereafter inhabits and guides Kyger's perception of Mexico, and much like the beautiful Desecheo species imbued with an aura that broadens, the Ambassador Butterfly offers Kyger a means of imaginative entry into the life of the place. She encounters it or its iridescent, prismatic energy over and over again, in various places and incarnations. The butterfly's color and motion are reflected in a full moon she describes as "red gold vehicle / for Sun's reflection, rising swiftly" (23). Kyger describes the spirit and sense of her Yucatan–inspired poetry as "that gold butterfly / wing[ing] from Palenque fly[ing] away from notebook / pages"

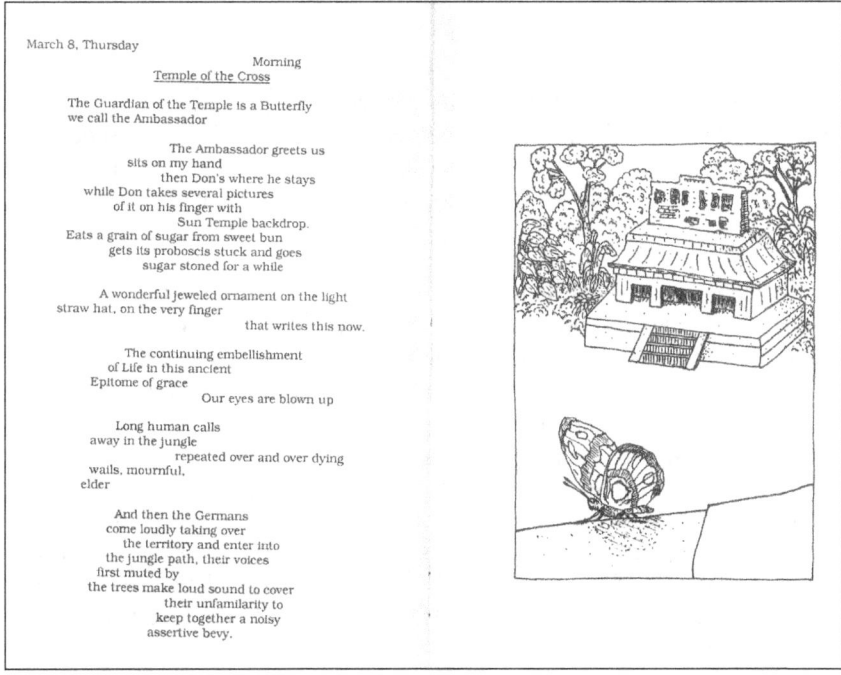

*Fig. 9.* Phenomenological *entry*

(20), and she positions as "parallel" her friend "Bill's last days" and her encounter with "the Butterfly Guardian," an encounter that results in "transcendental clarity" (24).

Kyger also finds imaginative entry into different places through dreams, which she views as "a constant activity of the mind, a parallel universe as it were" ("Conversation" 98). Dream entries in *Desecheo Notebook* merge Desecheo Island and Bolinas, reflect on the personalities of fellow island sojourners, and highlight her sense of difference from her male companions. One dream-record draws her ex-husband Gary Snyder, his second wife, and their son into her Caribbean experience to share food, conversation, and a sense of "belong[ing]" (14/117). In another, she resolves to eschew silliness and get "down to business" in serious and "abstract" thought, only to confront the material, complexities of daily experience as a woman living amongst men:

> Good lord I think I may / have buried some Tampax over there. There is / the son of the governor of Massachusetts turning over a / rock and looking sternly down. Gracious. We won't / mention that I'll just have to accept it as my kismet / on this desert Island stumbling around on rocks look- / ing for the ultimate lady-like way for the perfection / of toilet. (6/111)

Even though (or maybe because of) the submerged fears and conflicts excavated in dreams, Kyger credits her practice of "reporting dreams" in her notebook with enabling her to overcome the writer's block she had been experiencing prior to her Desecheo journey ("Conversation" 96), perhaps in part because dreams disrupt and dispute the waking mind's tendency to rend spirit from body, home from away, me from not-me.

Although, as Jane Falk points out, dream-record entries in *Desecheo Notebook* are distinguished by their structure—they tend to appear in "block paragraph format" ("Journal" 998)—no one but Kyger (and maybe not even she) can definitively identify which entries or parts of entries constitute dream-records. The impossibility of differentiating dreaming from waking states illustrates that Kyger found such distinctions finally irrelevant. She agrees with Carl Jung and other psychoanalysts who view dreams as keys to "understanding '[one]self'" ("Conversation" 98), and so affords dreams the same status and truth-value as conscious thought.[18] In fact, she suggests dreams provide access to truer, less filtered aspects of the self; because dreams are of the mind but not of the conscious mind, they reveal hidden "emotions and psychological states" and release "different languages and energies" ("Conversation" 98).

While some entries in Kyger's travel chapbooks consist entirely of dreams, others morph from waking to dreaming without warning or distinction. Still others self-consciously dissolve boundaries between conscious and unconscious experience, as in this early entry in *Mexico Blondé*, which begins with details of a weary train journey in the company of Guravich:

> The long night proves
> to be uncomfortable and crowded.
> Great complaints fall into sleep and
> dreams.   Suzuki Roshi and D.T.
> Suzuki are in the next room, Bill
> Berkson tells me.
>                   Well that's certainly
> enough to teach a little breathing
> patience.    Great gusty winds in
> mountain monastery forest drive me
> in temple door, red tori under arm
> to find Suzuki Roshi pounding
> great prajnaparamita sutra drum.
> I join in hesitantly because I can't
> remember it all. But the vibrations
> feel so good. (2)

Despite discomforts—crowded travel and uncertain participation in Zen practices—the train dream resolves both projects in "good" feelings.[19] The entry's fusion of "the vibrations" of the pounding drum and the movement of the train produces a seamless dreaming/waking experience that mimics the desired result of travel in the interpenetration of inner and outer worlds.

Many chapbook poems/entries that are clearly not dream-records are nevertheless imbued with a dreamy quality that partakes in the feeling of simultaneous motion and suspension which often accompanies travel. In the *Desecheo Notebook* poem "Thursday," for example, the traveling poet transforms into a "Superman" figure who merges different personas, locations, and modes of being:

> It's me too observing the dwellings by
> the train station as I fly by, carrying
> someone to this hotel room in Spain.
>    . . .
>
>        When spring comes to the
> ocean eggs.

> History of the Island, this
> movie, subjective feelings and objective
> actions.

> He exists outside time & is the son
> of the maternal unconscious. (13/116)

While Superman might seem above and beyond the world of human striving, his "low flight" keeps him in and of that world, able to see freely and expansively (13/116). Kyger's low flight pulls together opposites—"super" and everyday acts, male and female being, subjective and objective perception, dreaming and waking states. All constitute elements of the life-world that reasserts its own enduring motion in the return of spring. The poem ends in the company of Jung's archetype of the wise old man, a figure both paternal and maternal who exists, like Superman and the poet-in-flight, outside dualistic restrictions.[20]

Kyger's second published travel chapbook begins and ends with the sort of movement attributed to both Superman and the traveling poet in *Desecheo Notebook*. *Trip Out and Fall Back* opens with an entry/poem that compares driving cross-country with "space travel" (1/136) and concludes with an explicit link between motion and poetry, in her desire for the "bullet-like speed and precision" through which her "mind connects in ways of delight" and communicates "truth way beyond [her] individual voice" (17/144). Kyger's travel texts repeatedly and insistently construct metaphors related to movement to express connection with the wider life-world. "The obliteration of restrains," she observes in *Trip Out and Fall Back*, "cause[s] the room to become spaceless / hurtled far above the buildings," and frees her to "love…all" (13/142).

In Kyger's representation, travel mimics the mind's constant probing of its outermost borders, its search for new points of departure that might enable moments of integration and connection with the wider world. Travel "broadens" Kyger's scales of reference and prompts her to create in her chapbooks a new discursive means to account for perceptions that inspire the emergence of "something" that "transforms, transvalues, translates" (Bartkowski xxvi). For her, this "something" constitutes a felt experience of the "spirit[ual]" connections human beings never cease weaving with/in "world existence," "the delicate thread spun so finely / over and over thru the centuries, past back over the / Greeks" (*Desecheo* 15/118).

## Notes

[1] The original chapbook edition of *Desecheo Notebook* is unpaginated. I have assigned page numbers 1-30 to the text and also cite corresponding page numbers in Kyger's 2002 collection *As Ever*, which reproduces the entire *Notebook*.

[2] Kyger's view of the psyche as "a world existence" has obvious connections to "the Buddhist concept of mind—mind being this kind of larger, encompassing entity of which everything is a part" ("Conversation" 96). Zen Buddhism figures highly in Kyger's poetics. She studied in San Francisco and Japan, and taught at the Jack Kerouac School of Disembodied Poetics at Naropa University, generally considered the "institutional center of American literary Buddhism" (Whalen-Bridge 157).

[3] *The Japan and India Journals*, probably Kyger's best-known work, is not a chapbook (generally, chapbooks are twenty to thirty pages in length and contain a series of poems dealing with a common subject or theme). Due to this generic difference and to the differences in focus and form discussed above, I dedicate this essay to the travel chapbooks only.

[4] Kyger also shared with other Beat writers her habit of daily notebook writing. Nancy Grace points to the "Beat movement literary practice of self-disclosure and confession" manifested in "the publication of letters, journals, and other private papers both as adjuncts to and as art *tout court*" ("Places" 135). Jane Falk suggests that "the conversational tone of Kyger's journals...conveys a sense of being in the present without conceptualizing the experience," "provide[s] a solution to her concerns about poetry's artificiality," and "shows the interest in spontaneity that she shared with Kerouac and the Beats" ("Journal" 998).

[5] Despite her sense of gender-related difference, as Amy Friedman points out, Kyger has in common "with other Beat writers her contemplation of Eastern religions, the elevation of quotidian reflections in her art, the repeated mention of other Beat writers that creates a sense of familiar artistic community, and a suggested patina of spontaneity in the generation of her writing" ("Joanne Kyger" 75). Kyger's friend Bill Berkson asserts that her "connection with the Beat writers, aside from matters of plain friendship, is grounded on mutual understandings of tradition and sources, poetic and philosophical" (325). For discussion of Kyger's position as a female poet within male-dominated literary communities, see Freidman, Grace, Russo, and Shaw.

[6] In addition to her links to the Beat movement, Kyger is also associated with the poets of the second wave San Francisco Renaissance and with the Bolinas, California writers' colony—all, in their own ways, restless groups. Kyger herself was a life-long traveler with a "self-admitted drive for adventure" (Friedman, "Kyger" 184). After returning to San Francisco from Japan, she went to Europe, traveled back and forth across the United States, spent time in the Caribbean, and took repeated trips to Mexico.

[7] "I always try to write my line," Kyger remarked, "so it reflects some movement of inflection" ("Conversation" 112). She told Nancy Grace that she strives for "a tension of lines so when [the line] breaks there's a certain energy that keeps you moving; that holds the end of the line and picks up on the next—the kinetics of what a line movement on the page is" ("Places" 149). Kyger credited Charles Olson's "Projective Verse" with enabling her to see "that it was possible to chart the actual breathing of the human voice on the page" ("The Community" par. 1). Michael Davidson notes that Kyger intended "her poetry to be gestural, 'an extension of [her] arm'" (188), and Berkson points out that she expressed "her aesthetic" stance in broad, though emphatic, terms such as *energy, non-linear, line,* (and *generous line*), and *breath*" (325).

[8] *Pátzcuaro* is paginated 1-29; I cite corresponding page numbers in Kyger's 2007 collection *About Now*, in which the full text (with the exception of the final poem) is reproduced.
[9] Jane Falk notes that Kyger viewed the world "as one huge space, and the poet the recorder," a stance likely influenced by Olson, who was influenced in turn by Merleau-Ponty's view of the world not as "an object" but as "the *field*" of human experience ("Joanne Kyger" 125, 129-30).
[10] The original chapbook edition of *Trip Out and Fall Back* is unpaginated. I have assigned page numbers 1-17 to the text and also cite corresponding page numbers in Kyger's 2002 collection *As Ever*, which reproduces the full chapbook.
[11] The poem appears as an unbroken unit in *As Ever*.
[12] I have assigned page numbers 1-27 to *Mexico Blondé*. Only thirty copies were printed, which appear to be un-typeset copies of the actual notebook (see fig. 7), and the entry/poems are not reproduced elsewhere.
[13] Kyger endeavored, she explained, to share what she saw in lines that construct a "kind of space that vibrates its meaning" (Oppenheimer, Dorn, and Kyger 65)—a description that suggests a tangible, sensory medium of signification. Kyger likened her vibrating line to "the one-liner or the sampler on the wall....It just stays there for a long time. You can go back into that one line and it will keep giving off overtones, so it doesn't have to sit there and be connected. It's connected but it's a different kind of space" (65).
[14] Rejection of "concepts," as Kyger observed, is also a Buddhist precept. "Zen Buddhists pointed out that concepts, ideas, are just ephemeral, so what really exists is you in the moment" ("Conversation" 104). As other commentators have suggested, Kyger consistently resists dualistic thought in her work; Jane Falk notes that Kyger's attention to "the problematic nature of...'mind-body dualism'...originated in her college years" ("Joanne Kyger" 115). For discussion of intersections between Buddhism and phenomenology, see Park and Kopf.
[15] The original chapbook version of *Phenomenological* is unpaginated; I have assigned page numbers 1-30 to the text, which appears in *A Curriculum of the Soul*, published by the Institute of Further Studies. Only a few *Phenomenological* poems are reproduced in later collections of Kyger's work. When possible, I cite corresponding page numbers from *As Ever*.
[16] Neruda seems to share Kyger's view of the centrality of ordinary, everyday experiences, asserting that "the writer's task has nothing to do with mystery or magic, and the poet's, at least, must be a personal effort for the benefit of all. The closest thing to poetry is a loaf of bread or a ceramic dish or a piece of wood lovingly carved, even if by clumsy hands" (49). Neruda views himself as a product of place, and his detailed, passionate descriptions of various landscapes and geographies have much in common with Kyger's work, especially her later poems, which "place her among our most diligent of ecological poets" (Russo, "Precious" 28).
[17] A reader might expect the term "phenomenolog*ical*" to serve as an adjective or adverb, but the entity or an action it would modify is absent in the chapbook's title, leaving "phenomenological" to describe the book itself. Dan Coffey notes that "most of Kyger's non-poem works have been phenomenological in nature—using that discipline to reflect on the thought processes that are involved in observing the material world—but to actually call attention to that particular method in the book's title gives a self-consciousness to the work, above and beyond the self-consciousness of the 'I' in the text of the journal entries. In this case, however, Kyger is using phenomenology to analyze the phenomenological method itself" (par. 3). Lytle Shaw suggests that "Kyger's oscillation between a West Coast meditative poetics and an East Coast cultivation of dailiness is not so much a synthesis as it is a revelatory way of running one against the other—so that disembodied flights keep touching down into the gendered bodies and social contexts that make them possible" (81). *Phenomenological* was published in fulfillment of Kyger's "assignment" for the *Curriculum of the Soul* series, "a

collaborative text in twenty-eight books derived from 'A Plan for a Curriculum of the Soul' by Charles Olson" (Institute of Further Studies). Kyger described Olson's "Plan" as "a distinctive map with 223 names, subjects, ideas, topics, strewed across the page at all angles" ("The Community" par. 6). Publication of the series began in 1968 with Olson's *Pleistocene Man* (Institute of Further Studies). Following Olson's death, editor John Clarke "assigned topics from Olson's plan to selected poets" (Opstedal ch. 4). Titles in the now-complete text include Robert Duncan's *Dante*, Alice Notley's *Homer's Art*, Ed Sanders's *Egyptian Hieroglyphs*, John Thorpe's *Matter*, and Michael McClure's *Organism* (Institute of Further Studies).

[18] Kyger brought Jung's *Memories, Dreams, Reflections* with her to the island, and as a college student had been influenced by Erich Fromm, Robert Graves, and Joseph Campbell ("Conversation" 98; "Places" 143-44).

[19] Zen practices referenced in the dream-record include zazen, or seated meditation focused on breath—fundamental to Zen Buddhism. At points in her life, as Anne Waldman notes in her introduction to *Strange Big Moon*, Kyger "struggle[d] with" regulating her breathing and with "her…difficulty sitting still" (vii). Suzuki Roshi was a Buddhist monk and teacher with whom Kyger sat before going to Japan ("Joanne Kyger 2" par. 2). He played an important role in introducing Americans to Zen Buddhism. Kyger was acquainted with D.T. Suzuki, a Buddhist scholar whose books were also influential in the U.S. (see Kyger's *Crooked Cucumber* interview for details).

[20] The final sentence of the poem consists of a quote from Jung. Kyger had thought "he" referenced Jesus Christ ("Conversation" 95, 115)

# Works Cited

Barktowski, Frances. *Travelers, Immigrants, Inmates: Essays in Estrangement*. U of Minnesota P, 1995.

Belgrad, Daniel. "The Transnational Counterculture: Beat-Mexican Intersections." Skerl, pp. 27-40.

Berkson, Bill. "Joanne Kyger." *The Beats: Literary Bohemians in Postwar America. Dictionary of Literary Biography, vol. 16*, edited by Ann Charters, Gale, 1983, pp. 324-28.

Coffey, Dan. "'My phenomenology waits': Death and Rebirth in Joanne Kyger's *Phenomenological*." *Jacket Magazine,* no. 11, 2000. Accessed 28 Feb. 2012.

Davidson, Michael. *The San Francisco Renaissance: Poetics and Community at Mid-Century*. Cambridge UP, 1989.

Falk, Jane E. "Joanne Kyger 'Descartes and the Splendor Of': Bridging Dualisms through Collaboration and Experimentation." *The Philosophy of the Beats*, edited by Sharin N. Elkholy, UP of Kentucky, 2012, pp. 115-30.

———. "Journal as Genre and Published Text: Beat Avant-Garde Writing Practices." *University of Toronto Quarterly*, vol. 73, no. 4, 2004, pp. 991-1002.

Friedman, Amy. "Joanne Kyger, Beat Generation Poet: 'a porcupine traveling at the speed of light.'" Skerl, pp. 73-88.

———. "Kyger, Joanne." *Encyclopedia of Beat Literature: The Essential Guide to the Lives and Works of the Beat Writers*, edited by Kurt Hemmer, Facts on File, 2007, pp. 183-85.

Hansen, Miriam Bratu. "Benjamin's Aura." *Critical Inquiry*, vol. 34, 2007, pp. 336-75.

Hibbard, Allen. "William S. Burroughs and U.S. Empire." *The Transnational Beat Generation,* edited by Nancy M. Grace and Jennie Skerl, Palgrave Macmillan, 2012, pp. 15-30.

The Institute of Further Studies. *A Curriculum of the Soul.* Canton, New York, 2010.

Knight, Brenda. "Joanne Kyger: Dharma Sister." *Women of the Beat Generation: The Writers, Artists, and Muses at the Heart of a Revolution*, edited by Brenda Knight, Conari Press, 1996, pp. 197-204.

Kyger, Joanne. *About Now: Collected Poems.* National Poetry Foundation, 2007.

———. *As Ever: Selected Poems.* Penguin, 2002.

———. "The Community of THE CURRICULUM OF THE SOUL." *Harriet: A Poetry Blog.* Poetry Foundation, 2012. Accessed 4 Jan. 2016.

———. *Desecheo Notebook.* Arif Press, 1971.

———. Interview by Dale Smith. "Energy on the Page: Joanne Kyger in Conversation with Dale Smith." *Jacket Magazine,* no. 11, 2000. Accessed 28 Feb. 2012.

———. Interview by David Chadwick. "Joanne Kyger 2." *Crooked Cucumber.* 31 Mar. 2015. www.cuke.com/Cucumber%20Project/interviews/kyger-2.htm. Accessed 4 Dec. 2016.

———. Interview by Nancy M. Grace. "Places to Go." *Breaking the Rule of Cool: Interviewing and Reading Beat Women Writers*, edited by Nancy M. Grace and Ronna C. Johnson, UP of Mississippi, 2004, pp. 133-53.

———. Interview by Paul Watsky. "A Conversation with Joanne Kyger." *Jung Journal: Culture & Psyche,* vol. 7, no.3, 2013, pp. 94-116.

———. *Mexico Blondé.* Evergreen, 1981.

———. *Pátzcuaro.* Blue Millennium Press, 1999.

———. *Phenomenological: A Curriculum of the Soul.* Institute of Further Studies, Glover, 1989.

———. *Strange Big Moon: The Japan and India Journals, 1960-1964.* 1981. North Atlantic Books, 2000.

———. *Trip Out and Fall Back.* Arif Press, 1974.

Meltzer, David. Introduction. *As Ever: Selected Poems*, by Joanne Kyger, Penguin, 2002, pp. xvii-xxi.

Merleau-Ponty, Maurice. *Phenomenology of Perception.* 1945. Translated by Donald A. Landes, Routledge, 2014.

Neruda, Pablo. *Memoirs*. 1974. Translated by Hardie St. Martin, Farrar, Straus and Giroux, 2001.

Oppenheimer, Joel, Ed Dorn, and Joanne Kyger. "Three Versions of the Poetic Line." *Credences: A Journal of Twentieth Century Poetry and Poetics*, vol. 2, no. 1[4], 1977, pp. 55-66.

Opstedal, Kevin. *Dreaming As One: Poetry, Poets and Community in Bolinas, California 1967-1980*. Big Bridge Press, 2008.

Park, Jin Y. and Gereon Kopf. "Introduction: Philosophy, Nonphilosophy, and Comparative Philosophy." *Merleau-Ponty and Buddhism*, edited by Park and Kopf, Rowman and Littlefield, 2009, pp. 1-13.

Russo, Linda. "Introduction: A Context for Reading Joanne Kyger." *Jacket Magazine*, no. 11, 2000. Accessed 28 Feb. 2012.

———. "'Precious, rare, and mundane': Some Thoughts on the Work of Joanne Kyger." *About Now: Collected Poems*, by Joanne Kyger, National Poetry Foundation, 2007, pp. 25-29.

Shaw, Lytle. "Presence in the Poets' Polis: Hippie Phenomenology in Bolinas." *Among Friends: Engendering the Social Site of Poetry*, edited by Anne Dewey and Libbie Rifkin, U of Iowa P, 2013, pp. 67-86.

Skerl, Jennie, editor. *Reconstructing the Beats*. Palgrave macmillan, 2004.

Skinner, Jonathan. "Generosity and Discipline: The Travel Poems." *Jacket Magazine*, no. 11, 2000. Accessed 28 Feb. 2012.

Waldman, Anne. Foreword. *Strange Big Moon*, by Kyger, pp. vii-x.

Whalen-Bridge, John. "Poetry and Practice at Naropa University." *Writing as Enlightenment: Buddhist American Literature into the Twenty-first Century*, edited by Gary Storhoff and John Whalen-Bridge, State U of New York P, 2011, pp. 157-84.

Wiskus, Jessica. *The Rhythm of Thought: Art, Literature, and Music after Merleau-Ponty*. U of Chicago P, 2013.

# Big Sur Breakdown: Lew Welch and "Ring of Bone"

By Terence Diggory

Many readers first encounter Lew Welch (1926-1971?) as a fictional character in *Big Sur* (1962), the novel by Jack Kerouac (1922-1969), in which Welch is called Dave Wain. But Welch was a real person and an exceptional writer—Kerouac calls his character Dave Wain "a marvelous poet" (47)—who was, like Kerouac, haunted by his own fictional projection of himself to the point of self-destruction. Welch's disappearance in 1971 cannot be defined as suicide because his body was never found, but it is clear from his writing that he had long sought to disappear not only from others but also from himself.[1] As Beat movement writers, both Welch and Kerouac described experiences that were like suicide, insofar as they involved psychological breakdown, yet from which, they believed, grew a new spiritual awareness; a form of consciousness survived that was not ego-centered. The Big Sur wilderness on the central coast of California was the scene of such transformative experiences for both Kerouac and Welch. In what follows, I focus on the poem that emerged from Welch's experience, "Ring of Bone" (written 1962-63; published 1973), but I intend to "break down" that poem—reemploying that term in the sense of making an analysis—by reading it in the light of Kerouac's *Big Sur* and a number of other texts, including a report of Welch's Big Sur experience that he composed in the form of a 1962 letter to the poet Robert Duncan.[2] Comparison of the poem "Ring of Bone" and Welch's letter helps us to understand both the poet's breakdown and the experience of survival that remains available to the reader.

**I.**

"Ring of Bone" dates from Welch's stay in Big Sur during the summer of 1962, in solitary retreat at the same location as, but two years later than, the visit on which Welch had been one of Kerouac's companions. That Welch later chose "Ring of Bone" as the title poem for the collected edition that he prepared toward the end of his life as a kind of "spiritual autobiography" suggests the poem's centrality in Welch's thinking about both his life and his art (*Ring* 17). It is a brief poem, quoted here in its entirety:

> I saw myself
> a ring of bone
> in the clear stream
> of all of it

> and vowed,
> always to be open to it
> that all of it
> might flow through
>
> and then heard
> "ring of bone" where
> ring is what a
>
> bell does (*Ring* 91)

On a first surface reading, there seems to be none of the defiance of convention that is supposed to characterize Beat writing. The form observes modernist conventions, especially reminiscent of William Carlos Williams, an important influence on Welch (Phillips 74). But the imagery reaches back to traditions much earlier than modernism: for instance, to the myth of Narcissus, who fell in love with his image in a stream, and to the theme of *memento mori*, with the image of the skull ("a ring of bone") serving as a reminder of mortality. The final image of the bell reinforces that theme, recalling John Donne's explanation of "for whom the bell tolls."

The Beat literary twist on these conventions starts with the tone, which literally re-sounds with a strange doubleness, like the repetition of the phrase "ring of bone." Combined with the mood of depression implied by the theme of mortality (Narcissus, we recall, dies of unfulfillable longing), there is simultaneously a sense of relief, even release. Out of the contracted space defined within a "ring of bone" there grows an expansion, an opening to "all of it," even as the visual image of the ring dissolves into the sound of ringing. This is a combination of tropes characteristic of Beat literature, defeat (beat down) leading to ecstasy (beatific), though that movement is sensed only subtly in Welch's poem (Kerouac, "Beatific" 570-71). The full force of the movement comes through when the poem is read in the context of the visionary experiences that Big Sur provided first to Kerouac and later to Welch.

Kerouac retreated to the Big Sur wilderness in July 1960 in the hopes of controlling his alcoholism and getting in tune with a more natural mode of existence than the life of celebrity he had suffered since the publication of *On the Road* (1957).[3] He had met Welch in San Francisco in fall 1959 right after a disturbing episode of televised stardom, his appearance on *The Steve Allen Show* in Hollywood. Eager for escape, Kerouac was attracted to Welch as the sort of guy who knew how—and where—to get away: "that lean rangy red head Welchman with his penchant for going off in Willie to fish in the Rogue River up in Oregon where he knows an abandoned mining camp, or for blattin around the desert roads" (*Big* 47).[4] "Willie" was the name Welch gave to his car, a Willys Jeepster, in which he, Kerouac, and Albert Saijo (a San Francisco poet affiliated with Beat writers who features briefly in *Big Sur* as

# BIG SUR BREAKDOWN *Diggory*

"George Baso") took off for a cross-country trip in late 1959 to return Kerouac to his home in New York. The trip, which produced a series of collaborative haiku published under the title *Trip Trap* (1973), was a reprise of Kerouac's adventures with his hero Neal Cassady that had supplied the material for *On the Road*. Cassady and Welch were the same age, both born in 1926, four years after Kerouac. *Big Sur* explicitly compares Cassady and Welch, or the characters based on them, as "the two greatest drivers in the world" (71), and Welch, like Cassady, is "one of the world's best talkers" (47). Moreover, at the time of the events chronicled in *Big Sur*, Welch was more willing than Cassady to join Kerouac in a drinking binge (45, 57).

That is the solace that Kerouac sought after the solitude at Big Sur proved to be too much for him. He recruited Welch to drive him around the San Francisco Bay area, with frequent stops at bars and liquor stores in between visits with friends, including Cassady, whom Welch now met for the first time (*Remain* 2: 7). With Cassady's permission, Kerouac shared his mistress, Jacky Gibson (called "Billie" in *Big Sur*)—a form of Beat fraternity in which Welch and Kerouac also indulged, according to Welch, who does not identify the woman in question (*Remain* 1: 182). Kerouac, Gibson, Welch, and the poet Lenore Kandel, Welch's girlfriend at the time, ended up returning to Big Sur to stay in the Bixby Canyon cabin owned by Lawrence Ferlinghetti where Kerouac had attempted his earlier retreat. Having failed the earlier test of solitude, Kerouac now seemed to be testing his capacity for being in relationship. He failed once again, measured against the standards of Welch and Kandel. While the latter couple harmonized with the primal wilderness like "Adam and Eve" (*Big* 157), Kerouac and Gibson tore each other apart, plunging Kerouac into an experience of nightmare. It wasn't just the booze. Jack Duluoz, Kerouac's persona in *Big Sur*, says:

> I marvel that I cant be so useful and humanly simple and good enough to make small talk to make others feel better, like Dave [Wain, the character based on Welch], there he is long and hollow of cheeks from long drinking himself the past few weeks, but he's not complaining or moaning in the corner like me, at least he does something about it, he puts himself to the test—He gives me that feeling again that I'm the only person in the world who is devoid of human-beingness...(*Big* 168)

To be human, Kerouac seems to imply, is to be in, or at least to be capable of, relationship. Having failed to be in relationship with nature or with another person, Kerouac felt as if he had ceased to be, but that ending opened him to the possibility of a new mode of being.

At the conclusion of *Big Sur*, the narrative moves rapidly from the depth of despair to a sudden experience of illumination, from defeat to ecstasy. A single sentence toward the end of the book contains this whole movement: "suddenly hopelessly and completely finished I sit there in the hot sun and close my eyes: and there's the golden swarming peace of Heaven in my eyelids" (*Big* 187). The reference to Heaven is evidence of the persistence of Christian imagery in Kerouac's religious experience, like the image of the Cross that appeared in nightmare visions during the night preceding this moment of enlightenment. However, the word "golden," linked with "eternal" in the next-to-last sentence of *Big Sur*—"And it will be golden and eternal just like that" (188)—indicates that Kerouac is thinking of the "golden eternity" that was his personal take on Buddhist *nirvana*. A key difference between the two perspectives is the fate of the individual self, "saved" for eternal existence in Heaven by way of the Cross in Christian doctrine; dissolved into the continuous, undifferentiated process of Being in Buddhist teaching. The moment of awakening or enlightenment, called *satori* in Zen Buddhism, is accompanied by the death of the ego, so the Beat paradox of defeat and beatitude found ready corroboration, and indeed inspiration, in Zen.

Interest in Buddhism was another common bond between Kerouac and Welch, especially by way of their mutual acquaintance with Gary Snyder and Philip Whalen, who had been fellow students with Welch during his years at Reed College (1948-50). After returning to the East Coast from his experience at Big Sur, Kerouac wrote a joint letter to Whalen and Welch in which he expressed the full ambivalence of that experience: "It appears like I had my first serious nervous or mental breakdown this time but now that it's over I wonder if it wasnt some kind of satori, because I've changed" (*Selected* 265). Linked with the concept of *satori*, the change that Kerouac claims for himself implies a release from the drive either to escape or to punish himself through binge drinking. But a sense of ambivalence lingers in the doubtful expression, "I wonder." The ambivalence deepens when Kerouac's sense of what he felt is compared with Welch's understanding of what he witnessed in Kerouac's behavior.

## II.

Had Kerouac experienced breakdown or *satori*? On the evidence of Kerouac's behavior, and his own history of alcoholism and depression, Welch diagnosed a breakdown. In November of 1960 he wrote to Kerouac: "I knew you were having some sort of a breakup when we last saw each other [....] when the old body starts screaming for help like yours was: not letting you sleep and bringing on the scares and deep depressions (for there isn't any difference between mind/body)...then the only thing to do is slow down, feed yourself, get back in shape" (*Remain* 2: 19). In these last words of simple advice we can hear that concern "to make others feel better" which Kerouac attributes to Welch's persona Dave Wain in *Big Sur*.

# BIG SUR BREAKDOWN *Diggory*

Ominously, in his letter Welch goes on to warn Kerouac more bluntly: "to put it another way and to stop sounding like a nurse, you don't have the right to kill yourself, Jack—too many of us love you and need you around" (*Remain* 2: 19). Kerouac's eventual death in 1969 would seem like a kind of suicide by alcoholism, to judge by the standards that Welch applied to Dylan Thomas and Malcolm Lowry (*Remain* 2: 55). Sadly, despite Kerouac's claim to have changed after his experience in Big Sur, his self-destructive behavior persisted, further casting doubt on his characterization of that experience as a moment of *satori*. A similar doubt hovers over Welch's disappearance in 1971. The question of whether his action involved suicide is entangled in the question of what sense of suicide might apply.

*Satori*, as both Kerouac and Welch understood it, is accompanied by the dissolution of the ego, a kind of death. So if one engages in practice that leads to *satori*, is such practice a form of suicide? In his recalling the many writers who literally committed suicide, Welch drew a careful distinction:

> The really tragic thing about the drownings and gunshots and the irreclaimable madnesses is this:
> They, Poets all of them, missed the truth of it by a quarter of an inch.
> You do not have to do it with a gun. You do not really do it with a gun.
> (*Remain* 2:55)[5]

You do it with writing, as both Welch and Kerouac demonstrate. Through their writing, both aim directly at purging the ego, on the one hand, and indirectly at neutralizing the ego, on the other hand, through the discipline of observation. If Kerouac's *Big Sur* highlights the first method (purging), Welch's "Ring of Bone" highlights the second (neutralizing). In that poem, the self becomes simply a channel of perception, not even a filter, but an opening, "that all of it / might flow through."

In February 1960, shortly after he met Kerouac, Welch wrote a letter to Gary Snyder in which he placed that meeting in the context of several other "huge things" that had recently occurred in his life (*Remain* 1: 181). He had lost a job, given up on women, and even given up on himself. He was now intent on "getting Lew Welch all empty and gone. I am sick of him. He is weak, romantic, over-sensitive to others, afraid, wordy, too thin, too proud (really believes he is a Prince), moody, ashamed, unemployable, and vain. Not only that, he dreams and hopes" (*Remain* 1: 182). In response to his self-disgust, Welch invented an alter-ego called Leo, the name of his astrological sign and also a graphically significant transformation of his own name (replacing a "double-you" [*w*] with a zero [*0*]). If killing off Lew would be suicide, a mere act of destruction, the prospect of killing off Leo helped to stimulate Welch's creativity. He seems to have experimented first with writing

Leo into—and out of—a series of poems. "It is also possible to *uninvent* yourself," he states in "Entire Sermon by the Red Monk" (1960), one of these "Leo Poems" (*Ring* 43, Welch's italics). A draft apparently intended as the preface to a collection of these poems offers a succinct summary of Welch's view on writing as a form of suicide: "All Characters in this book are fictitious. The writer invented them for the sole purpose of exterminating himself, knowing that suicide is illegal, in every sense and State, but knowing, also, that what we think of as 'Self' is our chief enemy, and must be destroyed" (*Ring* 202). In addition to whatever self-disgust might underlie this project as a psychological motive, Welch's statement also implies an ethical motive that commits writing to telling the truth. The self is the writer's enemy because it is false, a fiction. To destroy the self in writing is, at least in part, to expose the self as a fiction.

Under the influence of his new friend, Kerouac, Welch soon turned to writing an autobiographical novel, to be titled *I, Leo*. However, no sooner had Welch begun writing his novel than Leo began "slowly dropping out of it," as Welch reported in his letter to Snyder (*Remain* 1: 182). The narrative concern shifted from Leo, as subjective focus, to the people Leo encounters, viewed more objectively. Of course, getting Leo to "drop out" was the original stimulus for writing, but the fading of that character deprived the novel of its center, so within a year Welch abandoned it in favor of a series of more objective short stories, without a narrating "I" (*Remain* 2: 20). When Kerouac published *Big Sur* in 1962, Welch had a chance to view himself as a character more objectively. He assured Kerouac that the portrayal did not upset him: "Say whatever you like about Lew Welch. I am tired of him" (*Remain* 2: 101). Although Welch claimed that Kerouac, too, was "tired of Leo" (*Remain* 1: 182), he surely did not mean that Kerouac was tired of Welch. Rather, each man was tired of *his* Leo, his ego. "Like you say about you, I'M [sic] tired of myself," Welch wrote to Kerouac (*Remain* 2: 23). Thus, it makes sense to read the novel *Big Sur* as the successful completion, on Kerouac's part, of the writing project that Welch attempted in *I, Leo* but eventually abandoned: the project of purging the ego. If Kerouac's experience at Big Sur felt like *satori* only in retrospect ("now that it's over"), as he reported in his letter to Whalen and Welch (*Selected* 265), it is because Kerouac, at the time of writing that letter, was beginning to take the writer's perspective on the experience of the man. Seeing the self as a fiction became a means of seeing through the self's illusions, freeing writing to serve as a medium of truth. Ultimately, I will argue, this is the reader's perspective on writing in which the writer has disappeared.

The terrors involved in the process of purging the ego were vividly portrayed in letters that Allen Ginsberg sent to both Kerouac and Welch in June 1960, shortly before Kerouac's first visit to Big Sur. Ginsberg was in Peru experimenting with the drug *ayahuasca* or yage, used by the indigenous people of the Amazon region to induce visions during ritual ceremonies. The purgative nature of the ceremony was viscerally enacted in the vomiting that accompanied consumption of the drug. After one particularly powerful session, Ginsberg became convinced that yage induced visions of death, though he quickly brought the terror of that experience under control by writing in his journal: "The struggle & Pain of Death is only the Soul being forced to recognize its Final nature & leave the Separate Individual Self" ("Appendix" 106). At the beginning of *Big Sur*, Kerouac explicitly compares the lessons of yage with the bleak vision he derived from alcohol, having "gone the way of the last three years of drunken hopelessness which is a physical and spiritual and metaphysical hopelessness you cant learn in school no matter how many books on existentialism or pessimism you read, or how many jugs of vision-producing Ayahuasca [yage] you drink, or Mescaline take, or Peyote goop up with" (*Big* 5). At the end of *Big* Sur, the scene of Kerouac's breakdown is staged as a ritual ceremony comparable to those that Ginsberg was reporting in his letters about yage. In place of the Amazonian *curandero*, the presiding shaman is Lew Welch. Gripped by paranoia, Kerouac's persona Duluoz asks about the characters based on Welch and Kandel, "are they members of a secret society that dopes people secretly the idea being to enlighten them or something?" (*Big* 172). The conclusion of the novel, as we have seen, suggests that Kerouac eventually accepted his encounter with death at Big Sur as a form of enlightenment.

While shamanism is one expression of the ecstatic sensibility that Ginsberg and Kerouac shared, it is very different from the more disciplined and detached attitude of Zen Buddhism cultivated by West Coast Beat writers such as Gary Snyder and Philip Whalen.[6] Welch showed his alignment with the latter when he responded to Ginsberg's reports from the Amazon in the guise, not of a shaman, but of a Zen master, or *roshi*. In a letter to Ginsberg dated July 27, 1960, Welch begins with a self-mocking posture: "Leo takes out his Roshi stick, assumes instructive face" (*Remain*: 219). The joke is of course that "Leo," as Welch conceived him, is as false a pose as that of the *roshi*. Welch is responding coolly to Ginsberg's report that after his yage experience he felt himself to be "a permanent fraud" (*Remain* 1: 219), a consequence of "the Soul being forced to recognize its Final nature & leave the Separate Individual Self" ("Appendix" 106).

As Welch explains it: "What is a permanent fraud is the accident, built by your baby, Allen (he calls himself) Ginsberg. He does not, and never has, existed. Ain't all us Zenboes convinced you of this yet?" (*Remain* 1: 219). Welch elaborates on the image of the baby in a poem included in the letter, a version of "The Entire Sermon by the Red Monk," to which I referred earlier: "Whatever I think I am is an accident, built by a baby, on all kinds of baby purpose" (*Remain* 1: 220).[7] But the letter also points ahead to a poem that Welch had not written yet, the poem built around the image of the "ring of bone," which seems to have derived from the imagery Ginsberg employed to describe his yage experience. It is typical of the complicated relationship that existed among the Beat writers, as readers of each other's work, that in a single exchange Welch could project an image against Ginsberg (the baby), yet at the same time take from Ginsberg images that Welch would turn to his own purposes (bell and bone).

Referring first to Ginsberg's experiments with "laughing gas" (nitrous oxide), then to the yage experience, Welch sums up the lesson of the *roshi*: "What actually exists is a void, such as you saw, gassed and laughing: or the gong-purity round inside of skull seen in Andean (and I'm sure) scary wilderness" (*Remain* 1: 219).[8] The images of a ringing bell (gong) and of a skull (a ring-shaped bone) occur throughout Ginsberg's writing from Peru, perhaps most forcefully in a passage from "The Reply":

> a dead gong shivers through all flesh and a vast Being enters my
>    brain from afar that lives forever
> None but the Presence too mighty to record! the Presence
>    in Death, before whom I am helpless
>       makes me change from Allen to a skull (*Collected* 257)

It is clear that, for Ginsberg, this is an entirely negative experience. The "dead gong" is solely a death knell, and the skull is no more than the conventional image of death. But from his Buddhist perspective, Welch reads such images in the positive sense of purification: "the gong-purity round inside of skull." The "change" that Ginsberg laments, "from Allen to a skull," could be a sign of awakening to a new mode of life, the *satori* that led Kerouac to claim, "I've changed," after his experience at Big Sur (*Selected* 265).

For Welch, the new mode of life corresponded to a different mode of writing, a mode of calm observation that contrasts with the frenzied purgation that Ginsberg expresses in his yage letters and poems and that Kerouac describes in the climax of *Big Sur*. Each mode of writing offered a means of cancelling the ego without requiring the literal cancellation of the life of the author in an act of suicide. However, the method of purgation opposed the ego with a kind of negative power that risked putting an end to the act of writing. The annihilating Presence that Ginsberg describes in "The Reply" is "too mighty to record." In the method of observation, recording is the whole purpose of writing, and the writer's self is not so much eliminated as absorbed into that purpose.

Although it is not the style for which either Ginsberg or Kerouac is remembered in the popular imagination, both of these writers in fact practiced a mode of observation. In *Big Sur*, the initial cleansing effect of Kerouac's isolation in the wilderness is reflected in brief notes of sense perception. Chapter 8 of the novel is composed entirely of such notes: "But there's moonlit fognight, the blossoms of

# BIG SUR BREAKDOWN                                  *Diggory*

the fire flames in the stove—There's giving an apple to the mule, the big lips taking hold" (*Big* 31). Ginsberg later composed two "Bixby Canyon" poems, named for the location of Ferlinghetti's Big Sur cabin, in a similar mode: "Bixby Canyon" (1968) and "Bixby Canyon Ocean Path Word Breeze" (1971), both in *Collected Poems* (497-98, 559-567). The individual notations in these poems read like haiku, the poetic form employed in Zen practice to focus perception so sharply that the observer comes to a realization of all that is not there. A haiku is "completely packed with Void of Whole," as Kerouac put it (*Portable* 451), offering another version of the void that Welch saw in Ginsberg's image of "the gong-purity round inside of skull" (*Remain* 1: 219). When Kerouac read Ginsberg's account of his yage experience, he was reminded of a haiku by Buson, in which the ringing of a bell is the central image:

> Coolness—
> the sound of the bell
> as it leaves the bell (Hass 81)[9]

    Haiku or forms of notation that are similar in spirit to haiku abound in Welch's poetry. As I mentioned previously, Welch collaborated in producing haiku with Kerouac and Albert Saijo during their road trip in 1959. The influence of haiku is palpable in the series of "Hermit Poems" that concludes with "Ring of Bone." For instance, at the end of the "Preface" to the series, a string of three phrases separated by white space reads like the three lines of a haiku fitted to a single line: "Robin bedraggled.     Warm rain finally.     Spring." (*Ring* 82). However, "Ring of Bone" itself is based on a different type of observation, less objective in relation to sense data, more self-reflective in two respects. There is, of course, the initial attention to the self as an object: "I saw myself" (*Ring* 91). But there is also the poem's attention to its own language: "and then heard / 'ring of bone.'" In Welch's practice, this sort of attention owes less to Zen than it does to the early influence of Gertrude Stein, the writer who first inspired Welch to become a writer (Meltzer 316-18) and the subject of his undergraduate thesis (1950), published in 1996 as *How I Read Gertrude Stein*. Ultimately, as Vincent Dussol has pointed out, the two influences appear to have merged: "Ground common to Stein and Zen is the erosion of one's self and the one might say concomitant wish to embrace 'it all,' perceive, think and write in terms of the whole" (167). If in Zen, the self is dissolved into the continuous, undifferentiated process of Being, then in Stein, the self is dissolved into the undifferentiated "stream of consciousness" to which Stein was introduced by her teacher William James (Meyer 234-37), and which seems to be reflected as literary artifice in "the clear stream" of Welch's poem "Ring of Bone."

    From the perspective of Stein, the act of seeing with which Welch's poem begins, "I saw myself," is paradoxical because when the writer is absorbed into the act of seeing he or she is no longer available as a subject to be seen. "I am I not any longer when I see," wrote Stein ("Henry James" 149), a maxim that Welch quoted no less than four times in his thesis (Shaffer xxxn2). "This sentence," Stein continued, "is at the bottom of all creative activity." The creator becomes fully absorbed in the act of creation. "We say we are 'lost in our work,'" Welch observed. "When we write very clearly we often say 'the writing wrote itself'" (*How I Read* 22). Welch was fascinated by the way the activity of "word, word, word, word, word" made itself visible in Stein's writing (Meltzer 318). In Stein's *How to Write*, for example, Welch examined the sentence, "A seated pigeon turned makes sculpture" (*How to Write* 58). "See," Welch explained, "the interesting thing about that one is, you don't know where the verb is until the very end. *A seated pigeon turned*—that's a sentence. Then you say *makes*, and *turned* is not a verb anymore" ("How I Work" 57). It is like listening to a Charlie Parker riff, Welch mused. To a lot of people it sounds like "all wrong notes," but some hear it and say, "Wow!" That exclamation signals not merely admiration but awakening to a new set of possibilities—what music (Parker) or language (Stein) can do—and ultimately to a new vision of reality (*satori*). Like haiku in Zen practice, words in Stein's texts do not merely perform; they transform the reader's consciousness.

In addition to envisioning the loss of the writer, in the image of the skull, "Ring of Bone" releases the transformative power of language, not just as writing but also as speech. "Language Is Speech" was the title Welch assigned to an essay about his goals in teaching poetry workshops (*Ring* 235-49). He had learned that lesson from his graduate studies in linguistics under James R. Sledd at the University of Chicago (1951-53), where he sought a more formal understanding of what he had intuited from Stein (*Ring* 238). When it echoes at the end of the poem, the phrase "ring of bone" is not seen, but "heard." And what is heard is quite literally a speech act, not in the technical sense defined by J. L. Austin, but simply as an instance of how words become active and interact with each other, taking on a life of their own; "the writing wrote itself," in Welch's formulation (*How I Read* 22). As in the transformation of "turned" from noun to adjective in the Stein example, what is first seen (read) as a noun ("a ring") in Welch's poem is then heard as a verb, "where / ring is what a / bell does."

For Welch, such ringing expressed the ground tone of language, the "deep structure" of feeling underlying the surface meaning of individual words. As early as 1954, he had captured this feeling in words that came to him, as if on their own, in a dream:

> Through the years of her speech
> a persistent gong
> told us how grief had
> cracked the bell of her soul. (*Ring* 225)

# BIG SUR BREAKDOWN  *Diggory*

Months later, Welch realized that he had been dreaming about his mother (*Ring* 246-47; Meltzer 300-01). However, the "persistent gong" of speech also had, for Welch, a collective dimension, which he called "the din of a Tribe" (*Ring* 236). Like the image of the "cracked bell" in the early poem, or the "ring of bone" in the later poem, the term "din" is deliberately ambivalent, fascinating yet harshly dissonant. Welch found himself drawn to it, but periodically he also felt compelled to withdraw from it. His withdrawal to Big Sur in 1962 came at a moment of crisis in this pattern of oscillation. "I cannot shut out the din anymore," he wrote from Big Sur. "I am afraid" (*Remain* 2: 51).

## III.

That confession appears in an extraordinary document that provides invaluable context for understanding "Ring of Bone." The document is a kind of poem in its own right, as Welch recognized (*Remain* 2: 54), but it takes the form of a letter addressed to Robert Duncan, written during Welch's retreat at Big Sur in 1962 but "neither completed nor sent" (*Remain* 2: 56), according to Donald Allen, who published the text in his edition of Welch's letters. It begins by denouncing the state of the culture, the din of the Tribe, that has driven Welch into retreat: "it has seemed that Everything is dedicated only to mocking MAWKING all that I know is good" (*Remain* 2: 51). As an example, Welch describes hearing on television "a fat trained fake-virile voice," whose "fake" virility must have seemed a mockery of the "good" virility that Welch valued. But very quickly Welch's focus turns inward, to the condition of his spirit, which gives him another reason to fear. The statement I quoted earlier about "the drownings and gunshots and the irreclaimable madnesses" that have ended the lives of other poets comes from this letter to Duncan (*Remain* 2: 55).

During the past five months, Welch writes in the letter (*Remain* 2: 51), he has descended into a state of depression owing to "the usual list" of personal troubles, which he does not bother to specify (*Remain* 2: 52); they would likely include his recent breakup with Lenore Kandel (Meltzer 322). Now at Big Sur he feels he has reached the bottom of this descent. Welch fears that his madness—"I am mad," he admits (*Remain* 2: 52)—may lead to the suicide that has doomed other poets, "the drownings and gunshots" that Welch distinguished from the preferable means available to poets for release from the illusion of ego. The drive for release feels like madness, but the poet has a special means of release that Welch sees, at least for the moment, as his salvation. "I am mad in the way Poet is always" (*Remain* 2: 52), he writes. Here, his special treatment of the word "Poet," with a capital letter and without a definite or indefinite article, hints at an idealization that became yet another obstacle on the path to salvation; he replaced one illusion (ego) with another

(Poet). At Big Sur, however, what mattered most was that being a poet offered Welch an alternative to suicide through the act of writing.

In his letter to Duncan, Welch quotes from a version of "Ring of Bone" as an example of such writing. Before the quotation, he introduces the poem as the product of a "radiant vision of openness" that he experienced at Big Sur, wrenched from the closure into which he had descended in his state of depression (*Remain* 2: 52, 54). As an alternative to seeing himself as "a ring of bone in a clear stream" (*Remain* 2: 54), as in the poem, he also envisions himself in the letter as "a mess of gates," understanding "that having Human Being is to have many many gates, that it *all* all flow through" (*Remain* 2: 52, Welch's italics).[10] Like the poem, the letter also records Welch's vow "never, ever, to close myself again" (*Remain* 2: 54), but the letter goes on to concede that this vow is impossible to fulfill. It "hurts too much," he confesses simply (*Remain* 2: 53). Although he experiences orgasmic ecstasy, a sensation of "fucking the world" (*Remain* 2: 53), during his moment of total openness at Big Sur, the longer such experience lasts, the more likely it becomes that the sensory overload it entails will be felt as intolerable pain.

Awareness of the hurt turns the experience of enlightenment into a "black satori" (*Remain* 2: 53). There is something in him that defends against the pain of openness by seeking closure, something that resembles the ego that dissolves in the experience of *satori*. "Whatever it is," Welch concludes in his letter, "*this* must be killed again and again!" (*Remain* 2: 55, Welch's italics). Is this the death sounded in the ringing of the bell at the end of Welch's poem? "What does that mean?" Welch asks after quoting the poem's conclusion in his letter. Then he writes, "All that is left to say, here, is that this is the moment of suicide" (*Remain* 2: 54). In the context of this letter, it is clear that this statement does not refer to literal suicide, but rather to the writerly suicide available to the poet, and perhaps essential to the poet's role as seer.

Throughout the letter, Welch alludes to Arthur Rimbaud to distinguish the special madness of the poet from ordinary, uncreative madness. Underlying his thinking must be Rimbaud's declaration of the "derangement of all the senses" necessary to become a "seer," who discovers the unknown by abandoning familiar sensation, including the familiar self, abandoned in a gesture that is metaphorically suicidal: "I is another" (Miller 80, 86, 102).[11] But what Welch actually quotes from Rimbaud emphasizes gain rather than loss, an illumination of meaning "literally and in all senses," as Rimbaud explained the meaning of *A Season in Hell* (*Remain* 2: 52, 53; Miller 100). The emphasis on literal meaning insists on the substantial nature of the vision. What is seen is fully present, not immaterial. In a later interview, to explain the nature of the vision he had at Big Sur, Welch put it this way: "A seer is a man who can see things that others cannot see. He is Prometheus, a man who goes into the void, and brings back something and shows it to you, so that that kind of void is forever illuminated" (Meltzer 320). Again, literal meaning is emphasized in the direct presentation of what has been brought back from the void. The seer does not merely tell you about it, he "shows it to you," Welch says. In turn, you, the reader, are invited to see.

Like Rimbaud, whose insistence on literal meaning was a response to his mother's inability to understand his work, Welch was frustrated by his readers' failure to see what his work presented, even when "we write down and down and down, as I have, almost getting to a plainness that obviates all poetry" (*Remain* 2: 53). In his letter to Duncan, Welch complains that the literalness of his poem "Wobbly Rock" (1960)—"it's a real rock" (*Ring* 68)—made no sense to a reader whom he identifies elsewhere as his sister. "I don't understand it," the reader objects. "Why don't you write so that everyone can understand it.? [sic]" (*Remain* 2: 53-54).[12] This is an aspect of the mockery that Welch associated with "the din of the Tribe." Such incomprehension ultimately led Rimbaud, Welch infers, to abandon the vocation of poet altogether. He disappeared in the wilderness of Africa, though not as completely as Welch disappeared in the Sierra foothills; after falling ill, Rimbaud returned to France where he died. Welch's letter to Duncan concludes, "Is Rimbaud's way the only way, in this vulgar age? That we must finally kill Poet out of our total contempt for this time that mocks us?" (*Remain* 2: 56). Thus, the impulse to "kill" expressed in Welch's letter leads in contradictory directions. On the one hand, the poet's role is to "kill" something inside himself that resists openness. On the other hand, the resistance he finds outside himself, in society, pressures him to "kill" or abandon his role as poet.

The idealistic value that Welch assigns to the role of poet in this letter—often signaled by the capital "P"—helps to explain the curious fact that the letter is addressed to Robert Duncan. That Welch himself regarded the fact as curious is acknowledged in the letter's opening sentence: "It is odd that I should want to write this letter to you, since I know so many of us better, who I respect as much" (*Remain* 2: 51). Welch may have first met Duncan in the late 1950s while residing at East-West House, a San Francisco Buddhist commune, where Joanne Kyger, another resident, organized a writing group that welcomed Duncan as one of several visiting mentors (Jarnot 166, 465n4). From then on, Welch and Duncan occasionally crossed paths, but they were never especially close.[13]

Welch seems to draw on the evidence of Duncan's writing rather than any intimate knowledge of his personal life when in his letter he identifies Duncan as "one who has gone through something as black as this, and who made it somehow—or at least is still there, operating his Human Being (your phrase) decently, as a poet" (*Remain* 2: 51).[14] Duncan refers to "human being" as a condition rather than a person in "Pages from a Notebook" (401, 407), which appeared in *The New American Poetry* (1960), Donald Allen's revolutionary anthology that also included two poems by Welch. Among the more substantial selection of Duncan's poems was "A Poem Beginning with a Line by Pindar," which retells the myth of Psyche as recovery from a depression such as Welch had suffered, "something as black as this," as he writes to Duncan. Duncan had written:

>                                    Psyche
>     must despair, be brought to her
>                                    insect instructor;
>     must obey the counsels of the green reed;
>     saved from suicide by a tower speaking,
>           follow to the letter
>           freakish instructions. (53)

Welch's projection of such experience onto Duncan is an inference drawn from the poetry: "you could not have this gift unless you often took trips as black as this, as painful" (*Remain* 2: 56). What counts is the gift, that is, the gift of being a poet, for it is "as a poet" that Welch addresses Duncan in his letter "written by a Poet to a Poet" (*Remain* 2: 54). Of the poets among Welch's acquaintance, Duncan was certainly the one who assumed most grandly the mythic role of Poet, with a capital "P."[15]

But what about Kerouac? Welch had frequently exchanged letters with him since they met in 1959. Although poetry was not his principal medium, Kerouac was certainly a "seer" in the tradition of Rimbaud, about whom he wrote a long biographical poem, "Rimbaud." His novel *Big Sur* records a visionary experience that Kerouac had in the same location as Welch's later experience. Why did Welch not address his letter to Kerouac rather than Duncan? The choice of turning either to Kerouac or to Duncan—though it may not have been a choice that Welch faced consciously—is like the choice examined earlier with regard to Kerouac's experience: was it breakdown or *satori*? In Kerouac, Welch had witnessed breakdown. Turning to Duncan and writing to him as "a Poet to a Poet" allowed Welch to avoid viewing his own experience as breakdown (*Remain* 2: 54). It was *satori*, though a strange kind of "black satori," he conceded (*Remain* 2: 53). In a letter to his mother written from Big Sur at the same time (dated July 18, 1962), Welch insisted rigorously on the distinction. "I have had a violent time of it spiritually," he wrote, "but it looks like I'm coming through. Breakdowns for others are breakthroughs for the Poet. It is one of our major jobs" (*Remain* 2: 51).

It could not, however, be a full time job, as Welch's life confirmed during the years following his vision at Big Sur. The simple explanation, "it hurts too much" (*Remain* 2: 53), applies once again. The demand for ecstasies "every day" gets to be "a drag," Welch discovered (Meltzer 324), and it eventually brought him down. A relationship with Magda Cregg, begun in 1964, sustained him for a while, but they broke up in 1971 amid what Welch recognized to be a breakdown like Kerouac's. He wrote to Cregg: "I really know now where Kerouac was—how the spirit dies so there isn't even fear anymore & the body dies so there isn't any love or courage possible. You can't stop because there isn't anything to stop *with*" (*Remain* 2: 180, Welch's italics). Such desolation would feel bad enough, but Welch was tortured additionally by the disparity between the desolate reality and the visionary ideal. In the final entry of his journal, the day before his disappearance, Welch wrote: "I had great visions but never could bring them together with reality. I used it all up. It's all gone" (*Remain* 2: 187).

It seems that one of his "great visions" was the ideal of being Poet. Although writing poetry served Welch as a means of killing, or neutralizing, the ego ideal that closed him off from the world, his self-image as Poet proved to be the ideal come back to haunt him. He knew there was something wrong. In his letter to Duncan, he wrote, "I begin to wonder how many more times I can kill this thing. Is he always going to grow? Will he always be that same shape? There is some error to the way I keep doing it" (*Remain* 2: 55). His error was to envision the role of Poet as the killer, when it was in fact just one more role that needed to be killed.[16]

While the ideal of the poet never relinquished its grip on Welch, in practice he seemed increasingly willing to relax his grip on the ideal of the poem. The process may have started with "Din Poem" (1961), which purposely lets the "din" in—in the form of song parodies, brand names, street talk, religious and political rhetoric (*Ring* 115-24)—rather than shutting it out as Welch felt he needed to do at the time of his retreat to Big Sur in 1962. Even in the letter that he wrote to Duncan during that retreat, there is evidence that Welch's writing may be moving toward greater openness of form, starting with his recognition that the letter itself "is a poem, a letter and a poem" (*Remain* 2: 54). If clipped, haiku-like effects distinguish the sequence of "Hermit Poems" that includes "Ring of Bone," a looser prose poetry distinguishes "The Way Back," a complementary sequence that marks a later stage in the "spiritual autobiography" that Welch traced in his poems (*Ring* 17).[17]

"The Way Back" includes a text written entirely in prose, entitled "He Begins to Recount His Adventures," in which the speaker describes a fantasy of falling through a hole to the center of the earth and being suspended there, oscillating back and forth over a distance of "only 50 feet or so" from a central position from which "every way is up" (*Ring* 108). This fantasy also appears in the letter to Duncan as an image for a different response to the various dilemmas that tormented him: openness versus closure, visionary ideal versus reality. Once he had killed off the ideal for the moment, perhaps his error was that "I try to come *back* from it, instead of resting on it, when I'm through with it, hanging there, as one would hang, poised, in the center of the earth" (*Remain* 2: 55, Welch's italics). The possibility gives an ironic twist to the title "The Way Back," but perhaps there was a way of resting *in* a dilemma, rather than constantly moving back and forth between its poles.

Although it offers this glimpse of a resolution, on the whole Welch's letter to Duncan moves between the poles of its dilemmas rather than resting in them. On the one hand, Welch commends the process of writing "down and down and down" as "almost getting to a plainness that obviates all poetry" (*Remain* 2: 53). On the other hand, the dominant thrust of the letter turns out to be away from plain "poetry" toward "Poetry" with a capital "P," following the vision that Welch finds himself groping to describe: "After the radiant vision of openness (which it will take me books to bring into words, for I thought at the time 'no poetry, do not stop the flow of it (snagged in flight) but let it go through you'—and, incidently [sic], realized that that is what's wrong with wrong writing: it stops us, whereas Poetry means only 'this is *flight*!!!! This is the open flow of it!!!'" (*Remain* 2: 54, Welch's italics). This ideal of Poetry shares a flaw with the ideal of the Poet that Welch was ultimately unable to reconcile with the reality he experienced, either of himself or of the world. Seeking to extend his vision "at the time," the Poet envisions Poetry as continuing all the time: "do not stop the flow of it." This is the very condition that "hurts too much" to be sustained in the poet's life.

In contrast to the letter that contains it, the poem "Ring of Bone" comes closer to resolving, or resting in, the contradictions that tore the poet apart. Although the poet's "I" is prominently placed as the first word of the poem, the "flow" to which the poem opens is no longer channeled through a "you." As expressed in the poem, the desire is "that all of it / might flow through," whereas the letter to Duncan retains a personal object for the preposition: "let it go through you." Removal of the "you," the self as object, increases the poem's openness. Perhaps even more significant is the poem's handling of time, which resolves, or suspends, the tension between the visionary intensity of the moment and the desire to continue that moment indefinitely. The first stanza presents the moment of vision: "I saw." The second stanza vows to continue: "always to be open to it." But rather than permitting time to flow continuously, the third stanza explicitly divides time by introducing a second moment, "then," that shifts to a different sense modality: from seeing the image of a ring to hearing the word "ring." Indeed, the way the poem draws attention to each separate word through its careful placement has the effect of suspending time, fixing in place a succession of moments. The impression is like that of the Zen garden of Ryoanji that Welch describes in "Wobbly Rock," an image of the ocean (perpetual flow) made out of rocks, "Precisely placed" (*Ring* 69).[18]

Like the image of hanging in suspension at the center of the earth, the title image of "Wobbly Rock" evokes dynamic equilibrium, a way of resting in a dilemma. Welch describes a "real rock" on Muir Beach in California that shudders when it is hit by waves, but remains firmly fixed in place: "Notched at certain center it /

Yields and then comes back to it" (*Ring* 68). This meaning would suffice to explain Welch's allusion to "Wobbly Rock" in his letter to Duncan, in which Welch wrestles with the central dilemmas of his life and work. But the letter suggests more specific links in a chain joining "Wobbly Rock," the dilemma of suicide (with a gun or with writing), and the poem "Ring of Bone." After quoting "Ring of Bone" in the letter, Welch declares:

> this is the moment of suicide (or, in my phrase:
> The instant
> After it is made (*Remain* 2: 54)

The latter quotation is from "Wobbly Rock," in the passage about the garden of Ryoanji, describing the experience of the monks who made the garden and:

> first saw it, even then, when finally they
> all looked up the
> instant AFTER it was made (*Ring* 69)

As Welch explained in a commentary on this poem, the monks saw "what they were doing" only after they were done ("How I Work" 81). As in "Ring of Bone," the crucial time-marker, "then," divides a continuous flow into separate moments, a moment of doing and a moment of knowing.[19]

If "this is the moment of suicide," as Welch claimed in his letter to Duncan, it may be because the writer ceases to exist when the moment of doing is over. The act of writing is complete, or the act of seeing, since the writer is a seer in the tradition of Rimbaud. Yet this mode of suicide does not bring simple annihilation because what was seen can now be heard in words, like the word "ring," and the words remain to be read. At the point in "Ring of Bone" when Welch writes, "and then heard / 'ring of bone,'" the writer is reborn as a reader. He achieves a perspective similar to that which Kerouac reported *after* his experience at Big Sur: "now that it's over" (*Selected* 265).

For both Kerouac and Welch, there is a complex relationship between the original vision that prompted the writing and what is given to the reader to see in the writing. There is a difference. "The poem is not the vision," Welch ultimately conceded (Meltzer 323). However, the poem is a different type of vision, specifically a reader's vision, that reproduces the freshness felt by the one who "first saw it." Later in "Wobbly Rock" (*Ring* 73), after the passage about Ryoanji, Welch humorously compares his vision of the Pacific at Muir Beach with that of the Spanish explorers when they first saw that ocean, as Keats envisioned them in "On First Looking Into Chapman's Homer." Although he is reading Chapman's translation, Keats feels he is seeing Homer's world with an immediacy similar to that of the Spanish explorers viewing the Pacific. For Welch, as for Keats, the reader's experience of words well placed recovers the freshness of vision.

It seems likely that Welch's body will never be recovered from the California wilderness where he disappeared in 1971, but he left behind a body of work that deserves to be recovered from the sort of incomprehension that Welch complained of in his readers, and that, as "the din of the Tribe," contributed to his breakdown at Big Sur. In contrast, his disappearance in his work, such as the poem "Ring of Bone," is a creative act that gives rise to the vision of a reader who is encouraged to see "all of it," including the work into which the poet has disappeared. Is such a reader any less of an ideal than the ideal of the Poet which proved to be such a problem for Welch? Welch has left that question to his real readers to decide.

## Notes

Lew Welch, "['I Saw Myself']" and excerpt from "Dream Poem/Mother" from *Ring of Bone: Collected Poems 1950-1971*. Copyright © 1979 by Donald Allen, Executor of the Estate of Lew Welch. Reprinted with the permission of The Permissions Company, Inc., on behalf of City Lights Books, www.citylights.com.

[1] "A Brief Chronology" in *Ring of Bone* is my basis for dates in Welch's life (251-54). It concludes: "On 23 May [1971], in a deep depression, he took his revolver and walked away into the forest leaving a farewell note. His body has not been found."

[2] Because Welch referred to "my poem called 'Ring of Bone'" (Meltzer 322), I refer to the poem by that title. *Ring of Bone* is also the title of a posthumous collection of Welch's poems first published in 1973 and of the "new and expanded edition" published in 2012. The latter edition presents the first line of the poem in square brackets as the title: "[I saw myself]" (*Ring* 91). For the draft letter to Duncan, I cite the text as it appears in *I Remain, vol. 2* (51-56). It is also available online (Welch, "Draft of a Letter to Robert Duncan").

[3] See T. Diggory, "Many Movies," which examines Kerouac's Big Sur experience in detail.

[4] My quotations from Kerouac silently reproduce his idiosyncratic spelling and vocabulary, since they are such well-known characteristics of his style.

[5] This is from the draft of a letter to Robert Duncan from July 1962, discussed below. Crane's suicide in particular is cited in similar contexts in a letter from Welch to Allen Ginsberg dated July 27, 1960 (*Remain* 1: 221) and in an undated draft preface for a collection of Welch's "Leo Poems" (*Ring* 202).

[6] See interviews with Ferlinghetti and Snyder in Meltzer (104, 288-89). On his property in the Sierra Nevada foothills, Snyder named the site devoted to Zen meditation Ring of Bone Zendo, in honor of Welch (Martien).

[7] Section 7 of "The Entire Sermon by the Red Monk" reads: "On all kinds of baby purpose, you invented whoever you think you are. Out of ingredients you couldn't choose, by a process you can't control" (*Ring* 43).

[8] Ginsberg's experience with laughing gas is recorded in the poems "Laughing Gas" (1958) and "Aether" (1960), the latter drafted during his trip to South America (*Collected* 189-99,

242-54). Other poems from that trip are "To an Old Poet in Peru," "Magic Psalm," and "The Reply" (*Collected* 239-41, 255-56, 257-58).

[9] See Kerouac's letter of June 20, 1960 (Kerouac and Ginsberg, *Letters* 450), in which Kerouac mistakenly credits the Buson haiku to Basho.

[10] Compare the tradition of the "gateless barrier [or gate]" in Zen (*Wu-men-kuan* in Addiss 89). Zen offers a way toward full openness to existence, but the way cannot be conceived as an opening (or gate), because such conceptualization imposes form, or closure. Welch's image of "a mess of gates" resists form through messiness and multiplication, whereas the Zen image works through purifying negation, but the goal is similar.

[11] My references to Rimbaud are cited from Miller because I believe this work is at least one of Welch's sources for Rimbaud. Miller's sources are Rimbaud's letter to Georges Izambard (May 1871) and Isabelle Rimbaud's memoir, *Rimbaud mystique* (1914), containing her brother's explanation to his mother that *A Season in Hell* must be taken "literally and in all senses." Rimbaud was also an important figure for Duncan, who taught a seminar on Rimbaud at Black Mountain College in 1956 (Jarnot 463n19); and for Kerouac, who wrote the poem "Rimbaud" (1960).

[12] Welch identifies his sister as the uncomprehending reader in "How I Work as a Poet" (77-78).

[13] According to the chronology in *Ring* (253), Welch helped Duncan organize a show called "Looking at Pictures with Gertrude Stein" in spring 1965.

[14] Compare Kerouac's persona Duluoz, on feeling "devoid of human-beingness" (*Big* 168). Lisa Jarnot rejects the suggestion that Duncan suffered from depression in his life (452n23). On the other hand, Peter O'Leary identifies depression as a key element in Duncan's poetics (151-60).

[15] See the opening paragraphs of Duncan's essay "The Truth and Life of Myth" (1968). Here, as Peter O'Leary notes (130-32), Duncan presents the experience of "the inspired poet" as both psychotic, aligning with Welch's account of madness in his letter, and shamanistic, aligning with Ginsberg's experience in Peru. Welch's description of his ecstatic experience at Big Sur recalls characteristic features of shamanism, particularly the sensation of flight (*Remain* 2: 54), which ultimately finds its fullest expression in Welch's late poem, "Song of the Turkey Buzzard" (1971) in *Ring* (147-51). Following Mircea Eliade, O'Leary (147) discusses shamanistic flight in connection with Duncan's poem "My Mother Would Be a Falconress" (1968).

[16] Compare Zen teaching about "killing the Buddha" (*Lin-chi Record* in Addiss 49-50). Although the Buddha represents emancipation, as a representation, he is just one more "form" from which one needs to be emancipated. In writing to Snyder about the need to purge "Leo," Welch had complained that Leo "really believes he is a Prince." I contend that Poet became for Welch a version of that Prince that needed to be purged.

[17] In *Ring*, "Hermit Poems" precedes "The Way Back," but both sequences are assigned the same range of dates, 1960-64. Thus, while the structure of the book suggests a linear narrative sequence, the overlapping dates of composition suggest repeated oscillation between two impulses, withdrawing from society and returning to it.

[18] Compare Snyder's image of words "like rocks. / placed solid" in "Riprap" (1959). In thinking about the "wobbly rock," Welch acknowledged that he had "on my mind" (*Remain* 1: 194) the image of the "unwobbling pivot" that Ezra Pound adopted from Confucian writings (*Chung Yung*). Welch's perspective, influenced by Zen, is more experiential—"it's a real rock" (*Ring* 68)—and less dogmatic ("unwobbling").

[19] The version of "Ring of Bone" quoted in the letter to Duncan seems to resist the division into two moments: it reads, "right now heard" (*Remain* 2: 54), instead of "then heard" (*Ring*

91). A fusion of the moment of doing and the moment of knowing is suggested in a formulation by Gertrude Stein that Welch liked to quote: "You know yourself knowing it" (Stein, "Poetry and Grammar" 320). See Welch, *How I Read Gertrude Stein* 16; "How I Work as a Poet" 52. References to Stein at the opening of "How I Work as a Poet" lay the groundwork for Welch's later discussion of the Ryoanji passage in "Wobbly Rock" ("How I Work" 78-81). In addition to the quotation from "Poetry and Grammar," Welch seems also to be thinking of a statement from "Composition as Explanation" which supports the division of moments: "they all really would enjoy the created so much better just after it has been made" (521). This is closer to "the / instant AFTER it was made" described in "Wobbly Rock" (*Ring* 69).

## Works Cited

Addiss, Stephen, Stanley Lombardo, and Judith Roitman. *Zen Sourcebook: Traditional Documents from China, Korea, and Japan*. Hackett, 2008.

Allen, Donald, editor. *The New American Poetry 1945-1960*. U of California P, 1999.

Charters, Ann, editor. *The Portable Jack Kerouac*. Penguin, 1996.

Diggory, Terence. "The Many Movies of Kerouac's *Big Sur*." *Beat Drama: Playwrights and Performances of the "Howl" Generation*, edited by Deborah Geis, Bloomsbury, 2016, pp. 309-26.

Duncan, Robert. "My Mother Would Be a Falconress." *Bending the Bow*. New Directions, 1968, pp. 52-54.

——. "Pages from a Notebook." 1953. Allen, pp. 400-407.

——. "A Poem Beginning with a Line by Pindar." 1958. Allen, pp. 49-57.

——. "The Truth and Life of Myth: An Essay in Essential Autobiography." 1968. *Collected Essays and Other Prose*, edited by James Maynard, U of California P, 2014, pp. 139-94.

Dussol, Vincent. "Lew Welch and Theory Or How Reading Gertrude Stein Impacted on a Beatnik Poet's (Views on) Poetry." *GRAAT,* no. 8, Aug. 2010, pp. 158-177. www.graat.fr/dussol.pdf.

Ferlinghetti, Lawrence. Interview with David Meltzer. 1999. Meltzer, pp. 96-106.

Ginsberg, Allen. "Appendix 6: From Ginsberg's June 1960 South American Journal." *The Yage Letters Redux*, by William Burroughs and Ginsberg, edited by Oliver Harris, City Lights, 2006, pp. 101-10.

——. *Collected Poems 1947-1980*. Harper and Row, 1984.

Hass, Robert, editor. *The Essential Haiku: Versions of Basho, Buson and Issa*. HarperCollins, 1994.

Jarnot, Lisa. *Robert Duncan: The Ambassador from Venus*. U of California P, 2012.

Keats, John. "On First Looking Into Chapman's Homer." *Selected Poetry*, edited by Paul de Man, Signet, 1966, pp. 84.

Kerouac, Jack. "Beatific: The Origins of the Beat Generation." 1959. Charters, pp. 565-73.
——. *Big Sur*. Penguin, 2011.
——. "Rimbaud." 1960. Charters, pp. 458-63.
——. *The Scripture of the Golden Eternity*. 1960. Charters, pp. 590-97.
——. *Selected Letters, 1957-1969*. Edited by Ann Charters, Viking, 1999.
Kerouac, Jack, and Allen Ginsberg. *Jack Kerouac and Allen Ginsberg: The Letters*. Edited by Bill Morgan and David Stanford, Viking, 2010.
Kerouac, Jack, Albert Saijo, and Lew Welch. *Trip Trap: Haiku on the Road*. Edited by Donald Allen, City Lights/Grey Fox, 1998.
Martien, Jerry. "Out Looking for Lew: Bioregional Poetics and the Legacy of Lew Welch." *Big Bridge* vol. 15, Spring 2011, www.bigbridge.org/BB15/2011_BB_15_FEATURES/2011_BB_15_WELCH_FEATURE/OUT_LOOKING_FOR_LEW.pdf
Meltzer, David. *San Francisco Beat: Talking With Poets*. City Lights, 2001.
Meyer, Steven. *Irresistible Dictation: Gertrude Stein and the Correlations of Writing and Science*. Stanford UP, 2003.
Miller, Henry. *The Time of the Assassins: A Study of Rimbaud*. New Directions, 1962.
O'Leary, Peter. *Gnostic Contagion: Robert Duncan and the Poetry of Illness*. Wesleyan UP, 2002.
Phillips, Rod. "'The Journal of a Strategic Withdrawal': Nature and the Poetry of Lew Welch." *"Forest Beatniks" and "Urban Thoreaus": Gary Snyder, Jack Kerouac, Lew Welch, and Michael McClure*. Peter Lang, 2000, pp. 71-102.
Pound, Ezra, translator. "*Chung Yung* (The Unwobbling Pivot)." 1947. *Confucius*. New Directions, 1969, pp. 93-188.
Shaffer, Eric Paul. Introduction. *How I Read Gertrude Stein*, by Lew Welch, edited by Shaffer, Grey Fox, 1996, pp. vii-xxxii.
Snyder, Gary. Interview with David Meltzer. 1999. Meltzer, pp. 276-93.
——. "Riprap." 1959. Allen, pp. 308-309.
Stein, Gertrude. "Composition as Explanation." 1926. *Writings 1903-1932*, edited by Catherine R. Stimpson and Harriet Chessman, Library of America, 1998, pp. 520-29.
——. "Henry James." 1947. *Writings 1932-1946*, edited by Catherine R. Stimpson and Harriet Chessman, Library of America, 1998, pp. 149-89.
——. *How to Write*. 1931. Dover, 1975.
——. "Poetry and Grammar." 1935. *Writings 1932-1946*, Catharine R. Stimpson and Harriet Chessman, pp. 313-36.
Welch, Lew. "Draft of a Letter to Robert Duncan, Bixby Canyon, July 1962." *Electronic Poetry Center*. epc.buffalo.edu/authors/welch/to_duncan.html.

———. *How I Read Gertrude Stein*. Edited by Eric Paul Shaffer, Grey Fox, 1996.
———. "How I Work as a Poet." 1971. *How I Work as a Poet and Other Essays/Plays/Stories*, edited by Donald Allen, Grey Fox, 1973, pp. 50-91.
———. *I Remain: The Letters of Lew Welch and the Correspondence of His Friends*. Edited by Donald Allen, Grey Fox, 1980. 2 vols.
———. Interview with David Meltzer. 1969. Meltzer, pp. 294-324.
———. "Language Is Speech." 1970. *Ring of Bone: Collected Poems*. Edited by Donald Allen, City Lights/Grey Fox, 2012, pp. 235-49.
———. *Ring of Bone: Collected Poems*. Edited by Donald Allen, City Lights/Grey Fox, 2012.

# Michael McClure: A Filmography
## By Jane Falk

### Introduction

From the late 1950s into the early 1970s, Michael McClure appeared in five underground films, four documentaries, had roles in several independent feature length films, included film as a component of several of his plays, worked on a screen play of his novel, *The Adept,* shot documentary footage himself, and wrote film criticism. Although the screen play was never optioned for a movie, and McClure's film of his mushroom-hunting trip with Sterling Bunnell to Mexico was never completed and is now lost, McClure's adventure with film is surely impressive and is the subject of this filmography.[1] David James in his study *Allegories of Cinema* considers the 1960s a key moment for underground film in the United States: "Growing variously from New York and from San Francisco's North Beach scene, the history of underground film was shaped by the history of the bohemian subcultures and the shifts in their ideological and aesthetic principles" (119). McClure was part of this San Francisco "bohemian" art scene, his own theories and poetic practices feeding into the collaborative and multimedia period during which he embraced film.

McClure was born in Kansas in 1932 where he went to high school with assemblage artist and filmmaker Bruce Conner. After attending college at the universities of Wichita and Arizona, he settled in the Bay Area in the early 1950s where he gravitated to poet Robert Duncan's circle through courses at San Francisco State University. There he met experimental filmmaker Stan Brakhage and, through him and Duncan, filmmakers such as Lawrence Jordan, who knew Brakhage from Denver where they had grown up. McClure was also part of the seminal 6 Gallery poetry reading where East and West Coast poets associated with the Beat Generation read together for the first time. Thus, he uniquely combines San Francisco Renaissance, Beat Generation, and Bay Area experimental art scenes, while later as a denizen of the Haight district during the 1960s, he became associated with the hippie scene. McClure's involvement with Bay Area artists demonstrates the importance of a West Coast psychedelic art approach and positions him in San Francisco's urban milieu in its transition from Beat to Hip.

Many of these connections are caught on film. This period also demonstrates the importance of the communitarian for McClure. For example, most of the directors as well as many of those he performed with were personal friends, and the films were more like collaborations. McClure's role was primarily that of poet and inhabitant of San Francisco, a charismatic city dweller. Alternatively, he was shown as a rebel, especially in his roles in independent film.

However, just as significantly, these Bay Area collaborations can be seen as an aspect of McClure's working methods, which shed light on the multimedia emphasis in his work. In an interview with Harold Mesch, McClure notes of Mesch's comments on the "structural similarities" in some of his books that "a primary process of our [human] thinking is to move away from a scene, to come back to the scene, to move away from it in another direction....We create an expanding field around the scene and that gives...other resonances, other connections, other possibilities" ("Writing One's Body" 19). In addition, McClure espouses and practices an embodied poetics, seeing poetry as body-centered and organic; this may be the impetus for including his poetry in the more physically-inhabited media of film, stage, and video. The expansion of media is thus another way that McClure and others expanded consciousness. Ultimately, these points of cinematic light combine with words of poems, plays, and essays to form new constellations by which to experience McClure's body of work.

The McClure filmography that follows is divided into five sections: Underground Film and Video; Independent Film; Documentary Film and Video; Films and Plays; and Miscellaneous Film-Related Projects. Entries begin with director rather than title of film to better emphasize the varied and esteemed directors with whom McClure worked. In the case of films with numerous actors, only the leading ones in addition to McClure are listed.

### Filmography: Underground Film

Underground film, as defined by David James, involves film as "home movies" with "alternative practices," for example the use of 8 or 16 mm film stock in comparison to commercial film's use of standard 35 mm film. Sheldon Renan, in *An Introduction to The American Underground Film,* characterizes such a film as "conceived and made by one person and is a *personal statement*....It is a film that dissents radically in form or in technique, or in content, or perhaps in all three." He adds that "made for very little money...its exhibition is outside commercial film channels" (17). Renan also makes the point that *underground* is more often applied to films of the 1950s and 1960s, while *avant-garde* and *experimental* are terms more often associated with earlier periods of film history (21-22).

Brakhage, Stan, dir. *Two: Creeley/McClure*. Perf. Robert Creeley and Michael McClure. 1965. Orig. 8 mm and 16 mm. 3 min. DVD. Commercially available as *By Brakhage: An Anthology, Criterion Collection.*

Similarly to other Beat writers during the heyday of experimental film, McClure was often portrayed as a poet and focus of the camera's eye. This is the case with

# MICHAEL MCCLURE: A FILMOGRAPHY  *Falk*

Brakhage's 1965 color silent film portrait, *Two: Creeley/McClure*. Part of a series, *15 Song Traits,* Creeley's portrait comes first, then McClure's.[2] Brakhage depicts Creeley with negative reverse tones, as well as positive, in a fairly static, seated manner with some abrupt cuts near the end. In contrast, McClure is presented more dynamically with staccato and diagonal movements of the camera, simulating poetic voice. A flicker effect is also created as Brakhage's camera jumps rapidly between McClure's face and that of an image of a lion, an animal persona McClure had taken on in his 1964 poetry collection, *Ghost Tantras,* with poems written in what McClure calls beast language.[3] McClure also makes a brief appearance in Brakhage's *The Songs: 23rd Psalm Branch,* 1967, where he plays the autoharp as part of the Brakhage domestic scene.

Conner, Bruce, dir. *Liberty Crown.* Perf. Michael McClure. 1967. 3 min. Video. Collection Pacific Film Archive, Berkeley, CA.

This 1967 experimental black and white video, part of KQED's series on Bay Area arts, presents McClure reading one of his poems, "The Screen is Red and Gold and White and Pink," from the collaboration *Mandala,* with poems by McClure and drawings by Conner, published by Dave Haselwood in 1966. McClure reads in a somewhat measured fashion, while Conner's camera work with feedback loops and distortions presents a more dynamic image of the poet, similarly to Brakhage's film. McClure even seems to project an aura at one point. Of the video, Conner states that he "'tried to use its electronic character to make it obvious that there were cameras there that might be moving to Michael'....McClure was seen reading the poem to his own image on the set screen, sometimes multiplied in the process of feedback going into the monitors" (qtd. in Reveaux 109).

Jordan, Lawrence, dir. *Spectre Mystagogic.* Perf. Michael McClure, Joanna McClure, and Mary Rexroth. 1957. Orig.16 mm. 8 min. DVD. Rental from Canyon Cinema, San Francisco.

Lawrence Jordan's *Spectre Mystagogic* begins with a quote from Dada artist Hans Arp's *On My Way,* which contrasts light and shadow, flames and waves, the dead and the living, space and time. The title of this film can be loosely translated as *ghostly presence* who initiates others into mysteries, a figure played by Michael McClure who moves between the contrasts Arp has described. Throughout, the camera cuts between the world of nature (city park with pond and playground) and the domestic (a flat with mother and infant). The film, in black and white and silent but for a Beethoven score, begins with a distance shot of McClure and a young girl approaching each other by the edge of the pond. They never meet, although at one point their paths cross and the girl throws her ball into the water as McClure stands nearby. In between, McClure moves rapidly and stealthily between park and flat, through flickering light and shadows of trees and stairways. Sitting briefly at a table opposite the infant's presumed mother, he smokes a cigarette, then returns to the park for the final scene with pond's rippled reflections of spectre and girl. Viewers see McClure as enigmatic and charismatic. Jordan describes this film as a "fairly complete portrait of Michael McClure."[4]

———. *Triptych in Four Parts.* Perf. Wallace Berman and family, Larry Jordan, Philip Lamantia, Michael McClure and John Reed. 1958. 16 mm. 12 min. Rental from Canyon Cinema, San Francisco.

*Triptych in Four Parts,* in color and silent but for a sitar sound track, exemplifies underground film as "shaped by bohemian subcultures," in James's words. It also demonstrates the interest in art as both expanded mind and mind-expanding for Jordan, McClure, and others. The first and last parts depict San Francisco artists, John Reed, the Berman family, McClure, and Philip Lamantia respectively, while the second and third feature drugs as spiritual mind expansion, including peyote harvesting with Jordan in Texas. Jordan characterizes the film as "'a spiritual drug odyssey seeking religious epiphany'" (qtd. in Sitney 164). McClure appears with the Bermans in their flat as a disembodied hand holding a cigarette. His association with peyote is suggested here, but is evident in both his essay "Drug Notes," containing descriptions of various mind-expanding drug experiences, and "Peyote Poem," written at about this time and published in 1958 in the third number of Berman's *Semina* magazine. According to McClure, Berman introduced him to peyote, while in turn, McClure introduced Jordan.[5] McClure's essay echoes the intense and saturated colors and chiaroscuro effects Jordan captures in this film, reflecting the visual effects that peyote afforded its users as described by McClure in his essay: "White hands speak to you in sign language on a screen of black velvet" (27).[6]

———. *Visions of a City.* Perf. Michael McClure. 1957/1979. Orig. 16mm. 8 min. DVD. Commercially available as *The Lawrence Jordan Album.*

This sepia-toned film, silent but for its impressionistic jazz score by William Moraldo, was shot in 1957, but edited in 1979. Jordan depicts McClure as a habitué of San Francisco, or in critical theorist Walter Benjamin's terms, an urban *flaneur*, as discussed in the latter's study of Baudelaire. Benjamin would go on to describe this type of urban character in "The Return of the *Flaneur"* as "the priest of the genius loci," who looks for "images wherever they lodge" (264). Jordan's camera finds McClure as one passerby on a crowded city street, following him as he walks amidst San Francisco's downtown bustle. Jordan focuses on visual effects with reflections of McClure in store or restaurant windows, the surfaces of cars, and even bottles. McClure is anonymous, but magnetic. The film ends as he gets on a bus with a parting shot of Victorian houses in a more residential district, where presumably the bus has stopped to let McClure on. McClure's appearance in a number of Jordan's films in this period may reflect their close physical proximity, living as they did for a time in the same building in San Francisco. In addition, according to Jordan, the two worked on several writing and film projects which never came to fruition.[7]

### Filmography: Independent Film

In contrast to underground film, independent film is characterized by James as "the American art film," which is "produced as commodities to be put on the industrial market," though funded by "a series of ad hoc entrepreneurial efforts" (281). For example, Norman Mailer, producer and director of *Beyond the Law*, bankrolled his films himself. Renan defines independent filmmakers as "commercial filmmakers who produce Hollywood-type films outside the studio system" (22).

Fonda, Peter, dir. *The Hired Hand.* Perf. Verna Bloom, Peter Fonda, Michael McClure, and Warren Oates. 1971. Orig. 35mm, 93 min. Universal Pictures. DVD. Commercially available.

*The Hired Hand* is a western directed by and starring Peter Fonda as Harry, a drifter. With his sidekick, Arch, Harry returns to the wife he had abandoned to go West, and she takes him back as a hired hand. McClure has a minor role as Ed Plummer, small town troublemaker. Harry encounters Plummer in the town bar, where Plummer makes insinuating remarks about Harry and the lady he works for. A violent fight ensues with Harry and Arch joining in, after which Harry and Arch are kicked out of the bar. The film ends as Harry goes back out West where he is killed avenging yet another comrade. In outtakes not included in the final cut of the film, Plummer is shown shooting it out in the bar with Harry and Arch, and Plummer is killed. According to McClure, he had met Fonda through Rip Torn who had directed McClure's play, *The Beard*, in its Los Angeles venue. McClure's appearance in this film demonstrates his connections to the alternative art scene in Los Angeles. The rebellious character he plays seems to allow for an association others make about him in real life.

Mailer, Norman, dir. *Beyond the Law.* Perf. Buzz Farber, Mickey Knox, Norman Mailer, Michael McClure, George Plimpton and Rip Torn. 1968. Orig. 35mm. 98 min. Supreme Mix, Inc. DVD.
Commercially available as *Eclipse Series 35: Maidstone and Other Films.*

Norman Mailer's independent feature length film, *Beyond the Law,* was shot over four days in October 1967, when McClure's play, *The Beard,* was opening in New York at the Evergreen Theater. McClure had met Mailer a few years previously through Allen Ginsberg and connected with him while in New York. The film's action takes place over one night in a police precinct where criminals are being booked and interrogated, and in a bar where the detectives recount their evening's adventures. Film critic Vincent Canby characterizes the film as "improvisational moviemaking," because the dialogue was ad-libbed by the actors per Mailer's direction (142). McClure plays a long-haired Hell's Angel named Grahr who is arrested by the police with his buddy, played by Torn. Interestingly, *grahr* is one of the most frequently used words in McClure's beast language. Supposedly on a bad LSD trip, Grahr acts violently toward the detectives trying to interrogate him, one of them played by Mailer. There are homosexual overtones as he is harassed, his hair pulled, while police call him beatnik, hippie, and long hair. Here McClure again plays a rebel, rather than being portrayed in the rebellious terms of experimental cinema. McClure's collaboration on an autobiography of Hell's Angel Freewheelin' Frank may also have had something to do with his casting as a biker.[8]

### Filimography: Documentary Film

Webster's Dictionary defines the term documentary "as recording or depicting in artistic form a factual and authoritative presentation as of an event or a social or cultural phenomenon; as a documentary journalist or film." Documentaries are usually considered to be objective, although they are certainly subjective constructions, and often used for educational purposes. Sheldon Renan compares the objective documentary film to the subjective "fictive and transformatory" film but notes that an underground filmmaker "tends to make films of things in actual life (documentary), but he usually transforms their appearances and their importance (fictive and transformatory) in the process of filming and editing" (25).

Moore, Richard, dir. *USA: Poetry.* Perf. Brother Antoninus and Michael McClure. 1966. 58 min. KQED/NET. Video.
Collection Harvard University, Lamont Library.

This black and white video, the first in a four-part program originally made by KQED-TV, San Francisco in collaboration with National Educational Television (NET), New York, features Brother Antoninus (William Everson) and Michael McClure. Both have 29-minute segments. McClure, taped primarily in his home, is dressed first in a Nehru jacket with beads and tambourine, then changes to a flowered shirt. Reading some of his poems as well as commenting on them, he describes himself as an "experimentalist," listing experiments with drugs, especially peyote, and the creation of his word decks.[9] Filmmaker Bruce Conner then makes a guest appearance demonstrating McClure's "Lion Fight Word Deck." McClure makes the point that he wants to write poetry where sound creates an image in the body; he reads from *Ghost Tantras,* his experiments with poems written in beast language. The video closes with McClure reading "Silence the Eyes" from that volume to lions at the San Francisco zoo. The video is as much an interview as it is a poetry reading.

———. *USA: Poetry: Outtakes.* Perf. Michael McClure. 1978. 45 min. Poetry Center, San Francisco State University. Video.
Collection Harvard University, Lamont Library.

This video, outtakes from the *USA: Poetry* series shot in 1966, was produced by the Poetry Center at San Francisco State University in 1978. It begins with McClure reading from *Ghost Tantras* to the lions at the San Francisco zoo, then segues to McClure at home displaying the words on his "Lion Fight Word Deck." When asked about his past, he provides a zany autobiography: he had three fathers and his mother was a Mongolian princess. Bruce Conner makes an appearance and they play music together, McClure on the autoharp and Conner on the harmonica. McClure continues to goof for the camera, as Conner and McClure simultaneously read random passages from Plato. McClure talks about finding the divine in daily reality, no matter how strange, adding that he does not want to be categorized. His wife Joanna McClure appears and listens as McClure reads from his novel, *The Mad Cub,* while the camera pans the room picking out among other images a poster of a Hell's Angels movie and a Wallace Berman photograph. In this outtake video, McClure is presented as more irreverent and spontaneous than in the original *USA: Poetry* video.

Scorsese, Martin, dir. *The Last Waltz.* Perf. The Band, Lawrence Ferlinghetti, and Michael McClure. 1976. Orig. 35mm.117 min. Last Waltz Productions, Inc. Video.
Commercially available as *The Martin Scorsese Film Collection.*

This music documentary presents the last performance of The Band, Bob Dylan's backup band, in San Francisco's Winterland Ballroom, November 1976. There are many other musicians featured performing covers of The Band's songs, as well as documentary footage of band members as they prepare for the concert. As San Francisco's unofficial poet laureates, both Ferlinghetti and McClure read poetry between acts, McClure reading from "The Prologue" to Chaucer's *Canterbury Tales*. He alludes to this in the poem "The Last Waltz" from *Simple Eyes* (1993), adding in the notes section that he "meant to go on and recite a poem of my own next, but there was such benign amazement in the auditorium that I stopped with Chaucer" (129). McClure's inclusion in this event also demonstrates his close association with the San Francisco music scene in the 1960s and 1970s.[10]

Williams, Dick, dir. *The Maze*. Perf. Michael McClure. 1967. Orig KPIX-TV. Video. 25 min. Web. 19 Oct. 2017. http://diva.sfsu.edu/bundles/189371. Available online, see URL.

McClure is host and narrator of this documentary, produced by KPIX-TV, taking viewers on a walking tour of Haight Ashbury at the height of the hippie influx in 1967, thus acting as its genius loci. According to McClure, KPIX asked him to participate in this program. A counter to the media's sensationalized Haight as a scene of drugs and free love during the Summer of Love that same year, McClure's Haight is a compassionate place where free food is distributed by the Digger group; a poster store displays the people's art; and cooperative living spaces are places to practice spiritual communion. We even look in on a rehearsal of McClure's play, *The Beard*, at the neighborhood Straight Theater. Interestingly, in a short piece called, "Tear Gas," published in Diane di Prima and LeRoi Jones/Amiri Baraka's *Floating Bear* magazine (1969), McClure would write about a more brutal experience in the Haight as he observes a night riot where police are tear-gassing a gathering of young people with no idea of how the riot started. This video demonstrates a strong connection between the Beat Generation and the Hippie movement.

### Filmography: Films and Plays

This category refers to both plays in which McClure includes film as part of the play's stage set, as well as films which include or document McClure's plays, themselves, especially his most controversial play, *The Beard*.[11] The filming of these works involves not only a record of the play but also an alternative way to view it. Interestingly, Renan notes underground film's "tendency to document other works of art or to use them as a springboard," giving as example Jonas Mekas's film of *The Brig*, performed by the Living Theater (27).

# MICHAEL MCCLURE: A FILMOGRAPHY  Falk

McClure, Michael. *The Beard.* Grove Press: New York, 1965. Print.

McClure's most controversial play, *The Beard,* a dialogue between Billy the Kid and Jean Harlow, was busted and banned as obscene at its first public performances in December 1965, and then exonerated in a San Francisco court room in 1966, five months after litigation began. However, subsequent showings in Berkeley, Cal State Fullerton, and Los Angeles, also came under scrutiny and harassment, while venues in New York and London went without incident. McClure included film in the second performance of this play at the Fillmore, a rock hall in San Francisco. McClure describes the Fillmore production in a 1966 interview, "Writing *The Beard,*" where the stage set was put on the Fillmore bandstand: "Tony Martin set up an enormous and beautiful light show with everything from movies of horses running through liquid projections to…movies of little girls skipping rope and clouds passing by.…So, although we were looking upward at the play, it was as if the universe or the ocean of images was behind it" (288-289). He notes that there was also a light show for the play in New York (292).

——. *The Raptors.* Santa Barbara: Black Sparrow Press, 1957/1969. Print.

An earlier example of McClure including film in one of his plays is his farce, *The Raptors,* written in 1957 but published in 1969. In one scene, the stage directions call for film footage to be played as the characters, The Rose, The Wolf, General Planarian, and The Shark, march around the stage. At this point, "a movie of a woman struggling with a monster or tied to a stake and being molested is projected on the back of the stage. The movie should be sexy and lascivious. None of the actors notice the movie" (35). The inclusion of the film clip here (presumably from a Hollywood B movie) gives the impression of a happening, as well as demonstrates the influence of filmmaker Bruce Conner, who used found-film footage in his underground films of the 1950s and 1960s. Questioning the conventional commodity aspect of film, this method allows experimental filmmakers to subvert the status quo.[12] In *The Raptors,* the specific subject matter of the found footage may also imply an ironic commentary because the mission of the General and the other raptors is to free purity (The Rose) from truth.

Varda, Agnes, dir. *Lions Love (…and Lies).* Perf. Shirley Clarke, James Rado, Gerome Ragni, and Viva. 1969. Orig. 35 mm. 112 min. Cine-Terminus. DVD. Commercially available as *Agnes Varda Collection: Toute Varda.*

French director Agnes Varda's film about making a Hollywood film features underground filmmaker Shirley Clarke playing Varda, and the actors Viva, James Rado, and Gerome Ragni (non-Hollywood stars) playing the main characters, who form a ménage à trois. The film begins as the threesome enters a theater where McClure's play *The Beard* is being shown. They return home to discuss the play, then act out the same scene in their empty backyard swimming pool for an audience of children. Varda also includes TV footage of Bobby Kennedy's assassination in Los Angeles and the shooting of Andy Warhol in New York. The film ends with each of the stars making a last statement to the camera. Varda describes her interest in *The Beard* in a 1971 interview with Andre Cornand, noting that the play "had provoked a big scandal." She adds that seeing the play had influenced her to make a "film about stars" (52). According to McClure, Varda did not contact him about using his play in her film. Ultimately, both the film and McClure's play present the fantasy of stardom, often synonymous with Hollywood, versus the American reality of sex and violence.

Warhol, Andy. *The Beard.* Perf. Gerard Malanga and Mary Woronov. 1966. Orig. 16 mm. 60 min. Video.
Limited access, Michael McClure funds, Contemporary Literature Collection, Special Collection and Rare Books, Bennet Library, Simon Fraser University.

Gerard Malanga, poet and assistant to Andy Warhol, originally arranged with McClure to shoot this film version of *The Beard;* Malanga subsequently starred in it as Billy the Kid opposite the Warhol-superstar, Mary Woronov, who played Jean Harlow. Tony Power, curator at Simon Fraser University which houses McClure's archive, describes the film: "The two actors read from the script, there are no sets or costumes or action, and the shot is standard Warhol fixed camera throughout."[13] Woronov believes the film was shot in Los Angeles and remembers wearing a paper beard, part of McClure's stage directions.[14] She recalls that the actors read from the script, but did not follow their lines closely, in the spirit of Warhol films which involve a degree of ad-libbing and spontaneity. As Woronov puts it, "no set, no blocking, no script."[15] McClure mentions his reaction to the film in a June 6, 1966, letter to Brakhage: "Warhol wrote via his apprentice Malanga asking permission to do *The Beard* as a seventy-minute sound film….At first it sounded good and then finally I said NO! Then I got a card from LA…saying they had gone ahead and done *Beard* anyway" (*Flame* 101). McClure went down to see the film and found it to be "bad." Even after seeing the film several more times, he was convinced it was unworthy of distribution and got an injunction from a lawyer in order to keep Warhol from showing the film publicly.[16] Perhaps, as with Varda, the play's controversial nature made it more appealing to Warhol.

# MICHAEL MCCLURE: A FILMOGRAPHY

**Filmography: Miscellaneous Film-Related Projects**

This last category refers to film-related writing by McClure, specifically film criticism and a film script. McClure also dedicated a number of poems to various filmmakers, such as "For Kenneth Anger" and "The Surge" for Stan Brakhage; and "The Artist," "The Child," "Centaur," "Short Song," and "Thumbprint," among others, for Bruce Conner.

Michael McClure. "Dog Star Man." *Film Culture* 29 (Summer 1963): 12-13. Print.

This review of Brakhage's film *Dog Star Man, Part One* appeared in *Film Culture,* the preeminent film magazine of the time, but was first published in *Artforum.*[17] The film depicts a woodsman, the protagonist, as he walks with his dog, struggling up a mountain in the snow. McClure describes this as man amidst the elements: "he faints, struggles and hallucinates becoming immortal in his striving." An important aspect here for McClure is that Brakhage makes no distinction between "a physical adventure or a spiritual one." He then extols the film's "dance of editing" and compares the film to "the flashing of verse" (12). The review concludes with the claim that *Dog Star Man* is "greater than a synthesis of [Brakhage's] earlier works" (13). In comparing the film to those of Sergei Eisenstein, the Russian master of montage, as well as to other films by Brakhage himself, McClure demonstrates his knowledge of both film history and the contemporary scene. In addition, the review signifies the close relationship between Brakhage and McClure as evidenced by *Lighting the Flame*, a collection of their correspondence from 1961-1978.

——. "Defense of Jayne Mansfield." *Film Culture* 32 (Spring 1964): 24-27. Print.

In this essay, reprinted in the *Film Culture Reader* (1970), McClure comes to terms with the Hollywood sex goddess, represented by blonde and voluptuous Jayne Mansfield. He begins by claiming that Mansfield is part of a "black American tradition," which includes Poe and Thoreau, defining this darkness as "LOVE that is driven under cover into their bodies or souls and spirits" (25). This is a suggestion of the dark power of sex in the American psyche. He extols the "mystery" of Mansfield's physical presence, as she shows her body to the crowd without shame. The essay's second part compares Mansfield to other American stars such as Jean Harlow, "*La plus blanche*—the most white," and Marilyn Monroe, "THE MAMMAL," adding that "Mansfield alone needs protection and a champion—but you are all creatures of love" (26). If Harlow and Mansfield are opposites, then Monroe "is a classical balance of men's desires....Monroe is neither black nor white—she's rosy" (27). He recalls a poem he wrote for Jean Harlow ("La Plus Blanche") as well as a poem he wrote for Mansfield, but burned.[18] The essay ends with the admonition that "[b]lackness, sexuality and freedom must not be denied in any shape—or they wither" (27). These lines recall his poems "Fuck Ode" and "Garland," which espouse sexual freedom. McClure's equation of Mansfield's body with spirit also validates his praise of the body and the idea of embodied poetry. Here McClure combines his poetics with his knowledge and interest in film.

McClure, Michael, and Jim Morrison. "St. Nicholas." 1969. TS. Courtesy Michael McClure Foundation (Ms A5), Contemporary Literature Collection, Special Collection and Rare Books, Bennet Library, Simon Fraser University.

This collaboration with rock star Jim Morrison began with Morrison's interest in playing Billy the Kid in a film version of *The Beard,* a project that fell through due to the controversial nature of the play. Morrison then read the manuscript of McClure's second novel, *The Adept,* the plot of which revolves around a drug deal gone bad, culminating with a murder in the desert. He showed interest in this as an alternative, and the two found a producer in Los Angeles and began work on the film script titled "St. Nicholas." According to McClure's interview with Frank Lisciandro, the two worked hard, isolating themselves from distractions, while creating a film script with too many extraneous details. Morrison ended up cutting down the script, but according to McClure, he "missed the point of the novel" ("Nile" 251). There are four drafts of this film script: the first and fourth drafts are 76 and 77 pages, respectively, and the second and third are each 195 pages, much of which closely follows the wording of McClure's novel.

## Notes

[1] Information about the lost film is from a telephone interview with Michael McClure on March 24, 2017. Unless otherwise specified, all comments by McClure come from this interview. For McClure and others, Stan Brakhage wrote filmmaking instructions as "A Moving Picture Giving and Taking Book," first published in *Film Culture* 41 (1966).
[2] Brakhage uses the term *filmtrait* in a letter to McClure of August 1965 (*Flame* 79).
[3] See the cover of *Ghost Tantras* for McClure as lion.
[4] This quote is from Lawrence Jordan's email to the author on September 28, 2017. In an email on November 2, 2017, he notes that McClure evolves from "everyman" in *Visions of a City* to "a personality" in *Spectre Mystagogic*. Thanks also to Jordan for providing the source of the Arp quote.
[5] This is according to a telephone interview with Lawrence Jordan on October 5, 2017. Unless otherwise noted, all comments from Jordan come from this interview.
[6] Jordan describes the subliminal influence of Baroque artist Caravaggio on his work at this time.

[7] According to an interview with Jordan and Kathy Geritz, when Jordan showed an early version of this film without a sound track, McClure and Lamantia read their poetry as accompaniment ("Venue" 81).

[8] McClure was to have had a part in Mailer's subsequent film, *Maidstone,* until the two had a falling out on set.

[9] McClure's "Personal Universal Deck" is an actual deck of card that functions to facilitate spontaneous self reflection, using words associated with the senses. The technique is akin to Tristan Tzara's Dadaist method of random construction.

[10] For more on McClure and the rock scene, see Warner's 2004 interview with McClure in *Text and Drugs and Rock 'N' Roll.*

[11] *The Beard* was particularly controversial because it featured the character of Jean Harlow performing fellatio on the character of Billy the Kid. Brakhage fantasized about making a color film of McClure's play, *The Feast,* but realized it would be too expensive to make ("To Michael McClure" 40). In the Phoenix Bookshop bibliography of McClure's work, compiled by Marshal Clements in 1965, there is an allusion to a short film of *The Blossom* by assemblage artist George Herms, who did the sets for McClure's play, but according to Herms only still photos exist.

[12] Conner also found it cheaper to buy old black and white films and collage them together than to buy new film, shoot, and have it developed. See Conner's interview with Scott MacDonald in which he also mentions briefly working with Fonda on *The Hired Hand.*

[13] Per an email to the author on July 14, 2017.

[14] In McClure's interview with Mesch, he explains *The Beard*'s title: "'Beard' is Elizabethan slang, and it means to quarrel with someone; it means to pull his beard..." (17).

[15] Unless otherwise noted, Woronov's comments here are from a telephone interview with the author on September 28, 2017.

[16] According to Richard Candida Smith in *Utopia and Dissent,* McClure was considering making a film of *The Beard* himself, but the deal fell through partly due to Warhol's film (509-510).

[17] The completed film of this name, shot from 1961-1964, includes a *Prelude* and four parts.

[18] He also wrote a poem in beast language for Monroe on her death; Harlow would reappear in "The Sermons of Jean Harlow and The Curses of Billy the Kid," as well as in *The Beard.*

## Works Cited

Benjamin, Walter. "The Return of the *Flâneur.*" *Walter Benjamin: Selected Writings, Volume 2, 1927-1934,* translated by Rodney Livingstone, edited by Michael Jennings, Howard Eland, and Gary Smith, Harvard UP, 1999, pp. 262-67.

Brakhage, Stan. "To Michael McClure." *Brakhage Scrapbook,* edited by Robert Haller. Documentext, 1982, pp. 40-42.

Canby, Vincent. "When Irish Eyes are Smiling, It's Norman Mailer." *Conversations with Norman Mailer,* edited by J. Michael Lennon, UP of Mississippi, 1988, pp. 139-44.

Candida Smith, Richard. *Utopia and Dissent.* U of California P, 1995.
Conner, Bruce. Interview with Scott MacDonald. *A Critical Cinema*, edited by MacDonald, U of California P, 1988, pp. 244-56.
"Documentary." *Webster's New Collegiate Dictionary.* 2nd ed., G and C Merriam, 1956.
Herms, George. Email to the author. 1 Oct. 2017.
James, David. *Allegories of Cinema.* E.P. Dutton, 1970.
Jordan, Lawrence. Email to the author. 28 Sept. 2017.
——. Email to the author. 2 Nov. 2017.
——. Telephone Interview with the author. 5 Oct. 2017.
——. "The Venue Vanguard." Interview with Kathy Geritz. *Radical Light: Alternative Film and Video in the San Francisco Bay Area, 1945-2000*, edited by Steve Auder, Kathy Geritz, and Steve Seid, U of California P, 2010, pp. 79-83.
McClure, Michael. "Drug Notes." *Meat Science Essays.* City Lights, 1963, pp. 23-41.
——. "Nile Insect Eyes: Talking on Jim Morrison." Interview with Frank Lisciandro. *Lighting The Corners*, U of New Mexico P, 1993, pp. 237-56.
——. "Notes." *Simple Eyes.* New Directions, 1994, pp. 129-34.
——. "Tear Gas." *Floating Bear*, vol. 37, 1969, pp. 545-47.
——. Telephone Interview with the author. 24 Mar. 2017.
——. "Writing One's Body." Interview with Harold Mesch. *Lighting the Corners*, U of New Mexico P, 1993, pp. 3-25.
——. "Writing *The Beard.*" Interview with Lee Bartlett. *Lighting the Corners,* U of New Mexico P, 1993, pp. 282-95.
Power, Tony. Email to the author 14 July 2017.
Renan, Sheldon. *An Introduction to The American Underground Film.* E.P. Dutton, 1967.
Reveaux, Tony. "A Legacy of Light." *Radical Light: Alternative Film and Video in the San Francisco Bay Area, 1945-2000*, edited by Steve Auder, Kathy Geritz, and Steve Seid, U of California P, 2010, pp. 104-10.
Sitney, P. Adams. "Moments of Illumination." *Artforum International*, vol. 47, no. 8 April 2009, pp. 162-69.
Varda, Agnes. "Lions Love." Interview with Andre Cornand. *Agnes Varda Interviews,* edited by T. Jefferson Kline, UP of Mississippi, 2014, pp. 50-52.
Woronov, Mary. Telephone Interview with the author. 28 Sept. 2017.

# Le Club Jack Kérouac and the Renaissance in Beat Scholarship on Kerouac's French Canadian Background
By Sara Villa

> Happy Dream of Canada, the illuminated Northern land—! I'm here at first on Ste. Catherine or some other Boulevard with a bunch of brother French-Canadians and among old relatives and at one point Nat King Cole is there talking to my mother...I've been close and talkative and like Saintly Ti Jean with everyone...I see it all [as] only an outsider American Genius Canuck can see...such a happy dream, it was Ti-Jean the happy Saint back among his loyal brothers at last.
> —Jack Kerouac, *Book of Dreams* (206-207)

This description, from one of Kerouac's oneiric memories, seems to perfectly capture the complex and nostalgic duality of the writer's identity. On the one hand, such a dream shows the profound emotional, cultural, and linguistic ties he had with the French Canadian and partly Iroquois heritage of his family. As discussed in all of the major Anglophone and Francophone biographies and biographical studies of the author, including those by Victor-Lévy Beaulieu, Ann Charters, Tom Clark, Jean-Christophe Cloutier, Gerald Nicosia, Paul Maher, Hassan Melehy, Maurice Poteet, Steven Turner, Eric Waddell, and others, his father, Leo, descended from the Kérouac families of Rivière du Loup, a genealogical branch originating from Maurice-Louis Alexandre Le Brice de Kérouac. Jack Kerouac's mother, Gabrielle Ange Lévesque, had been born in St. Pacôme de Kamouraska within a peasant family and was three quarters French Canadian and one quarter Iroquois (Charters, *Brother-Souls* 14). On the other hand, hidden in a dream, this reality appears much easier than the reality of doubleness and partial outsider status that the writer, like many Francophone immigrants, had experienced in New England (Lavoie 1-15).

Kerouac's childhood occurred in the blocks of the Québécois who had moved to Lowell, Massachusetts, searching for work in a town with five different Catholic parishes and a relevant community of French-speaking Canadian immigrants (Turner 29-32). This Christian, Francophone, Canuck background coexisted with his U.S. identity as the Beat writer who had revolutionized American literature with his spontaneous prose, highly influenced by bebop. He also learned English only at six years of age, something that led Tom Clark to argue that he was "arguably the most important writer since Conrad to adopt English as a second language" (Clark 3). The unusual, hybrid, multilingual heritage of Kerouac was mixed with the difficult reality of the Québécois diaspora to New England, where, as Joyce Johnson notes in

*The Voice Is All*, this immigrant group was defined by the Massachusetts Department of Labor as "The Chinese of America," though some "New Englanders had other names for them: *frogs, pea-soups, dumb Canucks, white niggers*," as Johnson notes, clearly showing the multiple levels of discrimination that the community faced while resettling (22).

Such a complex background is the reason that the writer's American biographers have always dedicated the initial chapters of their work to difficult and at times contrasting analyses of his existential "Canuck duality" (Maher, *Kerouac* 244). The first Kerouac biographer, Ann Charters, in *Kerouac: A Biography* (1973), describes the history of his family in Lowell, the years following the Great Depression of 1929, and the 1936 floods that destroyed Leo's printing shop, in parallel with references to or narrations of his childhood which have entered *Doctor Sax (Faust Part Three), Visions of Gerard, Maggie Cassidy, The Town and The City*, and the preface of *Lonesome Traveller* (20-32). Thus Charters shows in detail how the writer's heritage and memories of his youth have permeated so many of his most experimental works, something which the Québécois critic François Ricard had defined in 1980 as *vécriture*, a fictional style imbued with facts and derived from the French words *vérité* [truth] and *écriture* [writing] (Ricard 85). In *Memory Babe* (1983) Nicosia recognizes the importance of child saints, such as the Québécoise Marie-Rose Ferron (Creighton 156), in the Catholic Francophone culture of young Kerouac and the influence this had on his family's hagiographic attitude toward the early death of Gerard, Jack's older brother, who died in 1926 from rheumatic fever (Nicosia 12-28). The motto on the coat of arms of the Kerouac families—*Aimer, Travailler, Souffrir* [To Love, to Work and to Suffer] (Kérouac-Harvey 3)—seems to sadly mirror the existence of many Quebeckers in the first five decades of the twentieth century, both in their province and abroad. Child mortality was extremely high (Lavoie 1-15). *Survivance*, in fact, is the very term used by Québécois communities to describe their struggles to save their Francophone cultural heritage and language within a life of extreme economic difficulties. Clark in *Jack Kerouac: A Biography* (1984) specifically refers to Kerouac's Québécois French, constantly spoken with his mother and jotted down in many of his journals, even heard in his dreams. Clark, moreover, devotes an entire chapter titled "Visions in the Lowell Night" to explain the intricate paths of Kerouac's ancestors from Brittany, describing how the writer was interested in all of the facets of his genealogy, including his partly Native Canadian (Iroquois) blood (3-25). Finally, Steve Turner, in *Angelheaded Hipster* (1996) explores the influence of the nuns and Jesuits who educated Kerouac before he attended junior high school, where only English was spoken, and Turner considers the importance of the Francophone newspapers of Lowell and of New England, which kept the Québécois community together (Turner 20-38).

# LE CLUB JACK KÉROUAC  *Villa*

As this brief introduction shows, interest in Kerouac's origins was strong even before the writer's journals and diaries, filled with texts, notes, lists, short stories, and entire literary works in *joual*, were opened to researchers in 2007 at the New York Public Library (NYPL). However, as Lawrence Ferlinghetti and Charters point out during the *Rencontre Internationale Jack Kérouac* [International Jack Kerouac Gathering] held in Québec City on October 1-4, 1987, the first generation born in the U.S. to immigrant parents usually loses its language of origin (Ferlinghetti 3). Kerouac faced a similar fate. In a journal entry from the Kerouac archives at the NYPL, quoted by Jean-Christophe Cloutier in his introduction to *Jack Kérouac: La Vie Est d'Hommage* [Jack Kerouac: *Life is a Tribute* or *Life is a Pity*], Kerouac wrote that "[*i*]*l faut vivre en Anglais, c'est impossible vivre en Français*" [You must live in English, it is impossible to live in French], highlighting the necessity to linguistically assimilate experienced by Quebec immigrants in America (qtd. in Cloutier 38).

This context is important in explaining why, since the opening of the Kerouac archives at the NYPL, scholarly publications and editions of Kerouac's manuscripts written in French have blossomed. On the one hand, the NYPL archive offers a treasure trove of manuscripts. Consequently, the experimental nature of Kerouac's texts, which generated an innovative contemporary prose style in America, can be more thoroughly seen as influenced by his Francophone syntax by studying the corpus of texts he wrote in French, written in his unique phonetic orthography (Cloutier 26-27). Kerouac's Francophone manuscripts can be found in *La Vie Est d'Hommage*, edited by Cloutier, and published by the Québécois house Boréal; in English, in the collection of original texts curated by Todd Tietchen, titled *The Unknown Kerouac: Rare, Unpublished and Newly Translated Writings*; and in recent works including Hassan Melehy's *Kerouac: Language, Poetics, and Territory* and Véronique Lane's *The French Genealogy of the Beat Generation: Burroughs, Ginsberg and Kerouac's Appropriations of Modern Literature, from Rimbaud to Michaux*. In 2014, the Québécois Ici Radio Canada radio program *Sur Les Traces de Jack Kérouac*, moderated by Franco Nuovo and Gabriel Anctil, re-traced the Québécois-American geography of Kerouac's heritage from Rivière du Loup to Lowell, Massachussets, to New York City, with interviews with members of the Kerouac families, scholars, and close friends of Kerouac, including Robert Frank and David Amram. The radio show is accompanied by a well-researched, free e-book in French, which is available for download on the website of Radio Canada as *Sur Les Traces de Jack Kérouac*. Also in 2014, the International Festiblues of Montréal dedicated a section of its program to Kerouac, under the title "Montréal Kerouac Blues," following the "Québec Kerouac" events of the 2012 Québec Jazz Festival (Kerouac, *La Vie* 37).

Such contemporary unveiling of Kerouac's Québécois identity has been helped by studies, conferences, and publications organized by a Québécois cultural and scholarly association, Le Club Jack Kérouac, which was active from 1984 to 1990 and based in the city of Québec. The primary mission of this organization was to expand the scholarly investigation, work, conferences and publications on the Francophone roots of Kerouac while creating an international network of scholars and writers, poets, and actual members of the Beat Generation (such as Allen Ginsberg, Carolyn Cassady, and Lawrence Ferlinghetti) who would use their knowledge and research skills to shed more light on this aspect of the writer's life and work (Foundational Documents of Le Club Jack Kérouac; see fig. 1). One of the most interesting goals of Le Club Jack Kérouac was to research Kerouac's Francophone cultural background and the influence that its language, traditions, geography, and religion had on the author, as a man and as a writer. However, the ways in which the organizational team and the members of Le Club Jack Kérouac explored this initial research path was international, with members from the U.S., Canada, Italy, and Japan, who also contributed to the Club's research journal entitled, *N'Importe Quelle Route* [*No Matter Which Road*].

The foundation of Le Club Jack Kérouac carried the same double—i.e., Franco-American and international—flavor; the Secrétariat Permanent des Peuples Francophones, in association with the Université de Laval via the affiliation of Professor of Geography Eric Waddell, formed the basis of the club. Waddell suggested to Louis Dussault, the director of the secretariat, "the idea of establishing a Club littéraire Jack Kérouac as a modern way of highlighting relations between Québec and New England and of reading the continent though the eyes of a 'Franco.' Dussault's reaction was enthusiastic" (Anctil, Dupont, and Waddell xi). The secretariat had been created in 1981 by the government of the province of Québec led by René Lévesque to link the Francophone communities of Canada and America and to promote American Francophone culture in all its forms, including new studies on the communities of Québeckers who had immigrated to New England, as had Jack Kerouac's parents (Georgeault and Plourde 182-183). Le Club Jack Kérouac provided all the Francophone American writers influenced by Kerouac with a series of events and publications, including the bulletin of the association, through which to share their Kerouac-inspired works.

As the multi-authored foreword to *Un Homme Grand: Jack Kerouac at the Crossroads of Many Cultures* [*Jack Kérouac à la Confluence des Cultures*] points out, the historical climate at the time was favorable for a Québécois rediscovery of Kerouac: the political morale in Québec, especially regarding Francophone unity and identity, had been undoubtedly damaged by the results of their independence referendum held in 1980 and required a more positive focus. Nineteen eighty-three was also the year of publication of Nicosia's *Memory Babe* after the biographer's

# LE CLUB JACK KÉROUAC *Villa*

*Fig. 1. Foundational Document of Le Club Jack Kérouac, Fonds Club Kérouac, 1983, BANQ archives.*

visit to Trois-Pistoles, home of Victor-Lévy Beaulieu, author of the first major Francophone study of the relationship between Kerouac and Québec, *Jack Kérouac: Essai-Poulet* [*Jack Kerouac: A Chicken Essay*], published in 1975 in its English translation. Ten years after a 1972 special in the Québécois cultural journal, *Le Devoir*, on Kerouac's Francophone roots, the magazine *Moody Streets Irregulars* dedicated its Spring/Summer 1982 issue to the same topic, under the title *French Connection Issue* (Anctil, Dupont and Waddell x-xi). The cultural atmosphere was ripe and the institutional support was equally favorable for the growth of Le Club Jack Kérouac.

The scope of the association was threefold: 1) fostering a constant exchange between American and international Kerouac friends, readers, and specialists as well as the Québécois fans and scholars of his work, 2) organizing events based on Kerouac as a writer who spoke Québécois French and wrote about himself as a Canuck, and 3) issuing a specialized journal and other publications dedicated to Kerouac's French Canadian background as well as to Québécois and international artists influenced by his poetics. A leaflet sponsoring the activities of Le Club Jack Kérouac thus informed its future members:

> Our aim is to gather people who are interested in discovering and deepening the multiple facets of the writer and man Jack Kerouac, with a specific focus on his being part of the Francophone community of New England....By becoming a member of the club, with a yearly subscription cost of 10$ [sic], all the members can participate in its activities, have full access to its research centre, and receive the bulletin of the club, a quarterly entitled *N'Importe Quelle Route* [*No Matter Which Road*]. In addition, a dossier Jack Kerouac, which includes a biography, a bibliography, and a press kit containing various articles on the author, is available for 5$ [sic], while the poster of the association costs 3$ [sic]. (Official Leaflet, translation mine; see fig. 2)

The result was an enthusiastic reception throughout all the years of the club's activities, which can be discerned from letters in the archives of the association now housed at La Bibliothèque et Archives Nationales du Québec. For instance, William J. Colquhoun, a college student from Ocean City, New Jersey, wrote that he was glad to discover Le Club Jack Kérouac, and Danielle Houboly from Grig Harbour, Washington, requested to become a member of the organization and was also curious about similar associations based in the U.S. (Correspondence of Le Club Jack Kérouac).

It is evident, then, that the documentary and bibliographical aspect of the association was as important to its founders as it was to readers and scholars of

# LE CLUB JACK KÉROUAC

Fig. 2. Official Leaflet of Le Club Jack Kérouac, Fonds Club Kérouac, BANQ archives.

Kerouac's work. The research center, in the eight years that the club existed, managed to gather rare books (e.g., a collection of memories from the descendants of Maurice-Louis-Alexandre le Brice de Kérouac since 1730, edited by Raymonde Kérouac-Harvey); studies (e.g., *The Three Avant-Dire of the Rencontre Internationale Jack Kérouac* held in October 1987); videos of conferences (many of the panels of the *Rencontre Internationale Jack Kérouac*, as well as interviews with Kerouac, such as Fernand Seguin's for Radio Canada in 1967); correspondence, minutes of meetings, press releases, photographs (including a group picture of the founding committee of Le Club Jack Kérouac when it had been invited to Lowell, Massachussetts, for the opening ceremony in 1988 of the Jack Kerouac Commemorative in Kerouac Park; see fig. 3); copies of the Club's bulletin; and a selection of journal articles from Canada, the U.S., France, and Italy related to Kerouac, which fill nine boxes of original documents available for scholarly research in the BANQ Research Center.

One of the most interesting aspects of this archival material is the collection of copies of the association's journal, *N'Importe Quelle Route* [*No Matter Which Road*], which ran from 1987 to 1989 (see figs. 4-8); it was diverse in its textual and

*Fig. 3. Le Club Jack Kérouac, opening ceremony in 1988 of the Kerouac Park in Lowell, MA, BANQ archives.*

visual content. A close analysis of some sections can allow readers to more fully appreciate the multiplicity of authors who collaborated on it. Every issue featured poems, sketches, interviews, essays, and original writings by numerous Québécois (but also Anglophone Canadian, American, and international) scholars, writers, journalists, poets, artists, film directors, with interviews and anecdotes related to the Beat author. Across the years, there was a clear evolution from the simpler, more minimalist, black-and-white format of the first issue, published in March 1987 and paving the way for the International Jack Kerouac Gathering (October 1-4, 1987), to the more detailed and colorful style of the later issues, dated 1989. The journal covers in figures 4-8, for example, depict iconographic themes that are clearly Kerouacian: car parts, tires, stylized images of female bodies, abstract drawings, photographic portraits of several authors, sketches of the American continent, collages of crumbled paper, aquarelle drops, mechanical parts, multiple and scattered fonts reminiscent of the literary experiments of DADA and Modernist journals, Italian Futurists' publications, as well as the underground magazines printed in Beat literary circles, such as *The Floating Bear* and *Yugen* (Hayward), and in Francophone Québec

# LE CLUB JACK KÉROUAC

following the turmoil of France's 1968 political protests (Baille 30-31). The journal may have reminded many Quebeckers of the famous *Hobo-Québec*, which was a

> magazine of writing and images (1972-1981) [which] can be seen as an artistic magazine par excellence of Quebec counter-culture. Created by Claude Robitaille, soon assisted by André Roy, the magazine published visual art, poetry, and prose by the likes of Denis Vanier, Josée Yvon, Yolande Villemaire, Claude Beausoleil, Straram Patrick, Victor-Lévy Beaulieu, and many others: collages, texts, images, games, essays, criticisms and reflections. (Expozine)

Among the most constant contributors to *Hobo-Québec*, one notices names of Kerouac specialists such as Victor-Lévy Beaulieu, and major Québécois experimental poets including Denis Vanier and Josée Yvon, who had openly declared to have been influenced by Kerouac. The magazine welcomed avant-gardist writers who, like Kerouac, aimed at breaking stylistic and thematic taboos. Hence, the Autumn 1988 issue of Le Club Jack Kérouac's journal includes Vanier's "Kundalini Heavy-Metal." One year later, in Autumn 1989, the journal published

*Fig. 4.* N'Importe Quelle Route [No Matter Which Road], *October 1987, BANQ archives.*

*Fig. 5.* N'Importe Quelle Route [No Matter Which Road], *April 1988, BANQ archives.*

*Fig. 6.* N'Importe Quelle Route [No Matter Which Road], *Autumn 1988, BANQ archives.*

an untitled poem by Yvon, whose work addressed the gender spectrum, including transsexual and lesbian characters living a liberated sexuality, through openly anti-homophobic and feminist political perspectives.

Following this same desire to break the gender taboos related to experimental writing and to Kerouac, when she was asked to contribute to the International Jack Kerouac Gathering (see fig. 9), Yvon replied with a letter, also in Le Club Jack Kérouac's archives, in which she agreed by declaring that she would deliver a speech entitled "*Jack Kérouac et le féminisme [Jack Kérouac and Feminism]*." Her presentation aimed to define the problematic attitude of the writer towards women (including his many partners, his mother, his daughter, and Carolyn Cassady) and the lack of recognition that the women of the Beat Generation faced in a closed circle that seemed to be exclusively male (Correspondence of Le Club Jack Kérouac). This eventually became her experimental essay entitled, "Slab Bacon *Comme à Lowell ou Les Tendances Sexuelles de Jack Kérouac*" in *Un Homme Grand* (Anctil, Dupont, and Waddell 165-179.) It is sad to think that Yvon did not live long enough to see the development of scholarship on women Beat writers over the last half century.

The openness and politically active positions of *N'Importe Quelle Route [No Matter Which Road]* were not limited to a Québécois feminist approach towards the Beat generation and Kerouac—the magazine clearly wanted to fight discrimination of all sorts, almost as a reaction to the marginalization and feelings of being

*Fig. 7.* N'Importe Quelle Route [No Matter Which Road], *Spring 1989, BANQ archives.*

outsiders that many Quebeckers had faced while migrating in search of work. If the geographical starting point of the journal was Québec and Francophone America, the path that its writers wanted to take had no geographical boundaries, and it included a unique entry, written by Japanese poet Yusuke Keda, on the reception of Kerouac in Japan. In this essay, Keda reveals how the Japanese translations of Kerouac's works were limited to *On the Road*, *The Dharma Bums*, and *The Subterraneans*, and how the lack of translations of his other novels had a serious impact on the ways in which the Japanese audience perceived the author. Keda also writes, however, that Kenzaburō Ōe, a major Japanese writer, had publicly stated his love and admiration for Kerouac, thus encouraging many of his readers to discover Kerouac's works in translation, as well as in English (30-31).

Widening the borders of the research published in French and related to Kerouac also meant providing a publication space for both the research of Québécois scholars specializing in the relationship between the main Francophone province of Canada and Kerouac, and their reviews of the most recent American scholarly publications on the writer, which may have interested a French-speaking public. Consequently, the journal carried contributions by Maurice Poteet, professor of literature at the University of Québec, on "The Role of Québec in Kerouac's Fiction" and by Robert B. Perreault on "The Franco-American Side of Jack Kerouac."

Together with scholarly articles such as these, the Québécois journal of Le Club Jack Kérouac published reviews of American scholarly texts on Kerouac—such as Regina Weinreich's *Jack Kerouac's Spontaneous Poetics*—and close readings of Beat works, focusing, for instance, on the recurrent erotic fixation with hanging in William S. Burroughs's fiction. Other contributions to the journal tried to compare Kerouac's double identity with that faced by other communities in America. Dean Lourder's "*Americanité, Americanidad*, Americanness: *Pourquoi Pas?*" for instance, created a parallel between the double identity of Chicanos in the United States and that of Francophone immigrants, both—albeit with their unique cultural differences—trying to maintain two languages in addition to a family structure as well as their Catholic backgrounds and traditions (22-23).

The last type of contribution that *N'Importe Quelle Route* [*No Matter Which Road*] featured was a series of interviews with Québécois writers who had met and spent some time with Kerouac or who were collectors of Beat memorabilia, such as Rod Anstee, author of *Jack Kerouac: The Bootleg Era: A Bibliography of Pirated Editions* (1994). With regard to the encounters between Kerouac and the Québécois audience, the most famous and commonly cited one is the long interview dated 1967 in which Kerouac replied in French to the questions of Fernand Seguin during the television programme, *Le Sel de La Semaine* for Ici Radio Canada. A thorough translation by Paul Fortin and Eric Waddell, as well as a series of critical analyses

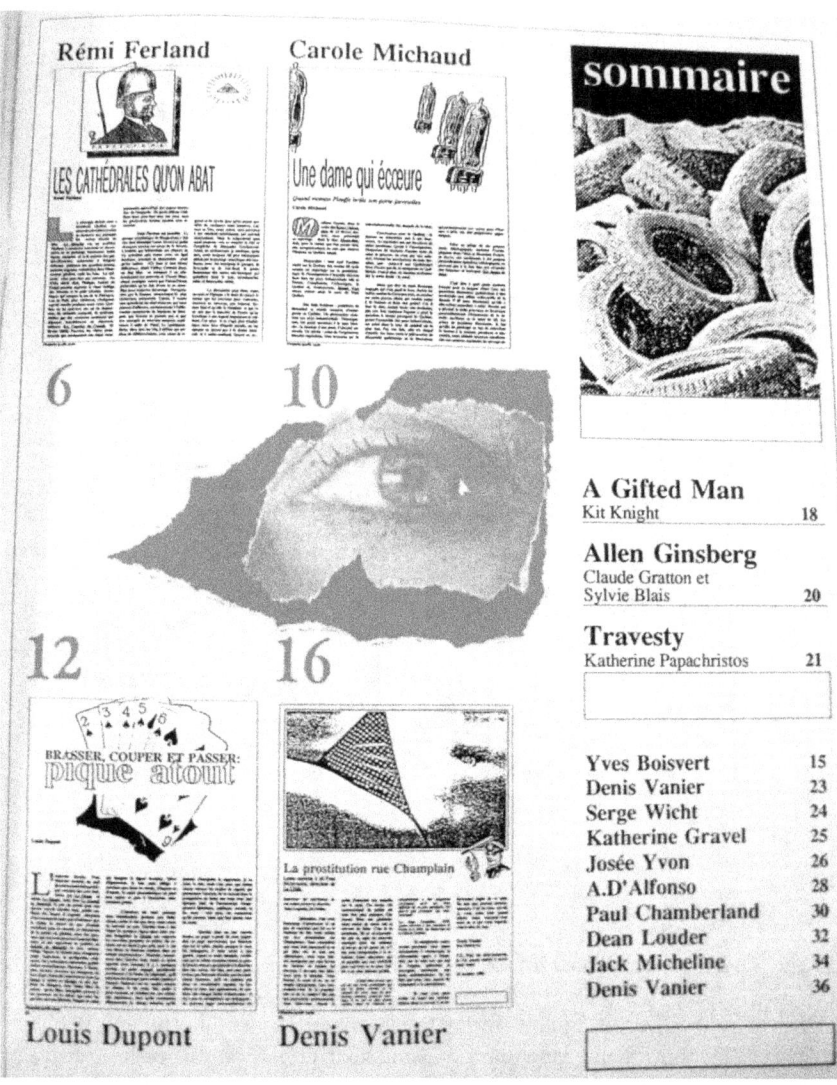

*Fig. 8.* N'Importe Quelle Route [No Matter Which Road], *sample table of contents, BANQ archives.*

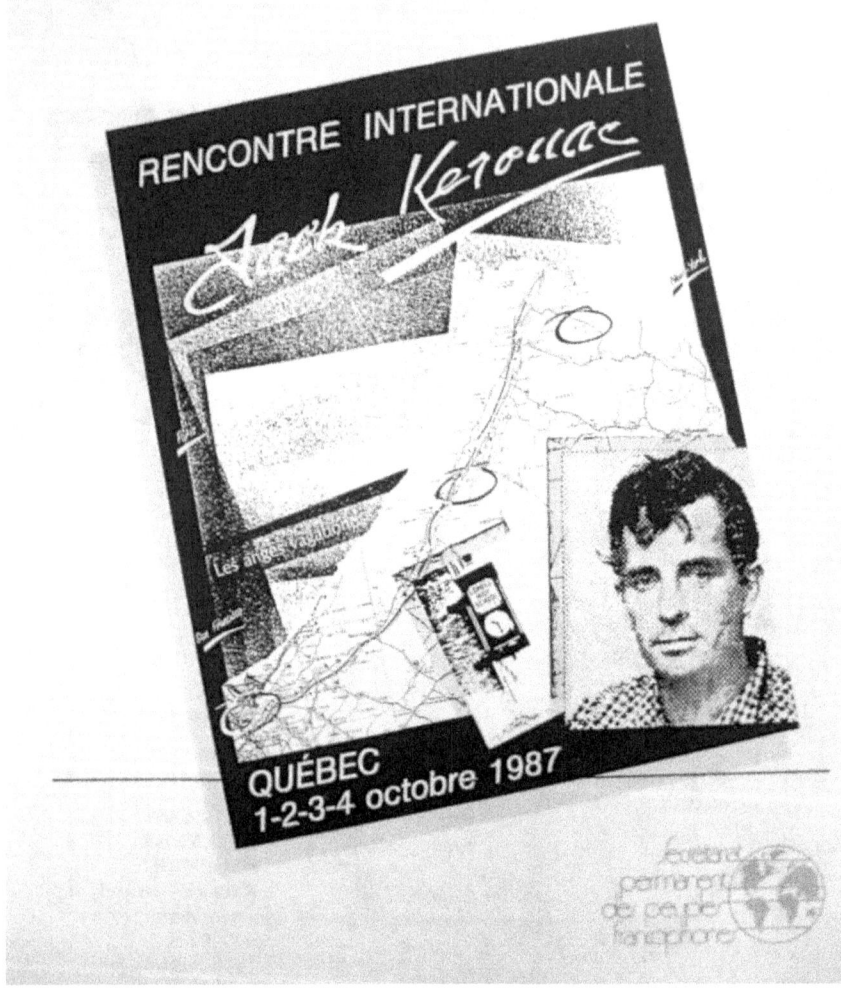

*Fig. 9. Jack Kerouac International Gathering leaftet, BANQ archives.*

of the references Kerouac made during the interview (also by Fortin and Waddell) are part of the third *Avant-Dire* that Le Club Jack Kérouac published in advance of its International Kerouac Gathering in 1987. The Québécois association also shared with a wider audience a less cited and earlier interview with Kerouac, in French, filmed in New York City by Pierre Nadeau and aired by Radio Canada in 1959. Here, a much younger Kerouac describes Céline as one of the most influential writers in his life and refers to Genet, as well, as a source of inspiration.

# LE CLUB JACK KÉROUAC Villa

Two Kerouac interviews conducted by André Major and Denis Vanier and published in *N'Importe Quelle Route* [*No Matter Which Road*] detail the time the two intellectuals spent with Kerouac. Major took Kerouac to a jazz club where he enjoyed a set by Lee Gagnon and his orchestra; the jazz saxophonist, flutist, and composer also discussed spontaneous prose with Kerouac. The evening concluded with a long conversation with Max Gros Louis, then Grand Chief of the Huron-Wendat Nation, with whom Kerouac discussed his Iroquois roots in his mother's line (Major 16). Vanier also took Kerouac to a jazz club called the Black Bottom in what was the home of Montréal's black artistic community at the time to listen to Canadian jazz guitarist Nelson Symonds. The night ended with Vanier and Kerouac at a nearby brothel, where Kerouac paid three women, while listening to a juke-box song by Billie Holiday, in order to simply talk to them about the difficulties of being a writer, without ever taking any of them upstairs for sex (Vanier 16-17). Both of these accounts reconfirm two aspects of Kerouac's interests that remained his focus until the end of his life. First is his genealogy and the hybridity of his identity, not only his Americanness and Francophone Québécois background, but also his Iroquois origins. Second is the omnipresence of jazz, its musicians, improvisations, and rhythms in his writing style.

It thus seems fitting that this musical genre was included in the multiplicity of events organized by Le Club Jack Kérouac from October 1-4, 1987, during the International Jack Kerouac Gathering. On October 2, a poetry performance featuring Allen Ginsberg, Alan Lord, Lawrence Ferlinghetti, Joy Walsh (editor of *Moody Street Irregulars)*, Paul Marion, Jack Micheline, John Montgomery, Herménégilde Chiasson (director of the movie *Le Grand Jack*), Patrice Desbiens, Josée Yvon, Lucien Francoeur (winner of the prestigious Émile Nélligan Prize for Québécois poetry), Indian poet Pradig Choudhouri (also editor-in-chief of the trilingual English-French-Bengali underground magazine PPHOO), and Italian experimental writer Pier Vittorio Tondelli, among others, included jazz accompaniment by pianist Dénis Hébert.

If *Un Homme Grand,* the bilingual edited volume stemming from this international gathering, became one of the most detailed contributions to scholarship on Kerouac's Francophone American identity, the material that accompanies it in Le Club Jack Kérouac archives at BANQ allows researchers to gather information on other events at the conference that were not documented otherwise. These included, together with the concerts and jazz poetry sessions, an exhibition of photographs and other rare materials titled *Canuck et Clochard Céleste: L'Univers de Jack Kérouac* at the Musée du Québec (see fig. 10), with images of Kerouac and other Beats by Robert Frank, Ginsberg, Charters, Walsh, Dave Moore (editor of *The Kerouac Connection*), Fred McDarrah, and George Durette; and rare materials, including first editions and copies of letters, of the Associations of the Families Kérouac, Le

*Fig. 10:* Canuck et Clochard Céleste: L'Univers de Jack Kérouac *at the Musée du Québec, BANQ archives.*

Club Jack Kérouac, and Rod Anstee. An exhibition of Lowell painters, artists, and illustrators inspired by "Jack Kérouac at Galerie Quatre Saisons" had also been opened to the public, thanks to the ties among Kerouac's friends in his Massachusetts hometown; the Lowell Preservation Commission; and Le Club Jack Kérouac. One of the Québécois association's trips out of the province, in fact, had been to Lowell, and the entire group was invited again by Paul Marion and the Lowell Historic Preservation Commission to the official opening of the Kerouac commemorative events in Kerouac Park (Official Program).

The visual aspect of the conference, together with photographs, illustrations, and paintings, also included film screenings of Frank's *This Song is for Jack*, and *Me and My Brother*, followed by a Q&A session with the director himself. The conference also featured the premiere of Chiasson's documentary, *Le Grand Jack*, produced under the auspices of the National Film Board of Canada, in a double bill with Frank's *Pull My Daisy*, followed by a reception which allowed the audience to meet and talk with the filmmakers.

One of the most enthusiastically received events planned for the International Jack Kerouac Gathering was a "Pilgrimage to the Village of Memère and of Léo

# LE CLUB JACK KÉROUAC

Alcide," organized by Le Club Jack Kérouac with the Association des Familles Kérouac and its president, Jacques Kérouac. The event, held on September 30, 1987, took the conference group to Cap Saint Ignace where Father Rodrigue Lagacé showed them the marriage records of Kerouac ancestor Maurice-Louis Alexandre Le Brice de Kérouac. The group then toured St. Pacôme de Kamouraska, where Kerouac's mother Gabrielle Lévèsque was born in a little farm house. In his review of the event for the magazine *Dolce Vita*, Tondelli reveals how the entire trip had some moving and nostalgic moments: many remembered lines from *Mexico City Blues* narrating the birth of Gabrielle, some quoted from the introduction to *Lonesome Traveller* in which the writer refers to his nationality as Franco-American, and at some point Réginald Ouellet started singing Francophone folk songs typical of Kerouac's childhood while several Québécois participants followed him in an improvised choir (8-10). The then-mayor of Lowell, Robert Kennedy, had sent an official copy of the keys of the city to Roger Ferland, the mayor of Saint Hubert, where Kerouac's father, was born, to symbolically stress the affective, cultural, and political ties between the Québécois town and the "Petits Canadas" of the Francophone inhabitants of Lowell (Tondelli 8-10).

This event is reconstructed through various letters, articles, and reviews of the International Gathering that are part of Le Club Jack Kérouac materials. On the one hand, the pilgrimage concretizes in a thorough historical, territorial, and cultural way the links between the Québécois borough that Kerouac had experienced in his childhood, and the province and towns that gave origin to the Francophone identity of his family. All this was condensed into a one-day experience open not only to specialists but also to all kinds of people who admired the writer. On the other hand, this pilgrimage stressed the importance in Kerouac's works of geography and the land, conceived not only in terms of his coast-to-coast "on the road" trips. This approach had characterized most Québécois studies of the writer, and it was one that the founders of Le Club Jack Kérouac, especially Waddell, had explored and written about earlier. Traditions and rituals of the Francophone communities in North America alongside Kerouac's descriptions of his Québec background constitute the dual analysis that Le Club Jack Kérouac undertook, hand-in-hand with American scholarship, ultimately leading to the recognition of Kerouac's original manuscripts written in French.

Note: The author thanks Professor Eric Waddell, co-founder of Le Club Jack Kérouac, for his kindness and generosity in sharing time, details, anecdotes, and knowledge during the writing of this article.

## Works Cited

Anctil, Gabriel, and Marie-Sandrine Auger. *Sur Les Traces de Jack Kérouac*. Ici Radio Canada, 2014, itunes.apple.com/ca/book/sur-les-traces-de-kerouac/id932063600?mt=11.

Anctil, Pierre, Louis Dupont, and Eric Waddell, editors. *Un Homme Grand: Jack Kerouac at the Crossroads of Many Cultures/Jack Kerouac à la confluence des cultures*. McGill UP, 1990.

Anstee, Rod. *Jack Kerouac: The Bootleg Era: A Bibliography of Pirated Editions*. Water Row, 1994.

Baille, Jean-Pascal. "*Apologie de l'analogique. À propos d'Hobo Québec: Journal d'écritures et d'images.*" *ETC*, issue 46, 1999, pp. 30–31.

Beaulieu, Victor-Lévy. *Jack Kerouac: Essai-Poulet*. Typo, 2004.

Charters, Ann. *Kerouac: A Biography*. Foreword by Allen Ginsberg, Third Mind, 1973, rpt. St. Martin's Griffin, 1994.

Charters, Ann, and Samuel Charters. *Brother-Souls: John Clellon Holmes, Jack Kerouac, and the Beat Generation*. UP of Mississippi, 2010.

Clark, Tom. *Jack Kerouac: A Biography*. Thunder's Mouth Press, 1984.

Correspondence of Le Club Kérouac. Fonds Club Jack Kérouac [195?]-1991 BANQ Archives Côte P922, BANQ, Québec, Canada.

Expozine, "Looking Back at Hobo-Québec: A Literary Touchstone" event held at Expozine in Montreal on 13 Nov., 2015, expozine.ca/en/blog/looking-back-at-hobo-quebec-a-literary-touchstone/.

Foundational Documents of Le Club Kérouac. Fonds Club Jack Kérouac [195?]-1991 BANQ Archives Côte P922, BANQ, Québec, Canada.

Georgeault, Pierre and Michel Plourde, et al. *Le Français au Québec: 400 Ans d'Histoire et de Vie*. Fides, 2010.

Gifford, Barry and Lawrence Lee. *Jack's Book: An Oral Biography of Jack Kerouac*. Penguin Random House, 1978, rpt. Penguin, 2012.

Hayward, Michael. "The Beat Generation in Print: The Underground Magazines and Presses." *Unspeakable Visions: The Beat Generation and the Bohemian Dialectic*, Simon Fraser University, 1991, sfu.ca/~hayward/UnspeakableVisions/InPrintUnderground.html.

Johnson, Joyce. *The Voice Is All: The Lonely Victory of Jack Kerouac*. Viking, 2012.

Keda, Yusuke. "Jack Kerouac au Japon." *N'Importe Quelle Route*, Autumn 1989, pp. 30-31.

Kerouac, Jack. *Atop an Underwood: Early Stories and Other Writings*. Edited by Paul Marion, Penguin, 2000.

———. *Book of Dreams*. City Lights, 1960, rpt. 2001.
———. *Good Blonde & Others*. Edited by Donald Allen, Introduction by Robert Creeley. Grey Fox, 1993, rpt. 2001.
———. Interview by Pierre Nadeau. *Jack Kerouac at Radio Canada*. Radio Canada, 1959. www. youtube.com/watch?v=q4BPacAbK4c.
———. Interview by Fernand Seguin. *Le Sel de la Semaine*. Radio Canada, 1967, www.vimeo.com/163981792.
———. *La Vie Est d'Hommage*. Edited by Jean-Christophe Cloutier, Boréal, 2016.
———. *Selected Letters, Volume One: 1940-1956*. Edited by Ann Charters, Penguin, 1996.
———. *Selected Letters, Volume Two: 1957-1969*. Edited by Ann Charters, Penguin, 2000.
———. *The Unknown Kerouac: Rare, Unpublished and Newly Translated Writings*. Edited by Todd Tietchen, Library of America, 2016.
Kérouac-Harvey, Raymonde. *Pensées des Déscendants de Maurice Louis Alexandre la Brice de Kérouac Depuis 1730*. Association Familles Kérouac, 1980.
Lane, Véronique. *The French Genealogy of the Beat Generation: Burroughs, Ginsberg and Kerouac's Appropriations of Modern Literature, from Rimbaud to Michaux*. Bloomsbury, 2017.
Lavoie, Yolande. *L'Émigration des Québécois Aux États Unis de 1840 à 1930*. Documentation du Conseil de la Langue Française, 1983.
Le Maître, Yvonne. "The Town and the City." *Le Travailleur*, 23 Mar. 1950.
Lourder, Dean, editor. *Le Québec et Les Francophones de la Nouvelle Angleterre*. Les Presses de l'Université de Laval, 1991.
Maffina, Stefano. *The Role of Jack Kerouac's Identity in the Development of his Poetics*. Lulu, 2012.
Maher, Paul. *Kerouac: The Definitive Biography*. Taylor, 2004.
Melehy, Hassan. *Kerouac: Language, Poetics, and Territory*. Bloomsbury, 2016.
Nation, Brian. "Charles Burke and The Black Bottom." *brian nation: the hot dog palace never closes 2010*, boppin.com/2006/04/charles-burke-and-black-bottom.html.
Nicosia, Gerald. *Memory Babe: A Critical Biography of Jack Kerouac*. U of California P, 1983.
Official Leaflet of Le Club Kérouac. Fonds Club Jack Kérouac [195?]-1991 BANQ Archives Côte P922, BANQ, Québec, Canada.
Official Program of the International Jack Kérouac Gathering. Fonds Club Jack Kérouac [195?]-1991 BANQ Archives Côte P922, BANQ, Québec, Canada.
Perreault, Robert. "The Franco-American Side of Jack Kerouac." *N'Importe Quelle Route*, Autumn 1989, p.28.

Poteet, Maurice. *Textes de l'Exode: Recueil de Textes sur L'Émigration des Québécois aux États Unis (XIX et XX Siècles)*. Guérin Littérature, 1987.

———. "The Role of Québec in Kerouac's Fiction." *N'Importe Quelle Route*, Autumn 1989, p. 29.

———, Robert Perreault, Eric Waddel et al. *Avant-Dire of the International Jack Kérouac Gathering.* March-August 1983, Fonds Club Jack Kérouac [195?]-1991 BANQ Archives Côte P922, BANQ, Québec, Canada.

Ricard, François. "Lire en Traduction: La 'Vécriture' de Jack Kérouac," *Liberté*, vol. 22, no. 2, 1980, p. 85.

*Sur Les Traces de Jack Kérouac.* Ici Radio Canada Radio Show, directed by Gabriel Anctil and Franco Nuovo, 21 Nov.-12 Dec. 2014, ici.radio.canada.ca/emissions/sur_les_traces_de_kerouac/2014-2015/index.asp.

Tondelli, Piervittorio. "Anche Lei È un Kérouac?" *La Dolce Vita*, no. 3, 1987, pp. 8-10.

Turner, Steve. *Jack Kerouac: Angelheaded Hipster*. Viking, 1996.

Waddell, Eric. "Le Désir Géographique...et la Réalité Québec-Amérique." *Géographie et Cultures*, issue 1, 1992, journals.openedition.org/gc/2544.

Yvon, Josée. "Poème." *N'Importe Quelle Route*, Autumn 1989, pp. 51-52.

# The Beat Interview
# Ed Sanders

*Ed Sanders reading at Beats & Beyond, June 2016, photo by Ann Charters*

# Interview with Ed Sanders
Jennie Skerl

### Introduction

Ed Sanders's multifaceted artistic career began when he read Allen Ginsberg's "Howl" as a high school student in Kansas City, Missouri. Inspired by Ginsberg's poetry and his powerful dissenting voice, Sanders hitch-hiked to New York a few years later in 1958 to enroll at New York University and became enmeshed in the Lower East Side poetry and arts scene—a distinctive avant-garde of the early 1960s peopled by second-generation Beat, New York School, and Black Mountain poets who read in coffee houses, painters who founded cooperative galleries, performance artists who created Off-Off Broadway, and underground film makers. Some noted artists who were part of the community are Andy Warhol, Jonas Mekas, Sam Shepard, Julian Beck and Judith Malina, Diane di Prima, Joyce Johnson, Rochelle Owens, and Ted Berrigan. The Lower East Side became a generational epicenter of artistic ferment, and Ed Sanders was a central figure whose work exemplified the art style of the period, later classified by critics as early postmodernism.

Sanders's art was inseparable from his politics and was a form of both protest and changing consciousness. His first published poem, *Poem from Jail* (1963), was written in jail after Sanders's arrest in a protest against nuclear submarines. From 1962 to 1965, Sanders was also an influential promoter and disseminator of avant-garde poetry through his self-published poetry magazine, *Fuck You/A Magazine of the Arts*, part of what Sanders called the mimeograph revolution. The magazine also served as a manifesto for free speech issues, sexual liberation, and legalization of marijuana. In 1964, Sanders opened the Peace Eye Bookstore, which sold small press poetry publications and provided a base for Sanders's diverse activities—the press, poetry, art shows, rehearsal space for his rock band, the Fugs (see fig. 1), work on his experimental films, and political organizing. Sanders was a participant in the 1965 Berkeley Poetry Conference, which was a seminal event for younger Beat and New York School poets.

The culmination of Sanders's border-crossing and communal art during the 1960s was his folk-rock band, the Fugs, co-founded with bohemian poet Tuli Kupferberg. Writing their own songs, the Fugs combined music with poetry, political protest, social satire, sex comedy, and an anarchic style that usually ended performances with a Dionysian kind of happening, such as the time when huge mounds of spaghetti (with sauce) were thrown at the audience. From 1965 to 1969,

*Fig. 1. The Fugs on stage at Astor Place Playhouse, 1966, Bill Beckman's stage design in the background (left to right: Pete Kearney, Vinny Leary, Ken Weaver, Ed Sanders, Tuli Kupferberg, Lee Crabtree), Ed Sanders archive.*

the band had a cult following in New York and beyond. In 1968, Sanders, with anti-war activists and Yippie movement founders, Jerry Rubin and Abbie Hoffman, organized a "Festival of Life" to take place in Chicago during the Democratic National Party Convention as a countercultural demonstration against the war in Vietnam. The Chicago police force violently opposed the gathering, and several organizers (David Dellinger, Rennie Davis, Thomas Hayden, Abbie Hoffman, Jerry Rubin, Bobby Seale, Lee Weiner, and John Froines, who came to be known as the "Chicago 8") were put on trial for conspiracy to cause civil disruption. Sanders was not charged but was called to testify for the defense in 1969.

Sanders's style in poetry, prose, and music employed the breakdown of hierarchies typical of arts of the period and was very much a part of the 1960s avant-garde program of democratization and accessibility. His work playfully combined elements from popular culture (such as cartoons, rock and roll), avant-garde art (such as open poetic forms and mixed media), and the poetic tradition of the lyric going back to the ancient Greeks, producing an idiosyncratic collage of high and low culture, an inter-art mix of verbal and visual elements, accessible language, and his own characteristic humor made up of comic hyperbole, satire, slang, and neologisms. The sexual body as the site of cultural struggle was prominent in Sanders's work of the 1960s, as displayed in some of his early poems ("Sheep Fuck Poem," "This is the Prayer Wheel and Vision"), the title of his poetry magazine (*Fuck You/A Magazine of the Arts*), and the sexual comedy of the Fugs. At the same time, ancient Greek literature informed his writing and music: during the time that Sanders was active in the Lower East Side avant-garde, he was also studying the classics at New York University, completing a degree in Greek in 1964. Sanders met his wife, Miriam Kittell at NYU; they were married in 1961, and their daughter was born in 1964 (see fig. 2).

*Fig. 2. Ed Sanders and his daughter, New York City, 1966, photo by Ann Charters*

As the 1960s closed, Sanders's life and work took a turn when he went to California in 1970 to report for the *Los Angeles Free Press* on the Manson Family murders, resulting in a highly respected book on the subject: *The Family: The Story of Charles Manson's Dune Buggy Attack Battalion* (1971; 1990). A few years later in 1974, he and his family settled in Woodstock, New York, where he continued to work as a poet, short story writer, political activist on environmental issues, a journalist, and a musician. He published several books of poetry in the 1970s and 1980s, culminating in *Thirsting for Peace in a Raging Century: Selected Poems 1961-1985* (1988). With the publication of his manifesto, *Investigative Poetry* (1976), and its counterpart in verse, *The Z-D Generation* (1980), Sanders defined a new poetics that led to historical and narrative poetry. Never abandoning the lyrical poetry of his earlier career, he began writing book-length biographical and historical poems, such as *Chekhov, A Biography in Verse* (1995); *1968, A History in Verse* (1997); *The Poetry and Life of Allen Ginsberg* (2000); and ultimately his longest work, *America: A History in Verse* (five volumes on the twentieth century published 2000-2009, with four more volumes to follow on earlier centuries). Sanders also developed a long-term prose fiction project: *Tales of Beatnik Glory*, a collection of semi-autobiographical short stories that memorialized the 1960s New York counterculture (published in four volumes from 1975 to 2004). This work was followed by his autobiography covering the same period, *Fug You: An Informal History of the Peace Eye Bookstore, the Fuck You Press, the Fugs, and Counterculture in the Lower East Side* (2011). In 1984, the Fugs began to perform annual reunion concerts, and Sanders continued to invent microtonal musical instruments (such as the Pulse Lyre, Talking Tie, and others) that accompanied his poetry readings, a project that began in 1968. In the 1990s, Sanders and his wife, Miriam, published the *Woodstock Journal*, a newspaper partially focused on environmental issues, later transformed into a website. Sanders remained linked to his Beat Generation origins through teaching in the summers at Naropa University, where he has taught courses on investigative poetry. Sanders conceives of investigative poetry as devoted to history and politics—the poet as chronicler of historical reality—supported by scholarly research and data gathering, and presented in modern poetic forms that include new technologies and performance. Sanders cites Ezra Pound, Charles Olson, and Allen Ginsberg as models.

Ed Sanders has received many honors and awards, including NEA fellowships for poetry, a Guggenheim fellowship for poetry, a Foundation for Contemporary Performing Arts fellowship, and the American Book Award for *Thirsting for Peace in a Raging Century*. His most recent poetry collection is *Let's Not Keep Fighting the Trojan War: New and Selected Poems 1986-2009*.

The interview published here took place on May 14, 1983, in my home, then located in Schenectady, New York. Sanders had received the Guggenheim fellowship and was temporarily living in the Albany area. I was primarily focused on studying Sanders as a poet and his connections with Burroughs and Ginsberg, since I was then researching Burroughs for my critical introduction to *William S. Burroughs,* 1985. Publications by Sanders referred to in this interview include *Poem From Jail* (City Lights, 1963); *Fuck You/A Magazine of the Arts* (1962-65); *Egyptian Hieroglyphs* (Institute for Further Studies, 1973); *Tales of Beatnik Glory,* volume I (Stonehill, 1975); *Investigative Poetry* (City Lights, 1976); *The Z-D Generation* (Station Hill, 1980); "Holy Was Demeter Walking the Corn Furrow" (first published in *20,000 A.D.*, North Atlantic, 1976); and "Sappho on East Seventh," a long narrative poem which was published several years after this interview in *Thirsting for Peace* (1987), and then included in *Tales of Beatnik Glory*, volume II (Citadel, 1990).

The interview summarizes many of Sanders's activities in the 1960s and his later commitment to investigative poetry. Since there were no other interviews with Sanders published in the 1980s, this conversation is informative about his then-perspective on his activities 20 years before (a man in his forties remembering his twenties) and his published poetry to date. It wasn't until the publication of *Fug You* in 2011 that he provided full details on his life in the 1960s. Also, it wasn't until the publication of *Thirsting for Peace* in 1987 that he began receiving attention for the body of his poetry. In this interview, he assesses his achievement as a poet. He also talks about continued work on *Tales of Beatnik Glory*, referring to volume II, which would not be published until 1990, and which would evolve into four volumes published in 2004. In volume II, as Sanders describes, he developed long narrative poems—"short story poems" of which "Sappho on East Seventh" is one—which provided an important transition to his later, historical and biographical book-length poems. Sanders speaks as he writes: informal, slangy humorous language combined with impressive erudition on the modern and ancient Greek poetic traditions.

**Jennie Skerl:** I was just reading through *Tales of Beatnik Glory*.[1] I don't think anyone could live in New York City like that anymore. It's too expensive.
**Ed Sanders:** Frankly, the civilization was brought about by two factors: one factor in the Lower East Side, or even the beatnik[2] ability to live in New York City was that the Lower East Side had been a slum for about 2000 years plus, and so it had a karma, a tradition, of being cheap. Also the rent controls of World War II were still in place in 1958, '59, '60, '61—all the way up to the end of the '60s. So there were really cheap apartments, and, at the same time, cheap food. That was all that was necessary.
**JS:** What about your friendship with Ginsberg?
**ES:** Yeah, well, I met all these people through *Fuck You/A Magazine of the Arts.*

**JS:** You didn't know them before?

**ES:** No. Well, I came to New York City as a trembling little guy who had read "Howl." And I had read a lot of Ezra Pound, and Dylan Thomas, and E. E. Cummings.

**JS:** So it is true what George Butterick said in his essay about you [in the *Dictionary of Literary Biography, volume 16*]—you read "Howl" on campus in Kansas and decided to go to New York City?

**ES:** You had a double choice, either you went to California or New York City. I got accepted by NYU, and Berkeley's acceptance came late, so I went to New York. Yeah, I read "Howl." I bought "Howl" at the [Missouri] university bookstore. I had it totally memorized, driving around, screaming it out there in the prairie. So, when I came to New York, I was very young. I thought I'd do a few years of research and studying language. I studied Latin, Greek, Egyptian.

**JS:** Oh, you actually studied Egyptian?

**ES:** Yeah, the state of my Egyptian has sort of dropped off in the last twenty years—but at one point I was able to read a sarcophagus. I was fairly adept. But Greek and Latin were my biggest subjects. Anyway, I wouldn't have approached these people in a million years back then. I used to go to all the Beat poetry readings, when I was 19 or so. I saw Kerouac and all those people. I saw Frank O'Hara and Ginsberg at the Living Theatre, say in '58. But it was all, you know, I'd see Ginsberg one year and see him the next year at another poetry reading, and he still had the same shirt on or something like that. I'd get some cultural inputs, but I wasn't prepared to approach any of these people for years. I didn't want to go the Rimbaud route. So, I just sat around there. Then when '62 hit, and I started putting out *Fuck You/A Magazine of the Arts*, I thought I was ready. I'd written a poem while I was in jail (I had tried to board a Polaris submarine on a peace demonstration: I swam out and tried to get on the submarine, and was arrested.)[3] I thought I had written a poem in jail that was as good as most of the poems that had been written by the Beat generation. Ferlinghetti printed it, *Poem From Jail*.

**JS:** So you had been writing and writing, and this was the first thing you had written that you thought was really good.

**ES:** Oh yeah, I had written lots of juvenilia—a thick stack of rewrites of Samuel Beckett, and rewrites of this and that, some good, some bad, crawling through the void puking and being young. So, in February, we got drunk one night after a Jonas Mekus movie, and I said I'm going to start a magazine called *Fuck You/A Magazine of the Arts*, and everybody was saying, "Sure, Ed, sure, yeah." So then I went the next day and bought a $30 mimeo and went down to the Catholic Worker where I used to eat (it was cheap) and went up on the second floor and typed it out on stencils, and they graciously gave me some of their paper, and I printed it. And then I thought of a great title, *Fuck You/A Magazine of the Arts*, a state of the art

title. Everybody thought I could go to jail. In '62, it was handcuff city. But I had been in jail for sit-ins, down south in civil rights demonstrations. I was getting arrested all over. No big deal. So I decided that I believed in what I was doing. I believed in my poetry at that time, *Poem from Jail*, because Ferlinghetti was going to print it. I thought, "Ferlinghetti is going to print my book! Hot stuff—this is it—big time—Ferlinghetti's Pocket Poets—City Lights!" It was a big thing because they printed William Carlos Williams, Corso, Ginsy—all my heroes. I was a 21-year-old ectomorph from the Midwest. It was like heaven. Like now getting a Guggenheim. If anybody had said to me in '58 I would ever get a Guggenheim, I would have laughed. So anyway at that time, to me, getting published by City Lights was the equivalent of a Guggenheim. [Sanders received a Guggenheim for poetry in 1983.] So I had a lot of confidence from being published by City Lights. I knew I had a good title: *FuckYou/A Magazine of the Arts*.
**JS:** Definitely, everybody loves that title.
**ES:** Here I was, trembling and shy and afraid. I'd go to these open poetry readings, and they'd say, "Let's put that skinny punk from the Midwest on at two in the morning." So everybody'd be reading, you know, "the green saliva of time," and I'd go on and read my poems. And then I put out *Fuck You/A Magazine of the Arts*, and they'd say, "Oh, when do you want to read, Ed? Just pick your time." So I learned corruption immediately. So everybody's groveling, wanting to get in: "Oh, here's some poems, Ed." They wanted to get in *Fuck You* because it became hot—all these people gave me articles to put in.
**JS:** How did you get all those really famous people to be contributors?
**ES:** I believed in what I did. I had a couple of semi-religious revelations, you know, from studying Egyptian and stuff. It was all happening right at the same time. So, I went into the Eighth Street Book Shop and I got some addresses. I made this list of people I would send *Fuck You/A Magazine of the Arts*: I sent it to Fidel Castro, Pablo Picasso, Samuel Beckett, Jean-Paul Sartre, Allen Ginsberg, Philip Whalen, Lawrence Ferlinghetti, Jack Kerouac. Of course, I would give it out, too. I had this endless list of people I respected, and I'd send it out to people just for the heck of it. Always first-class, because I was afraid of getting arrested, because it took a radical stance for its time. For instance, I wrote the first editorial advocating the legalization of marijuana, and everybody was saying, "Oh Ed (this was in late '62, early sixties), you can't. It's gotta be handcuff city."
**JS:** That was pretty early for that stuff.
**ES:** I was very honest. I was trying to live an open life. So, if my friend wrote poems for *Fuck You* Magazine and was also a drug dealer, I'd put it in the contributor's notes. So, anyway, I sent it to Ginsberg (I got his address in India), and he was apparently in a big depression, so he wrote back. Charles Olson wrote back, Philip Whalen wrote back, Gary Snyder, they all started writing letters back. And I was

just a trembling, little....So I said to myself, "you made your moves—you better get to know these people. Learn the language, get accepted as another beatnik schmo, just like a member of the club." So basically that's how it happened...that's how I met all those people. I did my apprenticeship, and I decided I was ready.

**JS:** But you were, I gather, really good friends with Ginsberg. He was involved with the Fugs.

**ES:** Yeah, well Ginsy and I got real close because I lived on the Lower East Side.

**JS:** So did he.

**ES:** Yeah. He always travelled a lot, but our apartments were pretty near, so I'd hang out. He's the one I got to know best of all of them because he was on the set. Allen's the one with whom I had the greatest rapport because he got me out of the Midwest. I still think he's a great poet. Some of his poems are American treasures. And poetry was always my greatest interest, too.

**JS:** What do you think is his greatest significance as a poet?

**ES:** He's got a really good ear. He's brilliant. He's one of the most intelligent people I know, and able to cope with insanity. He's a guy who has on occasion had full Blakean visions. Usually when you meet a writer or somebody and you know them for 20 or 30 years, you develop a kind of a standoff, sort of begrudging friendship—but I feel very close to him still.

**JS:** When did you first meet William Burroughs?

**ES:** I remember a party at Grove Press in '65....I have various memories....I remember seeing him around the campus [NYU] a lot....He was more of an influence to me, frankly, in the books. A piece that was a big influence was in a little magazine called *The Outsider*,[4] and also the books like *Exterminator* and *Nova Express*. Mainly, you got out of the early Burroughs things like you got from Sartre, from existentialism—"Existence precedes essence" and "Hell is other people"—apothegms. Burroughs was always interesting to me as a writer who was a distiller of apothegms—brilliant shards or fragments. We would all memorize stuff like that, or talk about Dr. Benway when *Naked Lunch* started coming out. So you picked up things then in segments when it came out in magazines. I couldn't afford to buy the book. Grove Press put it out for $5. In 1964, that was my weekly food bill.

**JS:** Did you know Burroughs's son?

**ES:** Yes.

**JS:** As I was reading *Tales of Beatnik Glory*, I kept comparing it to *Speed* [an autobiographical novel] by William Burroughs, Jr., because he portrayed the Lower East Side of the same era, around 1961, and there are a lot of parallels between your book and the amphetamine scene he described.

**ES:** Yeah, I had a lot of information about amphetamines. I made a documentary called *Amphetamine Head*.

*Fig. 3. Ed Sanders at The Bowery Electric, June 2016, photo by Ann Charters.*

**JS:** Yes, it's mentioned in *Tales of Beatnik Glory*.
**ES:** So I actually did it. The police took it. But I did do this film.
**JS:** They took the film?
**ES:** Yeah, they raided me. I had this little back building—one of those Lower East Side back buildings in the dark back courtyards, and they raided one night in 1965 in the summer and wiped out my film career. Some of it was pretty smutty. I did this film called *Mongolian Cluster Fuck*. I used to get all my friends, we'd drink, and I'd have them come over, and film. In *Amphetamine Head* I think I had some footage of Corso, and some of Joel Oppenheimer. Yeah, so, I rented this apartment on Allen Street, on the Lower East Side, a famous street in Lower East Side history. I bought a few ounces of amphetamines, and I strung lights all around, and I put this bag of amphetamines in the middle of the room, and put out the word. The only rule was that, whatever happened, I would be able to film it. It pretty much happened exactly as I wrote it in *Tales of Beatnik Glory*. There were a couple of sordid things that I didn't write about, but mainly it's all there. People drew murals all over the wall, and they took off the front door and put up a curtain. That's what the landlord really freaked about—what did they do with the front door? They probably used it as a staging area for art. They ripped the plumbing out to make plumbing flutes....These were hardcore A-heads. These guys were the ones that said, "Hell man, wow, I was up three weeks, wow, thirteen visions," you know. These guys that had stayed up for a couple of weeks had sleep-death, a terrible sleep-death....They would put India ink into hypodermic needles and squirt these arabesques. One or two of them were actually interesting artists. Most of the rest were just dopers—just burn-outs.
**JS:** Were they really young kids?
**ES:** There were old ones and young ones. Of course, with an A-head, you can't tell. If you go on amphetamines for a few weeks, you go kind of grey, and trembling, and skinny, and you don't know how old they are. They look like something casting called for cryptic movies [i.e., "from the crypt" horror movies]...
**JS:** What do you think is your most important work?
**ES:** I think it's a group of poems that will last...I guess I would say I'm a poet. I wrote a 23-page poem about the ghost of Sappho. ["Sappho on East Seventh" was published in volume II of *Tales of Beatnik Glory* in 1990.] I spent six months writing it last year. I would say there is a group of poems, beginning with *Poem From Jail*, and including a group of poems I wrote based on my studies of Egyptology, a series called *Egyptian Hieroglyphs*. I think those will last. And there are various other poems in my sex mania period that I think will probably last, at least they will always be of interest to collectors of erotica. So, I think, in an aggregate, I've written an important group of maybe 100-150 pages of poetry that I'm very interested in having survive. I think I'm a pretty good short-story

writer, too. *Tales of Beatnik Glory* was my first short stor[y] [collection], and since then I've written a whole bunch. In fact, I'm just now finishing volume two of *Tales of Beatnik Glory*, where I mix narrative poetry with prose—poetry that's really narrative—I call them "sho-sto-poes"—short story poems that mix prose with the poetry sections. There's no slack, no vague imagery, it's very direct, I'm kind of proud of those. I studied a lot of Yiddish-speaking socialists in the Lower East Side and compared those people that lived in the same buildings in 1895 with those of us who lived there in 1963, '64, '65, [which is] 60 years later, switching back and forth, comparing two years. So I think those will last. It's interesting, I've never had anybody ask that question before. I guess that's the answer. There's about 150 pages of poetry and some short stories. It's like the Dadaists in 1916, sitting in the Cabaret Voltaire in Zurich and spewing out some manifesto in five minutes, and that's what survives. And the rest of his life or her life they might have done 59 volumes of work, but, this is it, the manifesto. So, I don't know, maybe something I scratched on a tablecloth at Le Metro Cafe in 1964 in the middle of a poetry reading will be anthologized. It's like Robert Graves says, all he wants is two poems in *The Oxford Book of English Verse*...

**JS:** I like that poem about Demeter ["Holy Was Demeter Walking the Corn Furrow"]. Is that one you would save?

**ES:** That's one of the sex maniac ones. I wrote the first version in '67, when Joel Oppenheimer and I were reading at the Folklore Center, and I had to have something hot for that. So I just wrote it off one morning. Then I kind of rewrote it after I met Robert Bly. Yeah, that's not bad. That's a very metrical poem. I got interested in Greek meters.

**JS:** Well, that was a question that I wanted to ask you, about your concept of poetic form. Ginsberg always talks about breath as the basis for his line, I wondered if you were working within that concept. But you also seem to have a lot of visual elements in your poems, too, which is an entirely different thing.

**ES:** Well, it's a question of left brain and right brain. I think it's important to develop your right brain, and I think visual and spatial perception in poetry is a right brain phenomenon. It developed in the twentieth century by using the typewriter as a typesetting process, with guys like Pound, William Carlos Williams in his tercets, Paul Blackburn, Gary Snyder, Phil Whalen. Allen's not too much into that.

**JS:** So you think it's all related to the typewriter. For some reason I never thought of that before.

**ES:** Well, and calligraphy. Those guys—Whalen, Lew Welch, and Snyder—all studied calligraphy at Reed College. So, that's why when you get a letter from Gary Snyder, it's a work of art. Ditto for Phil Whalen. Whalen's a master of the calligraphic poem. Apollinaire was. Some of those other French guys experimented with the way a poem looks. And Robert Duncan, for example. To him it's all a very serious matter. When Olson said poem is field, the way it looks is part of the field. So I have never hesitated to used glyphs; it comes out of my study of Egyptian.

**JS:** Are those drawings in your poems actually Egyptian? Or are they your own?

**ES:** It depends on what poems....I'm going full color now. I've decided to go full color type. I think that typeface is going to go full color now, and therefore, since colors seem to relate to emotions, why not program the reading public to become sensitive to the mode and nuances of color typography? So that will come into poetry. Like color serifs. Serifs on a type font are a little hook, eye hooks that hook into a text. It's proven that that's an easier way to read, these hooks, so why not have color serif hooks?

**JS:** Are you using color symbolism?

**ES:** You can relate colors primitively, like red with blood, blue with water, but it's more sophisticated than that because you perceive more than 1500 color nuances, so you can relate them to emotions. Anyway, to me, it just goes to ability of your right brain in poetry, for your right brain to feed on as well as your linguistic half.

**JS:** So, you're really putting the two things together—the visual and linguistic?

**ES:** That's why I want full color...to go the Blake route...

**JS:** Related to that, I wanted to ask you if you participated in the printing of your books, because the visual part is so important.

**ES:** Oh, sure, my attitude about publishers is torture them until they respect you, especially if you have a visual sense. I have a very well-defined right brain. So I know to the micro-inch where I'd like to see these things go. And you have to get a little older and bolder to feel pushy enough to deal with the publishers. The best thing to do is to establish a cordial relationship and then force your will as much as possible on them, especially in spatial matters.

**JS:** I noticed you've been working with Open Studio.[5]

**ES:** They did the little manifesto of mine about the secret police, *The Z-D Generation*. It's great to work with them.

**JS:** So what is your concept of investigative poetry, which seems to be *The Z-D Generation*? It seems to me that's a whole new idea in your work.

**ES:** Basically, as a Newspeak précis, it's to keep poetry from becoming like Japanese flower arranging—not to trash Japanese flower arranging—but most people would rather be tortured than go to a poetry reading. I mean, if you go out there in the streets, people would maybe let you punch them in the face in lieu of going to a poetry reading, you know. At the same time, it's poetry's fault—it's a lot of gibberish. A lot of people are writing stuff that's just off the top of their heads—gibberish—without trying to take a step toward making it understandable. And it's really the fault of these brilliant guys like Apollinaire and Mallarmé.

Or, to go way back in time, the Greek dithyrambs—like Pindar—dithyrambs were just gibberish poems. But they were *sung*, you know, they had a chorus, so you can listen to the gibberish. It's like you don't really understand Wagner—most people don't—when it's sung, but it's beautiful and you don't mind. Same way in the dithyramb and just have somebody stand there—it's nod city....But that doesn't say much about investigative poetry. It's just a method, it's practical.

**JS:** You're saying it's a part of wanting to reach a larger audience, though.

**ES:** Well, another factor besides the gibberish factor is that poetry used to be the six o'clock news, it used to tell the frustrations and hopes and desires and myths and inner meanings and secrets of the civilization. That's the *Iliad* and the *Odyssey*. They used to recite poems at the Olympics. If you trashed the emperor, it was a big deal. Catullus trashed Caesar, and they wondered if he was going to get killed for it. Poetry had an intimacy with the civilization. Probably only because of numbers, I suppose, because poetry and rhythm and singing and recitations were the most apt way mnemonically to store the information. That was the tape recorder of ancient times—metrics. But when 2000 years go by, poetry is what? It's lost its relationship to civilization. So how would you, in a non-hokey, non-sellout, non-commercial, but in a socially and historically relevant way, bring poetry back to the position it had in ancient times? I thought one way would be by having poets write history and conduct investigations, using all the techniques from the last 200 years of French, German, and American poetry to write real time stuff—to do investigations to tell stories, to thrill a reader again, or the listener.

**JS:** In *The Z-D Generation* you're talking about investigating political issues.

**ES:** Yeah, another principle about investigative poetry is you don't have to drink the hemlock anymore. You throw the hemlock back in their faces. You say, "You drink the hemlock." It's like the Ginsberg line, "Now is the time for prophecy without death as a consequence,"[6] which is another principle of investigative poetry: that you can prophesy in a democracy. American democracy *does* remind me of Athens. Inside Athens is a great zone of freedom, while Athens would send out its triremes to kill: "Let's kill everybody in Lesbos because they didn't give us enough oil." So they would row off—to off the people of Lesbos. But within the walls of Athens there was a great freedom. If you wanted, you could be a drag queen, anything, whatever you wanted to do. As Aristophanes, you could write *Lysistrata* in the middle of the war. It reminds me of America. So, "it's time for prophecy without death" is valid. So, why not have a Z-D generation—after Zola and Diderot—where you do the equivalent of the encyclopedia—which changed France for the better?

**JS:** Were you really interested in war criminals? [*The Z-D Generation* proposes to expose war criminals in the U.S. government.]

**ES:** Yeah, I thought, what would shake America to the core just like the encyclopedia did? In my judgment, the way you do it is to go up to the war caste, which I devoted a lot of time to. There's this group of people hooked into the machinations of power that come right out of World War II and Korea and Vietnam and are down there in El Salvador right now. I want to investigate the bombing practices of Curtis LeMay and the building of the bomb, and go right back to find the scientist who invented the fragmentation bomb, and locate the people that were responsible for napalm, and just put them on the pickle fork of reality—write about them—poetry. So I thought that would be one project that would be equivalent [to the encyclopedia] because it would shake American civilization to the roots if you did it accurately.

## Notes

[1] At the time of the interview, only volume I of *Tales of Beatnik Glory* had been published (in 1975). A 30-year short-story project, volumes I and II were published together in 1990; volumes I-IV were published in 2004.

[2] "Beatnik" was a pejorative designation used by journalists (specifically the San Francisco columnist Herb Caen and derived from Sputnik, the Soviet satellite) to refer to Beat Generation writers and bohemians of the late 1950s and became part of popular culture. Many to whom it was applied rejected the label, but some, like Sanders, gladly adopted it to assert their nonconformity.

[3] The Committee for Nonviolent Action (CNVA), an anti-war, anti-nuclear weapons group organized a protest against nuclear-armed submarines in New London, Connecticut, in 1960. Sanders and others were jailed when they swam out to the Polaris submarines to prevent launching.

[4] *The Outsider* was a literary magazine published in the early 1960s by Loujon Press in New Orleans. The magazine published Beat writers, Charles Bukowski, and Henry Miller among others.

[5] Open Studio was a design, production, and training facility for writers, artists, and independent publishers in Rhinebeck, New York. The Studio assisted Sanders in designing and printing *The Z-D Generation*, which includes Sanders's drawings and a variety of typefaces.

[6] Allen Ginsberg's translation of a line from Apollinaire's "*Les collines*" ("The Hills"), which appears in the Ginsberg poem "Death to Van Gogh's Ear."

# Reviews

*Love, H: The Letters of Helene Dorn and Hettie Jones*
Helene Dorn and Hettie Jones
Duke University Press, 2016

*Love, H*, the correspondence of writer Hettie Jones (1934–) and sculptor Helene Dorn (1918–2004), has much in common with the epistolary novel. In fact, the vast majority of collected letters bears that resemblance since they are almost always a selection from a greater oeuvre (a transparent tease leaving us to wonder what has been omitted), constructed to present the narrative of a life and a portrait of the protagonist in the contexts of friends, family, colleagues, enemies, and others. Jones herself, who edited the volume and added commentary throughout, forthrightly acknowledges this editorial process, explaining that the letters were selected from "many exchanges…over 40 years," although she never calls the end product fiction (2). But the construct is a fiction culled from primary documents that more often than not speak to a life that was in reality messy, unplanned, and always in the process of becoming—anything but a coherent narrative.

Yet these very texts defy their own fictive construction. Most of us do not render letters solely to leave materials for an editor to affirm the importance of our presence on earth. Most often, they serve as tools to facilitate other actions and projects as part of someone's being in the world. We write letters to conduct business, to maintain or end relationships, to create new relationships, to express gratitude and sympathy, to remember the past and to imagine the future, to record our dreams, and so much more. Sometimes we write them to ourselves, sometimes to people we've never met, sometimes to our most intimate of confidants. The process of such writing requires that we shape and reshape the self that we wish to present to the Other(s), not undermining authenticity but acknowledging that at any given moment we can craft the self that we desire to be—and the self of the one to whom we communicate. It is against, and with, and through these artifacts that we reflect on our lives and check our memories alongside the greater documentation of fact. As such, letters when collected for publication simultaneously reify the epistolary novel and the memoir-auto/biography, the latter itself both fiction and fact.

This is what Ann Charters intended with her editing of Jack Kerouac's voluminous correspondence—to create a biography of the man himself—and this is what we find in collections such as Joyce Johnson's correspondence with Kerouac, Gary Snyder's correspondence with Wendell Berry, and perhaps even more so in William S. Burroughs's *Yage Letters*, based on his journals and correspondence with Ginsberg. It is also the kind of text readers immerse themselves in when they read *Love, H*, which weaves Jones's personal reflections on her friendship with

Dorn throughout the letters themselves. It is, as Jones states in her introduction, documentation of how her friendship with Dorn "kept [her] from sinking" during the difficult years chronicled in *How I Became Hettie Jones* (1990), while also telling the story of two women evolving in separate but similar ways, the twining narratives fashioned upon Jones's concern with "literature and art and our attempts to locate our own efforts within these disciplines." Trying, that is, "to be an artist in a woman's life" (3). In this respect, the collection fits comfortably in the long line of epistolary texts emerging in the 17th century as a feminized form in which self-expression, the affective, and everyday life dominate. But the book is so much more—which is not to trivialize self-expression, emotions, and daily occurrences, or Jones's magnanimous goals for the collection, but rather to emphasize the dynamism of the book as a whole.

With respect to Jones's focus on the female artist, their correspondence, which begins in 1963 and concludes in 2004 (the two first met in 1960), dwells on the often-brutal story of the intersection of race, class, sex, and gender as manifested in female friendship. As such, it differs markedly from the correspondence of many of the male Beat writers, in which they often celebrate their genius and engage in extended lectures on aesthetic philosophies. Throughout much of *Love, H*, both Jones and Dorn are divorced: Jones from the poet and playwright LeRoi Jones (Amiri Baraka), and Dorn from the poet Edward Dorn. Both women have children and both find themselves struggling to maintain their lives and identities as artists in tandem with their commitment to their families. Jones in this narrative develops as the more political and extroverted, dealing daily with both covert and unabashed racism; Dorn the more reserved and introverted. But together, as what Dorn called "discarded wives," they persistently affirm, decade after decade, the other's inherent self-worth and talents, encouraging and problem-solving along the way, while humbly and joyfully extolling the academic and professional successes of their children—and themselves.

What makes this particular story especially brutal, however, is the poverty that stalks them like a shadow self. It's always there. Jones is forever shopping at thrift stores, relying on freelance copyediting work and adjunct teaching jobs, and risking life and limb by driving across country in cars that belong in the scrap yard. Dorn repeatedly seeks decent housing in Gloucester, Massachusetts, her story the all-too-common one of a life descending from suitable living conditions to meager public housing. As in Ralph Ellison's *The Invisible Man*, we see cherished items from one of the homes she rented tossed unceremoniously onto the front lawn for garbage collection. Illness, alcoholism, and poor health care services plague her, and she mourns the loss of her hair as her health deteriorates. A photograph of her bundled up with head bowed down and pulling a cart of groceries through a January 1985 snowstorm symbolizes not only the resilience of both women—e.g., Dorn's long strides as she follows a car track down the middle of a snow-clogged Gloucester street (64)—but also the cruelty of lives forged in loneliness, on the precipice of extinction. Neither woman is homeless and without friends and family, but neither woman as she strives to be independent is without worries about her next meal, the possibility of eviction, and the fragility of her body.

The starving artist model, then, while a romantic possibility for the young, especially if one is white, male, and unattached, emerges in *Love, H* as potentially catastrophic. It's a common story, one that's been told over and over in fiction and nonfiction. Virginia Woolf resurrected it in *A Room of One's Own* as did James Joyce in *Dubliners*, *Portrait of an Artist as a Young Man*, and *Ulysses*; Bonnie Bremser Fraser told it in *Troia: Mexican Memoirs,* as did both Barbara Ehrenreich in *Nickle and Dimed* and Zora Neale Hurston in letters to artists such as Langston Hughes and Carl Van Vechten published as *Zora Neale Hurston: A Life in Letters*. But it is also a story that many seem all too willing to forget, or to ignore. So it is not surprising that both Jones and Dorn find a myriad of ways to express to each other the troubling question, "What is to happen to me/you/us?" as they face the blankness of their future at the end of each letter.

But face it they do, heroically, using humor, often self-deprecating, to bolster each other, sending one another book recommendations (Dorn spends much of her time in feminist self-education.) and, as the years pass, confronting head-on the invidious realities of aging in America. Holidays and birthdays mark the passage of time, the former—Christmas, as an example—being a celebration in reality more taxing than magical, something they wish they could "step over": Jones in a note dated December 12, 2003, comforts Dorn with the subtle irony of "[b]e of good cheer, my dear. Xmas will be over before we know it" (348-49). Their greetings are often accompanied by clippings of articles relevant to their temporal status. On March 27, 1996, approximately two months after Dorn's birthday, Jones sent Dorn a letter with an article from *Time* magazine about the word *old*. In her commentary on the article, Jones remembers that on the margins of the clipping she had written, "Got any thoughts?"—a prompt to Dorn to respond to the article's report that Americans are "'fearful of aging...thus giving rise to such euphemisms as 'senior citizen' and 'silver fox,' as well as more weighted words like 'elderly,'" biased terms that Jones notes are now frowned upon by most journalistic style manuals (151-52). Dorn replied the following day: "...it's all nonsense, of course. I call myself Helene Dorn. And respond to, and use, 'senior citizen' when it means a discount....'Mature American'—what bullshit!" (151-52).

Their back-and-forth reads as charming, sad, exciting, feisty, evasive, confusing, bittersweet, gutsy, and a mix of other qualities, all the while establishing love as the center of their world. In fact, their correspondence builds as a romance, hence the eponymous valediction, "Love, H," which signifies not only their unique identities but also the possible dissolving of those selves into a single spirit or the mirroring of one's self in the Other. Interestingly, Jones resists this trope in her commentary, stating that to correspond "isn't to duplicate but to harmonize" (3). In effect, she perceives that the one who emerges from the two is a creative illusion, art itself. But whatever one chooses to believe about the "I/You/We" nature of the linguistic chimera "Love, H," what remains stable throughout their correspondence is the fact that the writing of each letter functions as a metaphor for the one who is absent, the one upon whom love is projected. Jones and Dorn speak in secret at times; confide their dreams, hopes, and fears; remain silent on certain topics; and quickly build themselves into the other's confidante, comforter, and confessor, as they focus on what scholar Janet Gurkin Altman identifies as the "psychological nuance and the details of everyday life" (19), amidst which as partners in the romance they rely upon memory and expectation to keep the other alive and present (122).

*Love, H*, then, owes its dynamism not only to its honest exposition of poverty and its nimble elucidation of the heroism that can emerge from the romance of female friendship, but also to the fact that the book goes a fair distance toward sketching a theory of correspondence as genre. Jones never states this directly, but she does declare that "[l]etters stop time," that they "offer voices," that they "offer arrivals" (1-4). Her attentive introduction coupled with the letters themselves and her contemporary commentary direct readers to that which in everyday life remains invisible: the epistemological complexities of writing over time to the Other.

It is not my purpose in this short text to create that theory or comment on others' efforts to create their own such theories, so instead I will conclude by foregrounding a few components of Jones's hidden theory that drive *Love, H* to become what Ann Charters calls a Beat masterpiece, one which "'validat[ed] [her] own feelings about how difficult it must have been to survive and raise children as what Hettie calls the 'discarded wife' of a Beat author" (34). What Jones directly speaks about in her introduction but never fleshes out is the reader/writer relationship in a correspondence. *Love, H*, however, repeatedly reminds one that unlike conventional fiction and nonfiction texts, the epistolary text starkly dramatizes the reader/writer relationship—not simply as a one-way transaction, but as a complex dialectic amongst a potentially infinite number of participants in equally complex dimensions of time and space.

As a variant of first-person narration, the epistolary text at the most basic level features at least two first-person narrators (often more), each writing directly to the other, who is also the reader. The result is a text foregrounding as virtually equal the act of writing and the act of reading, a text in which one can see both actors struggling in their correspondence to make sense of their own actions and needs as well as those of the Other. For instance, toward the end of their relationship, Dorn writes to Jones that she's hobbled with a faulty printer, pouring rain, and an injured foot, but concludes, "Meanwhile bless you for writing! And I'll try [to write] later today, tho I ain't got much to say." Writing the following day, Jones reassures her, "Don't worry whether you have much to say, the point is just to get better so you can at least get out into the fresh air before it turns into hot air" (328). In this simple exchange, one that all good friends know extremely well, Dorn has not asked for reassurance—perhaps she can't admit in writing that she needs it?—but Jones as reader writes back explicitly to the what-was-not-said, a reading into the text based on long years of knowing her friend and thus accordingly adjusting her own writerly self.

Similarly, but from a different point in time, Jones splices their correspondence with a short, two-sentence comment on the significance of the phrase "years left" in their exchange: "That tossed off 'years left' stops me now. It didn't then; I simply refused to believe her"—a reference to Dorn who had written that she no longer wanted new books since "I've no place to put them, and don't have that many *years left* to get them read" (318, emphasis mine). As the reader of those words in 2003, Jones struggled with the reality of endings, realizing only years later in the act of editing that she as reader chose a particular response out of her own psychological needs, as we all do. The full effect is, again to quote Altman,

> very much like reading over the shoulder of another character whose own readings—and misreadings—must enter into our experience of the work. In fact, the epistolary [text's] tendency to narrativize reading, integrating the act of reading...at all levels (from a correspondent's proofreading of his own letters to publication and public reading of the entire letter collection), constitutes an internalizing action that blurs the very distinctions that we make between the internal and external reader. (88)

Simply put, the reader and writer share identities. By extension, no text ever emerges from anything other than a writer/reader union, since once published for a wider readership, a text is read by an unknown number of unknown readers who in the act of reading the correspondence become themselves agents and respondents in that very relationship. Jones alludes to this in her introduction, stating that the letter, be it a fax or email or postcard (all of which she and Dorn used), constitutes a message read not only by the addressee but also by others who may profit from the reading: specifically, Jones wonders what her readers can learn from the Hettie/Helene correspondence.

As the "years left" passage illustrates, the writer/reader construct in an epistolary text also highlights the temporality of epistolary statements, situating the writer and reader in a particular space as well. Those readers, for instance, who may learn from the Hettie/Helene letters exist in a world unplotted, while Jones and Dorn as the primary protagonists are resurrected by readers who move through the book in the imagined present moment in New York City and Gloucester, Massachusetts. Dorn and Jones's physical and metaphysical coordinates are complicated by the presentation of their physical and emotional conditions. Space and time fluctuate depending on when the letter was written, the date of composition (itself a somewhat unstable signifier), the date of arrival and of reading(s), and the condition of the letter (Did the ink smear? Is there a clipping of a *Time* magazine article enclosed?). In essence, the correspondence directs one to the present of someone's real life as it is repeatedly birthed—Jones and Dorn become a present reality for the Other each time they write a letter and each time they read the letter, while situating the reader/writer at the edge of the future. What will happen next?

Letters by their very nature are episodic, a complete whole that is a part of a larger whole signified by the blank separating each letter in the collection: physically on the page of the collection in book form, metaphysically in the present moment between the reading of one letter and the reading of a subsequent letter. Each letter-as-episode is akin to a snowflake, unique in its physical form, even when typed on the same typewriter or computer (e.g., Hettie and Helene's later correspondence). The space/time gap between them portends the unknown that faces their very physicality, that of both the letter and of its creator.

At some point, every correspondence must cease. Sometimes one writer/reader elects to end it, to the chagrin of the other; sometimes the nature of the correspondence dictates its cessation (e.g., the project was completed). Sometimes death itself forces closure, which is the case with *Love, H*. In a letter dated "Gloucester, 1/9/04," Dorn wrote excitedly about getting a small heater for her apartment, signing off with "That's all for now. Love, H," implying the continuation of life via another letter. In what may be one of the most powerful of literary endings, Jones from her position some ten years into the future remarks, "And that was all. For now and forever" (349). Helene never wrote again and passed away in May 2004.

*Love, H* testifies to the resilience of epistolary relationships. Even after they cease to exist, one can resurrect them through the very act of reading and rereading those letters, and by passing them along through publication for others to read. The collection's theoretical foundation upholds not only a narrative of letter writing itself, but also the narrative(s) of two extra/ordinary lives. These lives are most obviously those of Hettie Jones and Helene Dorn. But they are also the lives of any two individuals who have chosen to sustain their relationship, that hard journey home, through written discourse, to see themselves in Hettie and Helene, to write if only in their most private thoughts, "Such a story, our letters" (350).

—Nancy M. Grace, The College of Wooster

## Works Cited

Altman, Janet Gurkin. *Epistolarity: Approaches to a Form*. The Ohio State UP, 1982.

Charters Ann. "The Beat Interview." *Journal of Beat Studies,* vol. 5, 2017, pp. 29-40.

*The Poetry and Politics of Allen Ginsberg*
Eliot Katz
Beatdom Books, 2016

*The Poetry and Politics of Allen Ginsberg* is a fully-developed analysis of Ginsberg's political poetry; Eliot Katz deals directly with the political inspirations, implications, and influences of Ginsberg's bop prosody in a book-length study.[1] As might be expected of a poet with leftist political views, Katz writes for a general readership, not just for those steeped in critical theory. Using multiple approaches, Katz creates a portrait of Ginsberg that emphasizes his political commitment while defining the origins and ongoing influences of Ginsberg's politics, establishing a proper understanding of Ginsberg's contribution to political activism in his lifetime while expounding on how that contribution informs the twenty-first century.

The book began in the late nineties as a Rutgers University dissertation advised by Alicia Ostriker, a William Blake scholar, feminist, poet, and Ginsberg's colleague. Yet, the single biggest influence on Katz's work is Ginsberg himself; Katz met Ginsberg while a student at the Naropa Institute (now University) in 1980, and their relationship continued until Ginsberg's death in 1997. A personal relationship with an artist does not necessarily enhance one's analysis of that artist's work, of course. However, here the matter is both more complicated and possibly more relevant, as Katz's general subject is the conflation of the personal and the political.

Katz contextualizes the positions of literary critics in regard to political poetry, using the philosopher Jürgen Habermas and the literary critic Terry Eagleton to clarify his own theoretical position. Katz explains:

> According to Habermas, under postmodern theory "*all* genre distinctions are submerged in one comprehensive, all-embracing context of texts"....This "false pretense of eliminating the genre distinction between philosophy and literature," according to Habermas, only "robs both of their substance".... Instead, Habermas embraces a Kantian notion of sphere-differentiation, where the boundaries between disciplines are seen as drawn in dotted lines, something like semi-permeable membranes. Terry Eagleton defines this view as maintaining a "necessary differentiation of the cognitive, moral and cultural spheres," which are seen as "interrelated but not conflated".... In other words, art and politics are conceptually seen as different spheres which can interact, overlap, embrace, or stand apart in different historical contexts and different geographical locales. (16)

What connects the theories of Habermas and Eagleton to Katz's thesis about Ginsberg's political importance is not the political significance of his art, but rather that it can inspire others to get involved in larger political movements.

Katz rightly argues that the social movements often associated with the sixties owe a great debt to the Beat Generation and Ginsberg, in particular. As Lawrence Ferlinghetti attests, "[Ginsberg] had functioned as a great literary catalyst for the Beat Generation, just as Ezra Pound had done for his time, dragging a whole gang of writers into print with him, many of whom would never see print if it hadn't been for his insistence to editors" (284). Arguably, Ginsberg's networking and promotion of poets helped to create a recognizable body of writers who would be known as "Beats." And in another key way Ginsberg superseded the other prominent Beat writers, and the exploration of this decision is the core of this study. As Katz argues, "Ginsberg dismissed [the advice of Burroughs and Kerouac], writing about politics from the start and becoming a public activist beginning with his early 1960s participation in protests against the Vietnam War and remaining publicly and politically active throughout his entire life" (247). As a result, much of the political consciousness that has come to be associated with the Beat Generation owes a debt to Ginsberg's politics. While as Katz points out, "most of the Beat writers were politically progressive" (10), he also notes that when J. Edgar Hoover portrayed the Beat Generation in 1960 as one of the three most threatening subversive groups inside the United States, it was Ginsberg's political influence that concerned Hoover (250).

Echoing the volume edited by Jason Shinder, *The Poem that Changed America: "Howl" Fifty Years Later* (2006), which includes an earlier version of Katz's chapter on the poem, Katz calls "Howl" "the most influential American poem of the second half of the 20th century" (1), explaining that "'Howl' is structured like many meaningful projects in politics, psychology, or science. A problem is first examined, so that it can be identified. Once the problem is identified, a solution is proposed—and, if the solution seems like a potentially effective one, the project's designer celebrates" (51). Yet what truly makes "Howl" a politically important poem is not so much its creation but, as Habermas and Eagleton would argue, its impact. When the poem became the center of an obscenity trial, it made the poet and his work notorious, but the political impact of the poem on its readers made it historic. Katz notes that "[i]t is difficult to imagine what American culture, in the sixties and in subsequent decades, would have looked like without the impact of Bob Dylan and The Beatles," who were influenced by Ginsberg, and argues, "by extension, it is therefore difficult to conceive what it would have looked like without Allen Ginsberg and the Beat Generation" (2). The true heirs of Ginsberg's poetry, Katz posits, were not fellow poets but some of the most influential pop stars of the 1960s.

In addition, Katz points out the direct influence of Ginsberg on activists such as Abbie Hoffman, Al Haber, Tom Hayden, Roz Baxandall, Paul Krassner, Ed Sanders, and Jerry Rubin. Hoffman, for instance, saw Ginsberg as a prophet of social revolution. Rubin credits Ginsberg with the idea that protest could be theater: "[Ginsberg] suggested we march to Beatles' music.... He suggested there be huge floats. So instead of its being a march of 10,000 angry people who wanted to stop the war, it would be a parade....I think it was the first time I ever thought of politics being theatrical. Allen's ideas opened my mind to the possibility of what you might call, psychedelic politics, a politics that's inspired by imagination" (qtd. in Katz 5). Ginsberg also had an uncanny knack of being at the right place at the right time—not only participating but being a significant player in some of the most politically relevant events of his time, such as the 1968 Democratic National Convention in Chicago, where he was among the leaders of the protest movement into which he sought to instill peace rather than violence and famously chanted "Om" in an effort to ease tension at the fractious event. Katz also debunks Lee Siegel's October 2010 *New York Times Book Review* article that gave the false perspective that Ginsberg was mainly committed to personal freedoms rather than championing peace, egalitarianism, and ecological sustainability (10). As John Tytell says in one of the first works of Beat scholarship (1976), "Ginsberg sees his poetry as transmitting a sacred trust in human potentials...his role would be to widen the area of consciousness, to open the doors of perception, to continue to transmit messages through time that could reach the enlightened and receptive" (18-19). Catherine A. Davies in *Whitman's Queer Children* (2012) analyzes "the conflation of the personal and the political" in Ginsberg's poetry, finding this synthesis to be "a trope that Ginsberg returns to again and again in his writing." By way of example, Davies shows how in "America," Ginsberg seeks unconventional methods to simultaneously "protect and represent the nation," claiming a status that makes him at once an individual and a representation of the nation: "It occurs to me that I am America." Davies also sees significance in the physical placement of "America" adjacent to "Howl" in *Howl and Other Poems*, where it "speaks through a melding of the public and private, [offering] a more humorous and condensed politicization of the concerns voiced more obliquely in 'Howl'" (98-99).

Later in his chapter on "Howl," Katz quotes Kenneth Rexroth, the *pater familias* of the San Francisco Renaissance, who believed Ginsberg could be "the first genuinely popular, genuine poet in over a generation" (35). Rexroth's lines, "Three generations of infants / Stuffed down the maw of Moloch" (239) from his 1953 poem for Dylan Thomas, "Thou Shalt Not Kill," may have been (as T. S. Eliot says mature poets are apt to do) "stolen," as is suggested by Ann Charters (232), for his own use in "Howl" Part II. Ginsberg's Moloch also has a striking resemblance to the Moloch of Fritz Lang's anti-capitalist film *Metropolis* (1927), which Ginsberg recalls he may have seen as a child ("Author's Annotations" 140). Providing a broad context from which to grasp Ginsberg's most famous poem, Katz places "Howl" against the background of McCarthyism (and its homophobia), segregation, nuclear paranoia, Erich Fromm's emphasis on alienation, and the sociological work of C. Wright Mills. Katz calls the Moloch of Ginsberg's poem "the power elite" (72), President Dwight D. Eisenhower in his 1961 farewell address to the nation called it the "military-industrial complex," while Michael McClure called it the "military-industrial-corporate complex" (Aronson). Ginsberg himself called it the "military-industrial-nationalist complex" ("Author's Preface" xii)—and today I might call Moloch the "military-industrial-prison complex."

It is not insignificant, then, that the site of Ginsberg's first *reading* of "Howl"— with the emphasis on the *performance*, not the poet—is honored with a plaque in San Francisco. Katz believes:

> Ginsberg deserves primary credit for the exponential growth of poetry readings that first appeared in the late 1950s through the 1960s, and that has exploded more than ever since the last decade of the 20th century. This is especially significant in a consideration of poetry and politics, since in this television-and-internet age of so much stay-at-home entertainment, the resurgence of poetry readings has created new public spaces that provide additional opportunities for social meetings and public discussions, especially among young people. (45)

Kerouac's prose rhythms are credited by Katz for the sound of "Howl" Part I (55), which Tytell points out in *Naked Angels* were an even bigger influence than Whitman on the rhythm of the poem (216-17). Emphasizing Charles Kaiser's perceptive observation in *Gay Metropolis: 1940-1996*, Katz notes that "Ginsberg and other Beat writers were influential in large part because they were the first American writers to present gay themes as hip..." (98). Katz also reads "Howl" in light of William Blake's influence on Ginsberg, yet Katz distances his reading of "Howl" from what Tony Trigilio calls the influence of "Blake's Biblical revisionism" (125), which Trigilio sees as part of a grander deconstruction of the "impulse toward system-building" found in Ginsberg's work (174). "I think it would be a mistake," writes Katz, "to fit Ginsberg's ideas into a kind of postmodern 'anti-system' theoretical framework. Rather than opposing all notions of 'authority' and 'system-building,' it seems to me that it is the particular repressive characteristics of actually existing authority and systems that Ginsberg is criticizing" (68). In one passage, Katz writes, "[I]t is important to acknowledge that, as a result of social movements of the 1960s and 1970s, American culture has generally become far more open and tolerant than it was in the 1950s" (85-86).

In his chapter on "Kaddish," a poem thought by some to be Ginsberg's greatest achievement, Katz emphasizes the influence of Naomi Ginsberg's political commitment on her young son, which is expressed throughout the poem: "'Kaddish' functions, perhaps even more than 'Howl,' as a poem of witness" (104). Katz points out the stylistic differences between "Howl" and the staccato rhythm of "Kaddish: "[T]he lines seem choppier, more condensed or economical than the lines of 'Howl,' punctuated throughout by dashes reminiscent of Emily Dickinson....The short, choppy phrases of 'Kaddish' give the reader a sense of the fragmented life the poem describes—a fragmentation that is nevertheless connected to a whole poem and a whole, even though ill, psyche" (105-06). The choppiness of Ginsberg's lines in "Kaddish" reflects the psychological hesitancy between this masterpiece and the overflowing burst of energy characteristic of "Howl."

The fourth chapter moves on chronologically to the Vietnam War and Ginsberg's poem "Wichita Vortex Sutra." Katz reminds us that Ginsberg was publicly protesting the Vietnam War as early as October 28, 1963 (135), and that John Lennon and Phil Ochs had used lines similar to Ginsberg's declaration in "Wichita Vortex Sutra": "I here declare the end of the War!" (415). In December 1969, Lennon staged a "bed-in" with his wife, Yoko, as a statement of love and peace. Andrew Solt's documentary, *Imagine: John Lennon* (1988), captures an argument that occurred during this event between Lennon and a *New York Times* war correspondent, Gloria Emerson, who had just returned from an assignment in Vietnam and took issue with Lennon's form of protest. Emerson had seen the savagery of war up close while Lennon was writing songs in his hotel room. I believe that his songs did indeed save lives by inspiring young people not to join the military. According to Katz, Ginsberg's poetic impact was similar, with poet Andy Clausen, for instance, crediting "Wichita Vortex Sutra" for convincing him to leave the Marines in 1966 (154). Certainly, Ginsberg's pronouncement of the war's end in "Wichita Vortex Sutra" did not have an immediate magical effect, but as Katz states, "it did make an important cultural contribution toward the anti-war movement's long-term struggle to change the consciousness of many Americans and to force the U.S. government to eventually abandon its disastrous war policy in Vietnam" (161).

The last major poem that Katz focuses on is "Plutonian Ode," a poem calling attention to the destructive power of human-made plutonium, a key element of nuclear weapons. The cover photograph of Katz's book features a 1978 picture of Ginsberg on train tracks participating in a sit-in to stop the transportation of plutonium in Rocky Flats, Colorado. According to Katz, "Ginsberg's poetic and activist efforts were certainly at least a small part of the culture that educated the public about the dangers of nuclear power and that turned public opinion against the building of new nuclear power plants and toward treaties that at least somewhat reduced nuclear weapons stockpiles and nuclear waste" (183). There are few contemporary poets with the cultural cachet to bring national attention to such an act of sedition.

It is also important to note that Katz at times turns a critical eye to Ginsberg's shortcomings. Katz discusses the 1975 Naropa Institute scandal involving Ginsberg's guru, Chogym Trungpa Rinpoche, who ordered a forced stripping of the poet W. S. Merwin and his girlfriend, Dana Naone, by Vajra guards at Rinpoche's Halloween party. It must be noted that Ginsberg was not present at the event, but the ensuing debate about the unethical behavior of Rinpoche can be read about in *The Party: A Chronological Perspective of a Confrontation at a Buddhist Seminary* (1977), a report made by Ed Sanders's Investigative Poetry Group, and Tom Clark's *The Great Naropa Poetry Wars* (1980). Katz reveals that "[e]ven Ginsberg's own longtime guru, Chogyam Trungpa Rinpoche, is not spared in [Ginsberg's "Elephant in the Meditation Hall"], which alludes to a well-publicized 1975 scandal at Naropa Institute..." (207).

Katz also calls to task Ginsberg's less than exemplary involvement in the struggle for women's equality, believing that "it would be fair to acknowledge that Ginsberg does not explore or challenge dominant conceptions of gender with anything near the energy or insight with which he explores nearly every other key social and political issue of his time" (243). Regrettably, Katz avoids the greatest blemish in Ginsberg's career—his membership in the North American Man/Boy Love Association (NAMBLA). Ginsberg tried to dismiss this troubling misstep by proclaiming it as a defense of free speech in a hypocritical society that allowed heterosexuals to sexually objectify underage girls but denied this privilege to homosexuals. Perhaps it can be explained away by Bill Morgan's observation: "Deep down he enjoyed stirring up controversy..." (613). Yet, perhaps it cannot be so casually dismissed. If there is one thing that Katz should have addressed head on it is this troubling issue, which he probably avoided because there is no legitimate justification for this blunder. But then, too, Katz has opened the door to further study of Ginsberg's political activist perspectives, particularly volumes focused on Ginsberg as a gay activist and as a Jewish poet. Such studies are greatly anticipated, and their authors would be well advised to take Trigilio's and Katz's achievements as models of fine scholarship.

Ultimately, Katz views Ginsberg as promoting an inclusionary politics that calls for participatory democracy. Ginsberg's legacy, Katz says, is for progressive viewpoints—"internationalism, nonviolence, anti-racism, gay liberation, environmentalism, free expression, non-repressed sexuality, intersubjectivity, interpersonal solidarity, and opposition to the poverty and other economic injustices too often caused by unchecked capitalism" (231)—a spiritual social consciousness, the promotion of the poet as political participant, and an optimistic view of the potential for change based on an individual's actions. As Katz quotes Ginsberg from a 1995 interview about the victory of Beat Generation values:

> Many of these values have entered mainstream thought—e.g., ecology, grass, gay lib, multiculturalism—but haven't seen fruition in government behavior, so that now we have more folk in our prisons or under government surveillance than any country West or East....This "Beat generation" or "sixties" tolerant worldview has provoked an intoxicated right-wing "Denial" (as in AA terminology) of reality, codependency with repressive laws, incipient police state, death-penalty demagoguery, sex demagoguery, art censorship, fundamentalist monotheists televangelist quasi-fascist wrath, racism, and homophobia. The counterreaction seems a by-product of the further gulf between the rich and poor classes, growth of a massive abused underclass, increased power and luxury for the rich who control politics and their minions in the media. Prescription: more art, meditation, lifestyles of relative penury, avoidance of conspicuous consumption that's burning down the planet. (175)

Through Katz's explorations, it can be seen that Ginsberg melds politics and art, emerging as a poet who deliberately entwined his physical acts, his philosophical beliefs, and his art, creating a poetics that is at once personal and political.

—Kurt Hemmer, Harper College

## Notes

[1] Predecessors include Thomas F. Merrill's *Allen Ginsberg* (1969), which connects Ginsberg to the poetic canon; Paul Portugés's *The Visionary Poetics of Allen Ginsberg* (1978), which places Ginsberg's verse in the mystic tradition; *On the Poetry of Allen Ginsberg* (1984), edited by Lewis Hyde, which collects the competing voices debating Ginsberg's aesthetic value; Jonah Raskin's *American Scream: Allen Ginsberg's* Howl *and the Making of the Beat Generation* (2004), which provides a cultural context for Ginsberg's most famous poem; and Tony Trigilio's *Allen Ginsberg's Buddhist Poetics*, which studies questions of poetics, religious authenticity, and political efficacy in Ginsberg's poetry.

## Works Cited

Aronson, Jerry, director. *The Life and Times of Allen Ginsberg*. New Yorker Films, 2004.

Charters, Ann. "Kenneth Rexroth." *The Portable Beat Reader*, edited by Ann Charters, Penguin, 1992, p. 232.

Davies, Catherine A. *Whitman's Queer Children: America's Homosexual Epics*. Bloomsbury, 2013.

Ferlinghetti, Lawrence. *Writing Across the Landscape: Travel Journals 1960-2013*. Edited by Giada Diano and Matthew Gleeson, Liveright, 2015.

Ginsberg, Allen. "Author's Annotations." *Howl: Original Draft Facsimile, 50th Anniversary Edition*, edited by Barry Miles, Harper Perennial Modern Classics, 2006. pp. 121-46.

——. "Author's Preface: Reader's Guide." *Howl: Original Draft Facsimile, 50th Anniversary Edition*, edited by Barry Miles, Harper Perennial Modern Classics, 2006. pp. xi-xii.

——. "Wichita Vortex Sutra." *Collected Poems 1947-1997*, Harper Collins, 2006, pp. 402-19.

*Imagine: John Lennon*. Directed by Andrew Solt. Warner Brothers, 1988.

Morgan, Bill. *I Celebrate Myself: The Somewhat Private Life of Allen Ginsberg*. Viking, 2006.

Rexroth, Kenneth. "Thou Shalt Not Kill." *The Portable Beat Reader*, edited by Ann Charters, Penguin, 1992, pp. 233-41.

Trigilio, Tony. *"Strange Prophecies Anew": Rereading Apocalypse in Blake, H. D., and Ginsberg*. Fairleigh Dickinson UP, 2000.

Tytell, John. *Naked Angels: Kerouac, Ginsberg, Burroughs*. McGraw-Hill, 1976, rpt. Grove Weidenfeld, 1991.

# The Beat Index 2017

"The Beat Index" provides a chronicle of recent scholarship, including dissertations, in the field of Beat Studies. The artists and other Beat Generation figures represented here are core to the movement or are associated with then-contemporary and complementary avant-garde poetic movements. Unless otherwise noted, abstracts featured in the "Index" are publisher or author abstracts and may appear in excerpted form. Texts are organized alphabetically according to Beat author and chronologically by date of publication. While the focus is 2017, we have included more recent and earlier works not available at the time previous iterations of the "Index" were published. We intend the "Index" to be as comprehensive as possible. If we have omitted a title, we will greatly appreciate being informed of the omission so that we can include it in the next volume of the journal. Finally, note that some entries are repeated, either because they are joint authored or address more than one Beat author.

## The Beat Generation

Belletto, Steven, editor. *The Cambridge Companion to the Beats*. Cambridge UP, 2017.

> An in-depth overview of one of the most innovative and popular literary periods in America, the Beat era. Consummate innovators, the Beats had a profound effect not only on the direction of American literature, but also on models of socio-political critique that would become more widespread in the 1960s and beyond. Bringing together the most influential Beat scholars writing today, this *Companion* provides a comprehensive exploration of the Beat movement, asking critical questions about its associated figures and arguing for their importance to postwar American letters.

Belletto, Steven. "Five Ways of Being Beat, 1958-59." *The Cambridge Companion to the Beats*, edited by Belletto, Cambridge UP, 2017.

Calonne, David Stephen. *The Spiritual Imagination of the Beats*. Cambridge UP, 2017.

> The first comprehensive study to explore the role of esoteric, occult, alchemical, shamanistic, mystical, and magical traditions in the work of 11

major Beat authors. The opening chapter discusses Kenneth Rexroth and Robert Duncan as predecessors and important influences on the spiritual orientation of the Beats. Calonne draws comparisons throughout the book between various approaches individual Beat writers took regarding sacred experience. For example, Burroughs had significant objections to Buddhist philosophy, while Allen Ginsberg and Jack Kerouac both devoted considerable time to studying Buddhist history and texts. This book also focuses on Diane di Prima, Bob Kaufman, Philip Lamantia, and Philip Whalen. In addition, several understudied works such as Gregory Corso's "The Geometric Poem," inspired by Corso's deep engagement with ancient Egyptian thought, are given close attention. Calonne introduces important themes from Gnosticism, Manicheanism, and Ismailism to Theosophy and Tarot, demonstrating how inextricably these ideas shaped the Beat literary imagination.

Dickey, Stephen. "Beats Visiting Hell: Katabasis in Beat Literature." *Hip Sublime: Beat Writers and the Classical Tradition,* edited by Sheila Murnaghan and Ralph M. Rosen, The Ohio State UP, 2018.

Grace, Nancy M. "The Beats and Literary History: Myths and Realities." *The Cambridge Companion to the Beats*, edited by Steven Belletto, Cambridge UP, 2017.

—— and Jennie Skerl. "Standing at a Juncture of Planes." *Hip Sublime: Beat Writers and the Classical Tradition,* edited by Sheila Murnaghan and Ralph M. Rosen, The Ohio State UP, 2018.

Holladay, Hilary. "Beat Writers and Criticism." *The Cambridge Companion to the Beats*, edited by Steven Belletto, Cambridge UP, 2017.

Howard, Kristien. *The Beat Generation: Hatred for the Hipster.* Bokeh Bohemia, 2017.

> This essay, split into two arguments, demonstrates the importance of the Bohemian lifestyle and argues the extent of which the Beat Generation had an impact on political and social change.

Hrebeniak, Michael. "Jazz and the Beat Generation." *The Cambridge Companion to the Beats*, edited by Steven Belletto, Cambridge UP, 2017.

Inchausti, Robert. *Hard to Be a Saint in the City: The Spiritual Vision of the Beats.* Shambhala, 2018.

> Explores Beat spirituality through excerpts from the writings of the seminal writers of the Beat Generation, going deeper than the Buddhism with which many of the key figures became identified. Theirs is a spirituality where personal authenticity becomes both the content and the vehicle for a kind of refurbished American Transcendentalism.

Johnson, Ronna C. "The Beats and Gender." *The Cambridge Companion to the Beats*, edited by Steven Belletto, Cambridge UP, 2017.

Lane, Véronique. *The French Genealogy of the Beat Generation: Burroughs, Ginsberg and Kerouac's Appropriations of Modern Literature, from Rimbaud to Michaux.* Bloomsbury, 2017.

> The Francophilia of the Beat circle in the New York of the mid-1940s is well known, as is the importance of the Beat Hotel in the Paris of the late 1950s and early 1960s, but how exactly did French literature and culture influence in the emergence of the Beat Generation? French modernism did much more than inspire its first major writers. It materially shaped their works, as this comparative study reveals through close textual analysis of William S. Burroughs, Allen Ginsberg, and Jack Kerouac's use of French literature and culture, including the poetic realist films of Carné and Cocteau, the existentialist philosophy of Sartre, and the poems and novels of Baudelaire, Rimbaud, Proust, Gide, Apollinaire, St.-John Perse, Artaud, Céline, Genet, and Michaux.

Lee, A. Robert. "The Beats and Race." *The Cambridge Companion to the Beats*, edited by Steven Belletto, Cambridge UP, 2017.

———, editor. *The Routledge Handbook of International Beat Literature.* Routledge, 2018.

> Beat texts including *On The Road*, "Howl," and *Naked Lunch* are indisputably essentially America-centered Beat, but they have also had other literary exhalations, which invite far more than mere reception study. These are voices from across the Americas of Canada and Mexico, the Anglophone world of England, Scotland or Australia, the Europe of France or Italy and from the Mediterranean of Greece, the Maghreb, Scandinavia

and Russia, together with the Asia of Japan and China. This anthology of essays maps other relevant Beat voices, names, and texts. The scope is hemispheric, Atlantic and Pacific, West and East, giving recognition to the Beat inscribed in languages other than English and reflective of different cultural histories. Likewise the majority of contributors come from origins or affiliations beyond the United States, whether in a different English or languages spanning Spanish, Danish, Turkish, Greek, or Chinese.

Mackay, Polina. "The Beats and Sexuality." *The Cambridge Companion to the Beats*, edited by Steven Belletto, Cambridge UP, 2017.

Mitchell, Aaron Christopher. *Liminality and "Communitas" in the Beat Generation.* Peter Lang, 2017.

> Analyzes the literature and lifestyles of the Beat authors Jack Kerouac, William S. Burroughs, and Allen Ginsberg in regard to the anthropological studies of Victor Turner. The Beats partially separated from society by willingly entering the rites of passage. Liminal symbolism is apparent in their literature, such as in movement, time, space, pilgrimages, and monstrosities. In their liminal stage, they established "communitas" and developed anti-structure, questioning society and proposing to change it in their liminoid literature.

Mortenson, Erik. *Translating the Counterculture: The Reception of the Beats in Turkey.* Southern Illinois UP, 2018.

> Examines the reception of the Beat Generation in Turkey. There, the Beat message of dissent is being given renewed life as publishers, editors, critics, readers, and others dissatisfied with the conservative social and political trends in the country have turned to the Beats and other countercultural forebears for alternatives. Through an examination of a broad range of literary translations, media portrayals, interviews, and other related materials, *Translating the Counterculture* seeks to uncover how the Beats and their texts are being circulated, discussed, and used in Turkey to rethink the possibilities they might hold for social critique today. By focusing on the ways in which local conditions and particular needs shape reception, Mortenson examines how in Turkey the Beats have been framed by the label "underground literature"; explores the ways they are repurposed

in the counterculture-inspired journal *Underground Poetix*; looks at the reception of Kerouac's *On the Road* and how that reaction provides a better understanding of the construction of "American-ness"; delves into the recent obscenity trial of William S. Burroughs's novel *The Soft Machine* and the attention the book's supporters brought to government repression and Turkish homophobia; and analyzes the various translations of Allen Ginsberg's "Howl."

Murnaghan, Sheila and Ralph M. Rosen, editors. *Hip Sublime: Beat Writers and the Classical Tradition.* The Ohio State UP, 2018.

Despite their self-presentation as iconoclasts, the writers of the Beat Generation were deeply engaged with the classical tradition. Many of them were university-trained and highly conscious of their literary forebears finding in their classical models both a venerable literary heritage and a discourse of sublimity through which to articulate their desire for purity. In this volume, a diverse group of contributors explores for the first time the tensions and paradoxes that arose from interactions between these avant-garde writers and a literary tradition often seen as conservative and culturally hegemonic.

Ouakrim, Hassan. *Memoir of a Berber: Brian Jones, Jahjouka Rolling Stones, the Beat Generation in Morocco.* Fulton Books, 2017.

During the Beat Generation, Morocco saw a flourishing of arts, political change, and visits by distinguished guests from the West. Encounters between the aspects of the mystical/sacred traditions of Morocco's mixing cultures and emissaries from the West, many who indulged in the newly-opened freedoms and sacred traditions, led variously to works of genius, momentous cross-cultural encounters, and personal fame and ruin.

Polsky, Ned. *Hustlers, Beats, and Others.* 1967. Routledge, 2017.

This book, a reissue of Polsky's classic, analyzes deviant branches of American life, dispels misconceptions about them, and throws new light on sociological theory and method. Each chapter radically dissents from one or more mainstream opinions about deviance.

Raskin, Jonah. "Beatniks, Hippies, Yippies, Feminists, and the Ongoing American Counterculture." *The Cambridge Companion to the Beats*, edited by Steven Belletto, Cambridge UP, 2017.

Sterritt, David. "The Beats and Visual Culture." *The Cambridge Companion to the Beats*, edited by Steven Belletto, Cambridge UP, 2017.

Tietchen, Todd F. "Ethnographics and Networks: On Beat Transnationalism." *The Cambridge Companion to the Beats*, edited by Steven Belletto, Cambridge UP, 2017.

Tytell, John. *Beat Transnationalism.* Beatdom Books, 2017.

> Tytell examines the importance of Mexico to the Beat Generation, while recounting via letters from that period to his wife, Mellon, his own experiences in Oaxaca. Also included are essays on Bonnie Bremser, Lawrence Ferlinghetti, and Patti Smith, among others.

Torgoff, Martin. *Bop Apocalypse: Jazz, Race, The Beats, & Drugs.* Da Capo Press, 2017.

> Details the rise of early drug culture in America by weaving together the disparate elements that formed this new and revolutionary segment of the American social fabric.

Weinreich, Regina. "Locating a Beat Aesthetic." *The Cambridge Companion to the Beats*, edited by Steven Belletto, Cambridge UP, 2017.

Whalen-Bridge, John. "Buddhism and the Beats." *The Cambridge Companion to the Beats*, edited by Steven Belletto, Cambridge UP, 2017.

## Charles Bukowski

Bukowski, Charles. *Storm for the Living and the Dead: Uncollected and Unpublished Poems.* Ecco, 2017.

> Abel Debritto has curated poems from obscure, hard-to-find magazines, as well as from libraries and private collections all over the country—most of

which will be new to Bukowski's readers and some of which have never been seen before.

Johnson, Marguerite. "Radical Brothers-in-Arms: Gaius and Hank at the Racetrack." *Hip Sublime: Beat Writers and the Classical Tradition,* edited by Sheila Murnaghan and Ralph M. Rosen, The Ohio State UP, 2018.

## William S. Burroughs

Beaumont, Daniel. "Wake-Up Call: Žižek, Burroughs, and Fantasy in the Sleeper Awakened Plot." *Everything You Wanted to Know about Literature but Were Afraid to Ask Žižek,* edited and with an introduction by Russell Sbriglia, Duke UP, 2017, pp. 245-266.

Grattan, Sean Austin. "A Grenade with the Fuse Lit: William S. Burroughs and Retroactive Utopias." *Hope Isn't Stupid: Utopian Affects in Contemporary American Literature.* U of Iowa P, 2017.

Harris, Oliver. "William S. Burroughs: Beating Postmodernism." *The Cambridge Companion to the Beats*, edited by Steven Belletto, Cambridge UP, 2017.

Jarvis, Michael. "'All in the Day's Work': Cold War Doctoring and Its Discontents in William Burroughs's *Naked Lunch*." *Literature and Medicine,* vol. 35, no. 1, 2017, pp. 183-202.

> Treats the institutions and practices of science and medicine, specifically with regard to psychiatry/psychology, as symptoms of a bureaucratic system of control that shapes, constructs, defines, and makes procrustean alterations to both the mind and body of human subjects.

Lawlor, William. "Were Jack Kerouac, Allen Ginsberg, and William S. Burroughs a Generation?" *The Cambridge Companion to the Beats,* edited by Steven Belletto, Cambridge UP, 2017.

Reynolds, Loni. "'The Final Fix' and 'The Transcendent Kingdom': The Quest in the Early Work of William S. Burroughs." *Hip Sublime: Beat Writers and the Classical Tradition,* edited by Sheila Murnaghan and Ralph M. Rosen, The Ohio State UP, 2018.

## Gregory Corso

Olson, Kirby. "Beat as Beatific: Gregory Corso's Christian Poetics." *The Cambridge Companion to the Beats*, edited by Stephen Belletto, Cambridge UP, 2017.

## Robert Creeley

Selby, Nick. "Riffing on Catullus: Robert Creeley's Poetics of Adultery." *Hip Sublime: Beat Writers and the Classical Tradition,* edited by Sheila Murnaghan and Ralph M. Rosen, The Ohio State UP, 2018.

## Diane di Prima

Grace, Nancy M. and Tony Triglio. "Troubling Classical and Buddhist Traditions in Diane di Prima's *Loba*." *Hip Sublime: Beat Writers and the Classical Tradition,* edited by Sheila Murnaghan and Ralph M. Rosen, The Ohio State UP, 2018.

## Robert Duncan

Moul, Victoria. "Robert Duncan and Pindar's Dance." *Hip Sublime: Beat Writers and the Classical Tradition,* edited by Sheila Murnaghan and Ralph M. Rosen, The Ohio State UP, 2018.

## Bob Dylan

Barker, Derek. *Bob Dylan: Too Much Nothing.* Red Planet, 2018.

Carpenter, Damian A. *Lead Belly, Woody Guthrie, Bob Dylan, and American Folk Outlaw Performance.* Routledge, 2017.

> Carpenter traverses the unsettled outlaw territory that is simultaneously a part of and apart from settled American society by examining outlaw myth, performance, and perception over time. Focusing on the works and guises of Lead Belly, Woody Guthrie, and Bob Dylan, Carpenter goes beyond

the outlaw figure's heroic associations and expands on its historical (Jesse James, Billy the Kid), folk (John Henry, Stagolee), and social (tramps, hoboes) forms. He argues that all three performers represent a culturally disruptive force, whether it be the bad outlaw that Lead Belly represented to an urban bourgeoisie audience, the good outlaw that Guthrie shaped to reflect the social concerns of marginalized people, or the honest outlaw that Dylan offered audiences who responded to him as a promoter of clear-sighted self-evaluation.

Chicago, Danny. *Being Bob Dylan.* Bowker, 2017.

Dylan's musical expedition is written about through the eyes of a lifelong fan and Bob Dylan Tribute performer, Danny Chicago. Chicago micro-analyzes Dylan's songs, lyrics, and performances throughout his decades-long career, including his Greenwich Village days, early concerts at Carnegie Hall, the Last Waltz, the 30-Year Anniversary Concert at Madison Square Garden, and the Newport Folk Festival where Dylan blurred the line between folk and rock.

Dylan, Bob. *The Nobel Lecture.* Simon and Schuster, 2017.

On October 13, 2016, Dylan was awarded the Nobel Prize in Literature, recognizing his countless contributions to music and letters over the last fifty years. Some months later, he delivered an acceptance lecture that is now available in book form.

Goldberg, Michael. "Bob Dylan's Beat Visions (Sonic Poetry)." *Kerouac on Record,* edited by Simon Warner and Jim Sampas, Bloomsbury, 2018.

Goss, Nina, editor. *Tearing the World Apart: Bob Dylan and the Twenty-First Century*. UP of Mississippi, 2017.

This collection of essays participates in the creation of the postmillennial Dylan by exploring three central records of the twenty-first century—*Love and Theft* (2001), *Modern Times* (2006), and *Tempest* (2012)—along with the 2003 film *Masked and Anonymous,* which Dylan helped write and in which he appears as an actor and musical performer. It examines his method and effects through a disparate set of viewpoints. Readers will find a variety of critical contexts and cultural perspectives, as well as a range of experiences from members of Dylan's audience.

Heylin, Clinton. *Trouble In Mind: Bob Dylan's Gospel Years—What Really Happened.* Lesser Gods, 2017.

> Between 1979 and 1981, Dylan produced and released three of his most controversial albums—*Slow Train Coming, Saved,* and *Shot of Love*—toured the world, and played the most contentious shows of his career. Remarkably, this entire period was perhaps the most fastidiously well-documented of his career, with every studio session, every live show, and every single rehearsal recorded on Dylan's behalf. Serving as an invaluable companion to the latest Sony Bootleg Series (November 2017), *Trouble in Mind* is the first book to focus on the life and works of Dylan as a born-again Christian from the perspective of both his artistic growth and the development of his eschatological worldview. It will draw on previously undocumented song drafts, rehearsal tapes, and new interviews with engineers, musicians, and girlfriends.

Hudson, Robert. *The Monk's Record Player: Thomas Merton, Bob Dylan, and the Perilous Summer of 1966.* Eerdmans, 2018.

> In 1965, Thomas Merton fulfilled a 24-year-old dream and went to live as a hermit beyond the walls of his Trappist monastery. Seven months later, after a secret romance with a woman half his age, he was in danger of losing it all. Yet on the very day that his abbot uncovered the affair, Merton found solace in an unlikely place—the songs of Bob Dylan, who, as fate would have it, was experiencing his own personal and creative crises during the summer of 1966. In this parallel biography of two countercultural icons, Hudson explores Dylan's influence on Merton's life and poetry.

Lepidus, Harold. *Friends and Other Strangers: Bob Dylan Examined.* Oakamoor, 2017.

> A collection of more than 120 articles offering an informative and entertaining look at the people who have influenced, been influenced by, or simply hung around in Dylan's orbit at one point or another.

McCarron, Andrew. *Light Come Shining: The Transformations of Bob Dylan.* Oxford UP, 2017.

> Greenwich Village, the student movement of the 1960s and 1970s, Born Again Christians, the Chabad Lubavitch community, or English department

postmodernists, and specific intellectual and sociopolitical groups have repeatedly claimed Dylan as their spokesperson. But in the words of filmmaker Todd Haynes, who cast six actors to depict different facets of Dylan's life and artistic personae in his 2009 film *I'm Not There,* "The minute you try to grab hold of Dylan, he's no longer where he was." In *Light Come Shining*, McCarron uses psychological tools to examine three major turning points, or transformations, in Dylan's life: the aftermath of his 1966 motorcycle accident, his Born Again conversion in 1978, and his recommitment to songwriting and performing in 1987.

Renza, Louis A. *Dylan's Autobiography of a Vocation: A Reading of the Lyrics 1965-1967*. Bloomsbury, 2017.

Many critics have interpreted Dylan's lyrics, especially those composed during the middle to late 1960s, in the contexts of their relation to American folk, blues, and rock n' roll precedents; their discographical details and concert performances; their social, political and cultural relevance; and/ or their status for discussion as "poems." *Dylan's Autobiography of a Vocation* instead focuses on how all of Dylan's 1965-1967 songs manifest traces of his ongoing, internal "autobiography" in which he continually declares and questions his relation to a self-determined existential summons.

Savage, Craig. "Bob Dylan's American Adam." *ANQ: A Quarterly Journal of Short Articles, Notes and Reviews*, vol. 30, no. 3, 2017, pp. 194-197.

Schulte, Dilan Kale. "Ballad Form, Folk History, and Cubist Collage in Bob Dylan's 'Desolation Row.'" *NTU Studies in Language and Literature*, vol. 37, June 2017, pp. 77-113.

Thomas, Richard. *Why Bob Dylan Matters*. Dey Street, 2017.

When the Nobel Prize for Literature was awarded to Dylan in 2016, a debate raged. Some celebrated, while others questioned the choice. In *Why Bob Dylan Matters*, Richard F. Thomas, an expert on classical poetry, discusses his college course on Bob Dylan and makes a compelling case for moving Dylan out of the Rock & Roll Hall of Fame and into the pantheon of classical poets. Thomas offers an argument for Dylan's modern relevance, while interpreting and decoding Dylan's lyrics for readers.

Wolff, Daniel. *Grown-Up Anger: The Connected Mysteries of Bob Dylan, Woody Guthrie, and the Calumet Massacre of 1913*. HarperCollins, 2017.

> A tour de force of storytelling years in the making: a dual biography of two of the greatest songwriters, Dylan and Woody Guthrie, that is also a murder mystery and a history of labor relations and socialism, big business and greed in twentieth-century America—woven together in one epic saga that holds meaning for all working Americans today. In this cultural study, Wolff braids three disparate strands—Calumet, Guthrie, and Dylan—together to create a devastating revisionist history of twentieth-century America. *Grown-Up Anger* chronicles the struggles between the haves and have-nots, the impact changing labor relations had on industrial America, and the way two musicians used their fury to illuminate economic injustice and inspire change.

## Robert Frank

Smith, J.R. *American Witness: The Art and Life of Robert Frank*. Da Capo, 2017.

> The first comprehensive look at the life of a man who's as mysterious and evasive as he is prolific and gifted. Leaving his rigid Switzerland for the more fluid United States in 1947, Frank found himself at the social center of bohemian New York in the '50s and '60s, becoming friends with everyone from Jack Kerouac, Allen Ginsberg, and Peter Orlovsky, to photographer Walker Evans, actor Zero Mostel, painter Willem de Kooning, filmmaker Jonas Mekas, Bob Dylan, writer Rudy Wurlitzer, jazz musicians Ornette Coleman and Charles Mingus, and more. Frank roamed the country with his young family, taking roughly 27,000 photographs and collecting 83 of them into what is still his most famous work: *The Americans*. It was harshly criticized upon publication for its portrait of a divided country, but the collection gradually grew to be recognized as an American vision.

## Allen Ginsberg

Ginsberg, Allen. *The Best Minds of My Generation: A Literary History of the Beats*. Edited by Bill Morgan, Grove, 2017.

In 1977, 20 years after the publication of his landmark poem "Howl" and Jack Kerouac's seminal book *On the Road*, Allen Ginsberg decided it was time to teach a course on the literary history of the Beat Generation. Through the creation of this course, which he ended up teaching five times, first at the Naropa Institute (now University) and later at Brooklyn College, Ginsberg presented the history of Beat literature in his own inimitable way. Compiled and edited by Beat scholar Bill Morgan, and with an introduction by Anne Waldman, *The Best Minds of My Generation* presents the lectures in edited form, complete with notes, and paints a portrait of the Beats as Ginsberg knew them: friends, confidantes, literary mentors, and fellow revolutionaries.

**Grisafi, Patricia Ann. "The Sexualization of Mental Illness in Postwar American Literature."** *Dissertation Abstracts International*, vol. 77, no. 7, Apr. 2017.

Argues that writers during the Cold War period chose to use a rhetorical strategy that associated mental illness with sexuality in order to challenge power structures, especially those regarding gender norms. The dissertation focuses on Jim Thompson, Sylvia Plath, Anne Sexton, and Allen Ginsberg.

**Lawlor, William. "Were Jack Kerouac, Allen Ginsberg, and William S. Burroughs a Generation?"** *The Cambridge Companion to the Beats*, edited by Steven Belletto, Cambridge UP, 2017.

**Mortensen, Erik. "Allen Ginsberg and Beat Poetry."** *The Cambridge Companion to the Beats*, edited by Steven Belletto, Cambridge UP, 2017.

**Pfaff, Matthew. "The Invention of Sincerity: Allen Ginsberg and the Philology of the Margins."** *Hip Sublime: Beat Writers and the Classical Tradition*, edited by Sheila Murnaghan and Ralph M. Rosen, The Ohio State UP, 2018.

**Schumacher, Michael, editor.** *First Thought: Conversations with Allen Ginsberg.* U of Minnesota P, 2017.

With "Howl," Ginsberg became the voice of the Beat Generation. It was a voice heard in some of the best-known poetry of our time—but also in Ginsberg's eloquent and extensive commentary on literature, consciousness, and politics, as well as his own work. Much of what he had to say, he said in interviews, and many of the best of these are collected for the first time in this book. Here we encounter Ginsberg elaborating on how speech, as much as writing and reading, and even poetry, is an act of art.

Tusler, Megan. "American Snapshot: Urban Realism from New Deal to Great Society." *Dissertation Abstracts International*, vol. 77, no. 8, Feb. 2017.

> Argues that realism, however fraught the term, stages scenes of community in order to make claims upon the "real world" in the twentieth century. It identifies and analyzes forms of vernacular realism from 1941 to 1984 as well as aesthetic experiments that consider themselves to mimetically represent the "real world" to reconceive scenes of attachment and counter publics. The third chapter shows how the Beat collective and Allen Ginsberg deploy the photograph and narrative together to give permanence to the historical moment and its attendant political problems. Using Ginsberg's phototexts as primary multimedia objects, the dissertation asks how an aesthetic community "opts out" of its political present by turning to experiments in ways of being and an expansive model of documentation.

## Hettie Jones

Anderson, Stephanie. "Three Interviews on Small-Press Publishing: Hettie Jones, Margaret Randall, and Maureen Owen [Special Section]." *Chicago Review*, vol. 59, no. 1-2, 2014, pp. 78-112.

> The interviews with Jones, Margaret Randall, and Maureen Owen draw attention to the roles of women small-press publishers who were active between the 1950s and 1980s, specifically tracing geographical and temporal trajectories. Jones edited and co-published *Yugen* (1958-62) and ran Totem Press (1958-64) with LeRoi Jones/Amiri Baraka. Due in part to her connections at the *Partisan Review*, the magazine circulated more widely than other small press publications of the period and became an important venue for writers now associated with the Beat, New York School, and Black Mountain scenes. Randall founded *El Corno Emplumado* [*The Plumed Horn*] (1962-69) in Mexico City; issues 1-28 were co-edited with Sergio Mondragón and 30 and 31 with Robert Cohen. Owen founded the magazine *Telephone* and the press Telephone Books (1969) in New York; the magazine ceased publication in 1983.

# The Beat Index

## Joyce Johnson

Knight, Brenda. "Memory Babes: Joyce Johnson and Beat Memoir." *The Cambridge Companion to the Beats*, edited by Steven Belletto, Cambridge UP, 2017.

## Jack Kerouac

Beckett, Larry. "2nd Chorus: Blues: Jack Kerouac." *Kerouac on Record,* edited by Simon Warner and Jim Sampas, Bloomsbury, 2018.

Bliesener, Mark. "Driver." *Kerouac on Record,* edited by Simon Warner and Jim Sampas, Bloomsbury, 2018.

Burns, Jim. "Jack Kerouac's Jazz Scene." *Kerouac on Record,* edited by Simon Warner and Jim Sampas, Bloomsbury, 2018.

Field, Douglas. "'Straight from the Mind to the Voice': Spectral Persistence in Jack Kerouac and Tom Waits." *Kerouac on Record,* edited by Simon Warner and Jim Sampas, Bloomsbury, 2018.

Gair, Christopher. "'Thalatta, Thalatta!': Xenophon, Joyce, and Kerouac." *Hip Sublime: Beat Writers and the Classical Tradition,* edited by Sheila Murnaghan and Ralph M. Rosen, The Ohio State UP, 2018.

Garton-Gundling, Kyle. "Beat Buddhism and American Freedom." *College Literature*, vol. 44, no. 2, 2017, pp. 200-230.

> Investigates the influential cross-cultural adaptation of Buddhist traditions and practices in the works of Gary Snyder, Jack Kerouac, and Tom Robbins. All three promote Americanized Buddhism as an alternative to consumerism. Within a shared commitment to shaping American Buddhism, diversity exists: Snyder sees a harmonious merging of cultures; Kerouac struggles with unresolved conflicts; and Robbins combines cross-cultural openness with ethnically sensitive caution.

George-Warren, Holly. "Light is Faster than Sound: Texans, the Beats and the San Francisco Counterculture." *Kerouac on Record,* edited by Simon Warner and Jim Sampas, Bloomsbury, 2018.

Goldberg, Michael. "Bob Dylan's Beat Visions (Sonic Poetry)." *Kerouac on Record,* edited by Simon Warner and Jim Sampas, Bloomsbury, 2018.

Grace, Nancy M. "Detecting Jack Kerouac and Joni Mitchell: A Literary/Legal (not Musicological) Investigation into the Search for Influence." *Kerouac on Record,* edited by Simon Warner and Jim Sampas, Bloomsbury, 2018.

Hassett, Brian. "Jack Manifested as Music." *Kerouac on Record,* edited by Simon Warner and Jim Sampas, Bloomsbury, 2018.

Hemmer, Kurt. "Jack Kerouac and the Beat Novel." *The Cambridge Companion to the Beats,* edited by Steven Belletto, Cambridge UP, 2017.

Jago, Marian. "Duet for Saxophone and Pen: Lee Konitz and the Direct Influence of Jazz on the Development of Jack Kerouac's 'Spontaneous Prose' Style." *Kerouac on Record,* edited by Simon Warner and Jim Sampas, Bloomsbury, 2018.

Johnson, Ronna C. "From Beat Bop Prosody to Punk Rock Poetry: Patti Smith and Jack Kerouac; Literature, Lineage, Legacy." *Kerouac on Record,* edited by Simon Warner and Jim Sampas, Bloomsbury, 2018.

Jones, Jay Jeff. "Jim Morrison/Angel of Fire." *Kerouac on Record,* edited by Simon Warner and Jim Sampas, Bloomsbury, 2018.

Lawlor, William. "Were Jack Kerouac, Allen Ginsberg, and William S. Burroughs a Generation?" *The Cambridge Companion to the Beats*, edited by Steven Belletto, Cambridge UP, 2017.

Lee, A. Robert. "Art Music: Listening to Kerouac's 'Mexico City Blues.'" *Kerouac on Record,* edited by Simon Warner and Jim Sampas, Bloomsbury, 2018.

Marion, Paul. "Carrying a Torch for Ti Jean." *Kerouac on Record,* edited by Simon Warner and Jim Sampas, Bloomsbury, 2018.

Mills, Peter. "Hit the Road, Jack: Van Morrison and *On the Road.*" *Kerouac on Record,* edited by Simon Warner and Jim Sampas, Bloomsbury, 2018.

Morrison, Simon. "Tramps Like Them: Jack and Bruce and the Myth of the

American Road." *Kerouac on Record,* edited by Simon Warner and Jim Sampas, Bloomsbury, 2018.

Prince, Michael. "Beat Refrains: Music, Milieu and Identity in Jack Kerouac's *The Subterraneans,* the Metro-Goldwyn-Mayer film adaptation." *Kerouac on Record,* edited by Simon Warner and Jim Sampas, Bloomsbury, 2018.

Raskin, Jonah. "Jack Kerouac Goes Vinyl: A Sonic Journey into Kerouac's Three LP's." *Kerouac on Record,* edited by Simon Warner and Jim Sampas, Bloomsbury, 2018.

Sampas, Jim and Simon Warner. "The Tribute Recordings." *Kerouac on Record,* edited by Simon Warner and Jim Sampas, Bloomsbury, 2018.

Sullivan, James. "Punk and New Wave." *Kerouac on Record,* edited by Simon Warner and Jim Sampas, Bloomsbury, 2018.

Theado, Matt. "Kerouac and Country Music." *Kerouac on Record,* edited by Simon Warner and Jim Sampas, Bloomsbury, 2018.

Warner, Simon and Jim Sampas, editors. *Kerouac on Record: A Literary Soundtrack.* Bloomsbury, 2018.

> The leading light of the Beat Generation writers, Kerouac had a lifelong passion for music, particularly the mid-century jazz of New York City, the development of which he witnessed first-hand during the 1940s with Charlie Parker, Dizzy Gillespie, and Thelonious Monk at the fore. Most famous for *On the Road* (1957), Kerouac admired the sounds of bebop and attempted to bring something of their original energy to his own writing. Yet he was also drawn to American popular music of all kinds—from the blues to Broadway ballads—and when he came to record albums under his own name, he married his unique spoken word style with some of the most talented musicians on the scene. But Kerouac's musical legacy goes well beyond the studio recordings he made himself: his influence infused generations of music makers who followed. *Kerouac on Record* considers how the writer brought his passion for jazz to his prose and poetry, his own record releases, the ways his legacy has been sustained by numerous more recent talents, those rock tributes that have kept his memory alive, and some of the scores featured in Hollywood adaptations of the adventures he brought to the printed page.

## Henry Miller

Burnside, John. *On Henry Miller: Or, How to Be an Anarchist.* Princeton UP, 2018.

> The American writer Henry Miller's critical reputation—if not his popular readership—has been in eclipse at least since Kate Millet's blistering critique in *Sexual Politics*, her landmark 1970 study of misogyny in literature and art. Burnside argues that Miller's notorious image as a "pornographer and woman hater" has hidden his vital, true importance—his anarchist sensibility and the way it shows us how, by fleeing from conformity of all kinds, we may be able to save ourselves from the "air-conditioned nightmare" of the modern world.

Humphries, David T. "Going off the Gold Standard in Henry Miller's *Tropic of Cancer*." *Canadian Review of American Studies* [*Revue Canadienne D'Etudes Americaines*], vol. 47, no. 2, 2017, pp. 239-260.

> *Tropic of Cancer* (1934) provides a unique modernist representation of the economic warfare of the Great Depression, as evident in Miller's claims for "going off the gold standard." This essay explores what such claims reveal about the connections between economic regimes and the symbolic structures, which underpin both cultural production and the experience of everyday life. In his depiction of prostitution and embodied transactions, Miller offers alternate modes of circulation and currency. In his attempts to create a language and form that "flow," Miller reveals how nationalism, economic strictures, and literary conventions promote hoarding, create conflicts, and mask the experience of everyday life.

## Charles Olson

Fletcher, Richard. "Towards a Post-Beat Poetics: Charles Olson's Localism and the Second Sophistic." *Hip Sublime: Beat Writers and the Classical Tradition*, edited by Sheila Murnaghan and Ralph M. Rosen, The Ohio State UP, 2018.

## Maureen Owen

Anderson, Stephanie. "Three Interviews on Small-Press Publishing: Hettie Jones, Margaret Randall, and Maureen Owen [Special Section]." *Chicago Review*, vol. 59, nos. 1-2, 2014, pp. 78-112. See entry under Hettie Jones.

## Margaret Randall

Anderson, Stephanie. "Three Interviews on Small-Press Publishing: Hettie Jones, Margaret Randall, and Maureen Owen [Special Section]." *Chicago Review*, vol. 59, nos. 1-2, 2014, pp. 78-112. See entry under Hettie Jones.

## Kenneth Rexroth

Nisbet, Gideon. "Kenneth Rexroth: Greek Anthologist." *Hip Sublime: Beat Writers and the Classical Tradition,* edited by Sheila Murnaghan and Ralph M. Rosen, The Ohio State UP, 2018.

## Ed Sanders

Skerl, Jennie. "Sappho Comes to the Lower East Side: Ed Sanders, the Sixties Avant-Garde, and Fictions of Sappho." *Hip Sublime: Beat Writers and the Classical Tradition,* edited by Sheila Murnaghan and Ralph M. Rosen, The Ohio State UP, 2018.

## Gary Snyder

Calonne, David Stephen, editor. *Conversations with Gary Snyder.* UP of Mississippi, 2017.

> Snyder is one of the most distinguished American poets, remarkable both for his long and productive career and for his equal contributions to literature and environmental thought. *Conversations with Gary Snyder* collects interviews from 1961 to 2015 and charts his developing environmental

philosophy and his wide-ranging interests in ecology, Buddhism, Native American studies, history, and mythology.

Hunt, Anthony. "'Instructions' for Attentive Listening: The Rhythms of Gary Snyder's *Mountains and Rivers without End.*" *ANQ: A Quarterly Journal of Short Articles, Notes and Reviews*, vol. 30, no. 2, 2017, pp. 67-72.

> Explores the use of rhythm in Gary Snyder's long poem *Mountains and Rivers Without End,* arguing that the rhythmic aspects of the poem must be heard and studied in order for readers to fully connect to the poem. Snyder connects the use of sound and the Buddhist idea of enlightenment, and, Hunt argues, by listening to the "musical composition" of the poem and studying its patterns and sounds readers can better understand the poem's essence and wholeness.

Garton-Gundling, Kyle. "Beat Buddhism and American Freedom. *College Literature*, vol. 44, no. 2, 2017, pp. 200-230. See entry under Jack Kerouac.

Gonnerman, Mark. "Both Sides Now: On Gary Snyder's *This Present Moment.*" *ANQ: A Quarterly Journal of Short Articles, Notes and Reviews*, vol. 30, no. 2, 2017, pp. 88-92.

> Gonnerman walks readers through Snyder's *This Present Moment,* and its main themes. *This Present Moment* focuses on simplicity and Snyder's Thoreau-like beliefs and dedication to minimizing unnecessary materials, as well as his emphasis on connecting to the wild in order to more fully understand the world and its truths. The article explores Snyder's Buddhist beliefs and the ways in which they appear in his poems.

Martin, Julia. "The Path Which Goes Beyond: *Danger on Peaks* Responds to Suffering." *ANQ: A Quarterly Journal of Short Articles, Notes and Reviews*, vol. 30, no. 2, 2017, pp. 81-87.

> Investigates Gary Snyder's reaction to suffering, both personal and "eco-social," in his poem *Danger on Peaks.* The author argues that Snyder's works, despite increased personal and ecological pain, "foreground lightness and tenderness."

Murphy, Patrick D. "Complexity Integration, Ecocritical Analysis, and Gary Snyder Studies." *ANQ: A Quarterly Journal of Short Articles, Notes and Reviews*, vol. 30, no. 2, 2017, pp. 93-100.

> Describes complexity integration, or the recognition that fields of study, focusing on literary critics, build on various perspectives and other fields of study in order to gain the most complete understanding of a work. Snyder's works require this detailed approach to avoid reductionism that would distort the meaning. The article also details ecocritical analysis and its relationship to Snyder's works.

Murphy, Patrick D. "Gary Snyder Studies [Special Issue]." *ANQ: A Quarterly Journal of Short Articles, Notes and Reviews*, vol. 30, no. 2, 2017, pp. 63-131.

Qiao, Guoqiang. "'The Power-Vision in Solitude': Gary Snyder's Poetic Exploration." *ANQ: A Quarterly Journal of Short Articles, Notes and Reviews*, vol. 30, no. 2, 2017, pp. 112-117.

> In an interview with Gene Fowler, Snyder advanced the idea of "the power-vision in solitude." For Snyder, the power-vision is 1) the knowledge of self, which for Snyder is power of no-power, 2) the practice of Zen, and 3) the thing that is beyond or "larger" than Zen. These three aspects might not be separate as such but are interrelated and interacting. It is the aim of this essay to arrive at both a specific and a composite view of Snyder's idea of power-vision in his poems.

Qiu, Yan. "'Off the Trail': Ecophilosophy and Gary Snyder's Idea of 'The Wild.'" *ANQ: A Quarterly Journal of Short Articles, Notes and Reviews*, vol. 30, no. 2, 2017, pp. 101-111.

> Examines the meanings of the term "the wild" in Snyder's works and argues that "the wild" as a concept incorporated multiple ideas, including environmental, Buddhist, and Daoist philosophy, as well as Amerindian mythology, and that this ideological multiplicity is one of the core concepts in Snyder's ecophilosophical thought.

Tan, Joan Qionglin. "Walking on Walking: A Coded Ku in Gary Snyder's Mountains and Rivers without End." *ANQ: A Quarterly Journal of Short Articles, Notes and Reviews*, vol. 30, no. 2, 2017, pp. 73-80.

Whalen-Bridge, John. "Death and Destruction in Snyder's Twenty-First-Century Poems." *ANQ: A Quarterly Journal of Short Articles, Notes and Reviews*, vol. 30, no. 2, 2017, pp. 118-128.

> Explores the way in which Snyder's later works explore death, destruction, and the emptiness that relates to these experiences. It also gives additional background on the Buddhist notion of *shunya,* or emptiness, and how this notion appears in Snyder's works.

## Anne Waldman

Carruthers, A. J. "'Music for Posterity': Afterlives for the Score in Anne Waldman's *The Iovis Trilogy.*" *Notational Experiments in North American Long Poems, 1961-2011: Stave Sightings*. Palgrave Macmillan, 2017.

## Philip Whalen

Falk, Jane. "Philip Whalen and the Classics: 'A Walking Grove of Trees.'" *Hip Sublime: Beat Writers and the Classical Tradition,* edited by Sheila Murnaghan and Ralph M. Rosen, The Ohio State UP, 2018.

# Essay Abstracts

### A History of Diane di Prima's Poets Press
by Jolie Braun

This essay draws on archival material to tell the story of Diane di Prima's Poets Press. Founded by the most prominent woman poet of the Beat Generation and one of the rare women-run presses of the era, Poets Press published more than two-dozen volumes, including works by major underground poets of the second half of the 20th century as well as the first publications of important new writers. This essay explores the history of Poets Press, its books, as well as its successes and shortcomings.

### Joanne Kyger's Travel Chapbooks: A Poetics of Motion
by Mary Paniccia Carden

"Joanne Kyger's Poetics of Travel" argues that Kyger's travel chapbooks constitute a unique genre that merges poetry, journal, and dream diary as a means of investigating the relationship between the individual "psyche" and "world existence." In *Desecheo Notebook* (1971), *Trip Out and Fall Back* (1974), *Mexico Blondé* (1981), *Phenomenological* (1989), and *Pátzcuaro* (1999), Kyger develops the travel chapbook into a personal genre of expression aimed at forming new "points of departure" for conceptualizing human being and/in the world. Like other Beat-associated writers, she experiences movement as a liberating and liberated state, in which writers explore the limits of consciousness as they explore new spaces and places. This article analyzes Kyger's travel chapbooks by focusing on her practice of daily journal writing, her interest in dreams, her transformation of the everyday into occasions of truth and transcendence, and her attention to productive relationships between the human mind and the wider world. Ultimately, the chapbooks posit travel as a metaphor for human consciousness.

### Big Sur Breakdown: Lew Welch and "Ring of Bone"
by Terence Diggory

This essay provides an occasion for reevaluating Lew Welch's place in the canon of Beat literature by reading his poem "Ring of Bone" in a variety of contexts: biography, autobiography, literary history, and spiritual quest. Welch's relationship to Jack Kerouac, and particularly the transformative visions that each man experienced in the Big Sur wilderness of California, provides a key point of comparison, leading to consideration of additional influences including Allen Ginsberg, Gertrude Stein, Robert Duncan, and Zen Buddhism. Against a simplistic reduction of Welch's life to its end in supposed (but never proven) suicide, a careful reading of his work reveals a practice that writes through psychological breakdown to open a form of consciousness that is not ego-centered.

## Michael McClure: A Filmography
by Jane Falk

From the late 1950s into the early 1970s, Michael McClure was featured in numerous underground films and documentaries, had roles in several independent feature-length films, included film as a component of several of his plays, worked on a screen play of his novel, *The Adept,* shot documentary footage himself, and wrote film criticism. The screen play was never optioned for a movie, and McClure's film of his mushroom-hunting trip with Sterling Bunnell was never completed and is now lost.

McClure uniquely combines San Francisco Renaissance, Beat Generation, and Bay Area experimental art scenes in his person, and many of those connections are caught on film. In fact, most of the directors as well as many of those he performed with were personal friends, and the films were more like collaborations. Such collaborative practices can also be seen as an aspect of McClure's working methods, shedding light on the multimedia emphasis in his work. Ultimately, these points of cinematic light combine with poems, plays, and essays to form new constellations by which to experience McClure's body of work. The filmography is divided into five sections: Underground Film and Video; Independent Film; Documentary Film and Video; Films and Plays; and Miscellaneous Film-Related Projects.

## Le Club Jack Kérouac and the Renaissance in Beat Scholarship on Kerouac's French Canadian Background
by Sara Villa

The recent publication of original manuscripts written by Kerouac in French, and particularly *joual*, reveals a renaissance of scholarly interest in the Francophone roots of this major Beat author. This double culture is, indeed, one of the most pronounced and powerful identifying elements in Kerouac's personal and artistic life. Considering the renewed research focus on the writer's French Canadian production, this essay reconsiders within the context of the scholarship—mostly written in French—research, symposiums, and publications on the Beats in Québec, especially from 1984-1994, centered around Le Club Jack Kérouac. This association was created to promote research on the Québécois background of the writer and

## ESSAY ABSTRACTS

organized a major symposium on the subject in 1987. Their work paved the way for subsequent research on Kerouac's Francophone background. Original materials from the Le Club Jack Kérouac and from the Archives of the Libraries of Québec form the basis of the analysis.

## Notes on Contributors

**Jolie Braun** is the curator of American literature at The Ohio State University. Her research interests include women writers and publishers, self-publishing, and the Beat Generation.

**Mary Paniccia Carden** is professor of English and chairperson of the Department of English and Philosophy at Edinboro University of Pennsylvania. She is the author of *Sons and Daughters of Self-Made Men* and co-editor (with Susan Strehle) of *Doubled Plots: Romance and History*. Her study of the autobiographical practices of Beat-associated women writers, *Women Writers of the Beat Era: Autobiography and Intertextuality*, is forthcoming from the University of Virginia Press.

**Terence Diggory** is emeritus professor of English at Skidmore College. His books include the *Encyclopedia of the New York School Poets*, *The Scene of My Selves: New Work on New York School Poets* (co-edited with Stephen Paul Miller), *William Carlos Williams and the Ethics of Painting*, and *Yeats & American Poetry: The Tradition of the Self*.

**Jane Falk** is retired from the University of Akron, where she served as a senior lecturer. Her research and scholarship focus on Joanne Kyger, Philip Whalen, Zen Buddhism and the Beats, and Beats and independent film.

**Nancy M. Grace** is the Virginia Myers Professor of English at The College of Wooster and the author of *Jack Kerouac and the Literary Imagination*. She co-edited (with Ronna C. Johnson) *Girls Who Wore Black: Women Writing the Beat Generation*, and *Breaking the Rule of Cool: Interviewing and Reading Beat Women Writers*, as well as *The Transnational Beat Generation* (with Jennie Skerl).

**Kurt Hemmer** is a professor of English at Harper College, Illinois. He is the editor of the *Encyclopedia of Beat Literature* and with filmmaker Tom Knoff has produced *Janine Pommy Vega: As We Cover the Streets*; *Rebel Roar: The Sound of Michael McClure*; *Wow! Ted Joans Lives!*; *Keenan*; and *Love Janine Pommy Vega*. His essay, "'The natives are getting uppity': Tangier and *Naked Lunch*," appears in *Naked Lunch@50: Anniversary Essays*.

**Jennie Skerl** is a founding member and past president of the Beat Studies Association. She has published *William S. Burroughs* and *A Tawdry Place of Salvation: The Art of Jane Bowles*; edited *Reconstructing the Beats*; and co-edited

# NOTES ON CONTRIBUTORS

*William S. Burroughs at the Front: Critical Reception*, 1959-1989 (with Robin Lydenberg) and *The Transnational Beat Generation* (with Nancy M. Grace).

**Sara Villa** is a professor of English at John Abbott College (Saint-Anne de-Bellevue, Quebec, Canada). She is the translator into Italian of *Windblown World: The Journals of Jack Kerouac 1947-1954* (edited by Douglas Brinkley), and she has published articles on Virginia Woolf, Anglo-American Cinema, and Jack Kerouac. Her monographic volume dedicated to the film adaptation of Woolf's *Orlando* (*I due Orlando: Le poetiche androgine del romanzo woolfiano e dell'adattamento cinematografico*) is published by CUEM, Milan.

## Editorial Policy

The *Journal of Beat Studies* invites articles on the works of Beat movement writers and their colleagues, especially New York School, Black Mountain School, and San Francisco Renaissance writers, as well as those connected to these movements, in the United States and globally. The *Journal* intends to represent the breadth and eclecticism of critical approaches to Beat generation writers and welcomes new perspectives and contexts of inquiry.

Articles that are deemed appropriate are sent for review anonymously to a member of the Editorial Board and at least one other reader. Manuscripts should not be under consideration elsewhere, and we do not publish previously published work. It is strongly advised that those submitting work to *JBS* be familiar with the journal's content. Among criteria on which evaluation of submissions depends are whether an article demonstrates recognition of and thorough familiarity with scholarship already published in the field, whether the article is written clearly and effectively, and whether it makes a genuine contribution to Beat studies.

## Preparation of Copy

1. Articles are typically between 25 and 30 pages, and do not exceed 9000 words, including notes and works cited. Inquiries about significantly shorter or longer submissions should be sent to the editors.

2. A separate page should include the article's title, author's name, address, telephone & fax numbers, and e-mail address. The author's name and identifying references should not appear on the manuscript to preserve anonymity for our readers.

3. All submissions must include an abstract of no more than 250 words.

4. The manuscript should be in Times New Roman 12, double-spaced, and should adhere to the most recent MLA style.

5. Submissions may be sent by email as word documents ("doc" only, not "docx") to Ronna C. Johnson (ronna.johnson@tufts.edu) and Nancy M. Grace (ngrace@wooster.edu) simultaneously. Mailed submissions should be sent to Ronna C. Johnson at Department of English, East Hall 102, The Green, Tufts University, Medford, Massachusetts 02155. For mailed submissions, please send three copies of the article and abstract.

# EDITORIAL POLICY

6. Submissions may also be sent via the online submission form at http://www.beatstudies.org/jbs/submission_guidelines.html.

7. Authors of accepted manuscripts are responsible for any necessary permissions fees and for securing any necessary permissions.

8. All editorial, review, and advertising inquiries should be addressed to ronna.johnson@tufts.edu and ngrace@wooster.edu.

9. Inquiries concerning orders should be addressed to PaceUP@pace.edu.

# Mosaic
## an interdisciplinary critical journal
**Upcoming Issues**

**51.3 (Sep. 2018): Scale**

Given the scale of such issues as climate change and of factors contributing to it, must theory, too, undergo a transition from local and individual to global perspectives? In what might a global imaginary consist, and how might it relate to existing critiques of globalization as but a label for the hegemony of Western culture? This issue considers "greening" theory, ecocriticism, the Anthropocene, climate change, and environmental and animal ethics.

**51.4 (Dec. 2018): *Living On* Symposium proceedings**

This issue comprises papers presented at *Mosaic*'s 50th-anniversary *Living On* symposium, held at the University of Manitoba on March 9-11, 2017. Taking its theme and title from Jacques Derrida's "Living On/Borderlines," the issue reflects on the continuing life of tinterdisciplinary research.

**52.3 (Sep. 2019): Numbers**

How pervasive is the rule of numbers? What are the challenges to calculability? Out of what set of variable examples will the limits to the rogue power of numbers emerge? As a supplement to its own special issue on Letters, *Mosaic* invites submissions on numbers in literature, art, music, theoretical texts, and the world at large. Possible themes include: finitude, multitude, technics, contingency, and economy.

Mosaic, an interdisciplinary critical journal
University of Manitoba
208 Tier Building
Winnipeg MB R3T 2N2 Canada
Email: mosasub@umanitoba.ca
Submit: umanitoba.ca/mosaic/submit

The sixth volume of the *Journal of Beat Studies*
was published in Spring 2018
by Pace University Press

Cover and Interior Layouts by Elliane Mellet
The journal was typeset in Times New Roman and AmerType Md BT
and printed by Lightning Source in La Vergne, Tennessee

## Pace University Press

Director: Sherman Raskin
Associate Director: Manuela Soares
Marketing Manager: Patricia Hinds
Design Consultant: Sara Yager
Production Editor: Stephanie Hsu

Graduate Assistants: Elliane Mellet and Bryan Potts
Student Aide: Erica Magrin

www.ingramcontent.com/pod-product-compliance
Lightning Source LLC
Chambersburg PA
CBHW061449300426
44114CB00014B/1909